Risk-Based Performance Management

Risk-Based Performance Management

Integrating Strategy and Risk Management

Andrew Smart

Chief Executive Officer, Manigent

and

James Creelman

palgrave
macmillan

First published 2013 by
PALGRAVE MACMILLAN

Palgrave Macmillan in the UK is an imprint of Macmillan Publishers Limited,
registered in England, company number 785998, of Houndmills, Basingstoke,
Hampshire RG21 6XS.

Palgrave Macmillan in the US is a division of St Martin's Press LLC,
175 Fifth Avenue, New York, NY 10010.

Palgrave Macmillan is the global academic imprint of the above companies
and has companies and representatives throughout the world.

Palgrave® and Macmillan® are registered trademarks in the United States,
the United Kingdom, Europe and other countries.

ISBN 978–0–230–30132–0

This book is printed on paper suitable for recycling and made from fully
managed and sustained forest sources. Logging, pulping and manufacturing
processes are expected to conform to the environmental regulations of the
country of origin.

A catalogue record for this book is available from the British Library.

A catalog record for this book is available from the Library of Congress.

To all the risk-takers

Andrew Smart

To the memory of three close friends who left us too soon. The world is a poorer place without them. John Harvey (1962–1993), Lynne Brookfield (1960–2007), Peader Lawless (1958–2010)

James Creelman

Contents

List of Figures, Tables and Boxes		xi
Foreword		xv
Acknowledgements		xviii

1	**Continuous Turbulent Times: The Case for Risk-Based Performance Management**	**1**
	The early 21st-century revolution	1
	New models for managing organizations: Introducing Risk-Based Performance Management	3
	Learning from the past: The industrial revolution	5
	The impact of Taylorism	6
	Total quality management	7
	The knowledge or digital age	11
	Globalization	11
	The Credit Crunch	14
	The impact of sub-prime lending	15
	Avoiding a great depression	17
	The "psychology of denial"	17
	The failure of risk management	18
	Poor understanding of risk appetite and risk profiles	20
	Risk and business strategy	20
	Conclusion: Integrating strategy and risk	21
2	**Risk-Based Performance Management: An Explanation of This New Strategic Paradigm**	**23**
	Shifting paradigms	23
	The emergence of the Risk Master	26
	Critical capabilities – The experts' consensus	30

RBPM: An integrated approach   30
Set strategy   32
Managing performance   33
Managing risk   37
Aligning risk-taking with strategy   38
Conclusion   44

**3   RBPM: Integrating Risk Frameworks and
    Standards with the Balanced Scorecard   53**

Introduction   53
The Balanced Scorecard framework explained   54
Risk Management frameworks   70
Integration models   80
Conclusion   83

4   Defining Strategy: The Question of Appetite   85

Introduction   85
Defining strategy   85
RBPM: From formulation to execution   92
The strategic importance of appetite   94
Defining risk appetite   100
Creating a risk appetite statement   104
Measuring risk appetite   116
Cascading risk appetite   118
The statement is not the end-goal   119
Conclusion   119

**5   Understanding the Relationship between the
    Three Types of Indicators: KPIs, KRIs
    and KCIs   120**

The obsession with metrics   121
Measurement as an "end in itself"   121
Key indicators and a performance conversation   123
An integrated set of indicators   124
KPIs   126
KRIs   126
KCIs   127
Three indicator scorecards   127
How indicators work together   130

Leading and lagging indicators   130
Leading and lagging across indicator types   132
Indicators and behaviour   133
RAGAR colour coding   134
Conclusion   136

6 Managing Performance   **137**

Introduction   137
Managing Performance sub-components   137
Strategic objectives   138
Understanding key terms   144
Performance Scorecard   148
Selecting KPIs   148
Selecting targets   154
Strategic initiatives   157
Manigent approach   163
Processes   164
Conclusion   166

7 Managing Risk   **167**

Introduction   167
The Risk Management discipline and function   168
The birth of enterprise risk management   173
Defining risk   176
Identifying and defining key risks   177
Risk assessment   182
KRIs   187
Risk tolerance   188
A Risk Scorecard   192
Key controls   193
Initiatives   199
Conclusion   200

8 Aligning Risk-Taking to Strategy   **201**

Binding together strategy and risk   201
Appetite and set strategy   202
Appetite and managing performance   202
Appetite and managing risk   203
Three maps that align risk-taking with strategy   203
Explaining the Appetite Alignment Matrix   204

The Appetite Alignment process   209
Aligning risk-taking to strategy: From the technical to
    the cultural   213

9   Governance   **215**

Introduction   215
Governance and the Credit Crunch   215
Board oversight – post-Credit Crunch   219
Defining governance   220
The authors' definition of governance   224
Governance and risk management   225
The RACI model   226
Conclusion   230

10 Culture and Communication   **231**

Introduction   231
A strategy-focused, risk-aware culture   233
The 5 "Cs" of communication   242
Conclusion   248

11 The Enabling Role of Technology   **249**

Change and the role of technology   249
Technology: An enabler of RBPM   251
Technology and making the case for change   254
Technology and culture   257
Visualization: The role of dashboards   258
Thirteen required technological capabilities that enable
    effective RBPM   262
Conclusion   264

12 Conclusion and Change Roadmap   **266**

Introduction   266
Change roadmap   268
End note: May you live in continuous turbulent times   284

Notes   285

Index   293

Figures, Tables and Boxes

Figures

1.1	The RBPM framework	3
1.2	The circle to the left of the RBPM framework	4
1.3	The circle to the right of the RBPM framework	5
1.4	The Malcolm Baldrige national quality framework	9
1.5	The EFQM excellence model	9
2.1	The RBPM framework	25
2.2	The left cirlce of the RBPM framework	32
2.3	An example of a Strategy Map	34
2.4	An example of a conventional Balanced Scorecard schematic	35
2.5	A Four Perspective Risk Map	36
2.6	The Appetite Alignment Matrix	38
2.7	An implementation roadmap for the left circle of the RBPM approach	40
2.8	The right circle of the RBPM framework	41
2.9	HML conceptual Strategy Map	50
2.10	HML scorecard indicators for the process perspective	51
3.1	The RBPM framework	54
3.2	An example Strategy Map	55
3.3	Ashghal Corporate Strategy Map 2012	57
3.4	Initiative sheet used by Ashghal	60
3.5	A schematic of a conventional Balanced Scorecard	62
3.6	The five principles of the strategy-focused organization	64
3.7	The six steps of the "Execution Premium" model	66
3.8	A risk management process from the Australian and New Zealand Standards of Risk Management: AS/NZ 4360:2004	74
3.9	ISO3100 risk management principles, framework and process	79

4.1	The RBPM framework	86
4.2	Risk appetite should be integrated into the organizational strategic framework	93
4.3	The *Orange Book*: *Management of Risk – Principles and Concepts*: Overall risk management model	102
4.4	A SWOT analysis organized by Balanced Scorecard perspectives	106
4.5	Elements of a PESTEL analysis	107
4.6	The Business Model Canvas	109
4.7	An example of business drivers for a bank, with time horizons (and appetite levels for each time frame) and the capacity limit	110
4.8	The critical linkage between strategy execution and risk management is made at the objective setting stage	111
4.9	Risk appetite is a multidimensional construct, which changes depending on the organizational entity and its objectives	113
4.10	A risk appetite statement summarized according to strategic perspectives, strategic themes and risk categories	116
4.11	An appetite versus exposure result for the "increase investment returns by 25%" objective	118
5.1	RBPM framework	123
5.2	An example Performance Scorecard	128
5.3	An example Risk Scorecard	128
5.4	An example Control Scorecard	129
5.5	RAGAR model	135
6.1	RBPM framework	138
6.2	An example Strategy Map	140
6.3	An example Strategy Map	141
6.4	Saatchi and Saatchi Strategy Map (1998)	142
6.5	An example Performance Scorecard	149
6.6	City of Christchurch Strategy Map	154
6.7	Mapping Initiatives to Objectives, Palladium	161
6.8	An example initiative template	162
6.9	An Initiative Alignment Matrix	163
6.10	A Process Alignment Matrix	165
7.1	RBPM framework	168
7.2	Risk Management framework from ISO3100	175
7.3	Risk Management process from ISO3100	176
7.4	Categories of risk	178

7.5   NAICOM categories of risk   179
7.6   The Risk Bow-tie   180
7.7   Documenting risks from the risk name through to risk
      description   182
7.8   An example Risk Map   183
7.9   Four Perspective Risk Map   186
7.10 Translating risk appetite into risk tolerance   189
7.11 An example Risk Scorecard   193
7.12 An example Control Map   195
7.13 Exposure versus Control Effectiveness Matrix   196
7.14 Appetite Alignment versus Control Effectiveness   197
7.15 An example Control Scorecard   199
8.1   RBPM framework   202
8.2   Appetite Alignment Matrix   205
8.3   How a Strategy Map, Four Perspective Risk Map and
      Appetite Alignment Matrix work together in
      providing a robust summary of the present state of
      strategy execution   205
8.4   Appetite and Exposure Alignment Matrix   206
9.1   RBPM framework   216
9.2   How the RACI model might support a Strategy Map   229
10.1 RBPM framework   232
11.1 The RBPM framework   250
11.2 A screenshot of the StratexSystem solution   253
12.1 RBPM framework   267
12.2 An example Strategy Map   274
12.3 An example Risk Map   275
12.4 Appetite Alignment Matrix   276
12.5 Process Alignment Matrix   278
12.6 Initiative Alignment Matrix   278
12.7 The RBPM Maturity Model   282

Tables

1.1   The global GDP share of the big four economies
      (at purchasing power parities)   14
2.1   Performance dimensions of Manigent Financial
      Services study   27
2.2   Key dashboards and management questions   45

3.1 Research into the financial impact of using the
     Balanced Scorecard   69
7.1 Example risk likelihood rating   184
7.2 Risk categories and their descriptions   184
7.3 Key controls and their KCIs   198

Boxes

2.1   Seven key RBPM tools   45
2.2   HML case study   47
3.1   Ashghal case study   56
4.1   The failure of RBS: Strategy and risk appetite   94
4.2   COSO's overview of managing risk appetite   99
7.1   Managing Loss Events   169
10.1 IIR defines a successful risk culture   237
10.2 The role of internal and external communication,
      according to ISO3100   244
11.1 The question of spreadsheets   259

Foreword

Risk. It's talked about all the time, often in serious tones and accompanied by sage nods around the room. It's an issue that is in the media every day, usually accompanied by words such as "reckless", "mismanaged" and "greed". Risk permeates everything that we do, not just in business but in most aspects of our lives. And yet the debate about how best to manage risk is often simplistic, riddled with statements of the obvious and focused on describing the problem rather than a solution.

Despite the events of the last few years, we have made very little progress in getting to grips with what risk management means and how it can be integrated into the way we do business. By picking up this book, you are doubtless looking for some answers, some ideas to help you think about risk management in a way that can lead to tangible improvements within your organizations. You are in safe hands.

Andrew Smart and James Creelman have combined their experience to provide us with a wonderful opportunity to make some long overdue progress. Andrew has dedicated more than a decade to help organizations integrate risk management into the execution of strategy. His philosophy is based on pragmatism, clear thinking and passion to make risk management a source of competitive advantage for his clients. His passionate belief in the use of technology as a true enabler of business performance has made this book a real labour of love!

James is one of the pre-eminent thinkers and researchers in the whole field of "business performance management". He thinks deeply about these issues, and yet remains well grounded in the operational practicalities. His insights are based on rigorous research and close collaboration with organizations, managers and leaders all over the world.

In *Risk-Based Performance Management*, Andrew and James provide us with a set of tools, mental models and a language to enable us understand what opportunities proper risk management can create and how it can enhance an organization's performance. By the end of this

book, you will be equipped to engage in a far more informed and pro-
ductive conversation about what risk-based performance management
means and how it can work for your organization.

Risk is too often seen as an addendum to the agenda, a checklist
to be applied after the main business discussion. Risk Directors are
appointed because, as a bank CEO once told me, "then at least one
person is going to take risk seriously". And yet we all know that the
identification and management of risk is everyone's responsibility.

I started my career in military aerospace, designing air to air mis-
siles – a proverbial rocket scientist. My colleagues and I would have
laughed at the idea that we needed someone to remind us about the
risks of what we were doing. It was built into everything that we did,
every calculation that we made, every design specification that we drew
up. And yet when I started working in financial services, I was aston-
ished to learn that there was a separate risk department to make sure
risk was "taken into account".

Similarly, I often hear that many organizations, when implementing the Balanced Scorecard, decide to add "Risk" as a fifth perspective
to the traditional four (namely finance, customer, process and people),
because "risk is so important to what we do". Ironically this creates an
impression that risk is removed from financial results, customer experience, process capability and people management. In fact risk is part
of every Balanced Scorecard objective. Risk adds a dimension to everything that we do. It cannot be set to one side and thought about as a
separate agenda item. Few people understand this as well as Andrew
and James, and the Risk-Based Performance Management (RBPM)
framework provides a pragmatic model that is long overdue.

But this book is about more than the presentation of a new framework. There is no danger of presenting nice diagrams and then leaving
us to work out what to do next! While they are far too experienced to
propose a single answer for every organization, instead Andrew and
James help us build the organizational capabilities that we need to
adapt and learn in response to ever-changing social, market and regulatory changes. The nature of risk is that it is changing all the time,
and whatever controls and processes we put in place today may not be
right forever. It is vital that we can spot for ourselves when we need
to update or challenge what we do in response to external or internal
changes.

As Andrew and James set out so clearly in the very first chapter,
it is very clear what getting risk management *wrong* looks like and
what the implications can be. But we don't often talk about what

getting risk management *right* can mean – securing competitive advantage and delivering benefits to all stakeholders, customers, staff and shareholders, as well as regulators and society.

Risk is not bad per se. We will always look to take risks because that is what it is to be creative and innovative and secure competitive advantage. The sin is not to take a risk, but to take a risk that we don't understand and cannot manage. That is our challenge and our opportunity. And *Risk-Based Performance Management* is the starting point.

Dr Jonathan Chocqueel-Mangan
Managing Director, Tyler Mangan Consulting Ltd
London, August 2013

Acknowledgements

I would like to thank my colleagues and clients at Manigent and StratexSystems for their support and feedback during the development of the Risk-Based Performance Management approach. In particular I would like to acknowledge and thank Gillian Weatherill, Rick Warley and Nicholas Hawke for their input and James Prior for his support.

Andrew Smart

As always, thank you to my family and friends for their support during the writing of this book. I would also like to thank my ex-colleagues at Ashghal, Qatar, for their support and advice, in particular Mohamed Al Ansari, Thamer Al Sharam, Jehan Alagappan, Jason Anagnostopoulos, Koushik Banerjee, Angel Bright, Peter Downe, Ashraf Hafez, May Hashim, Vinod Kambrath, Lambros Karavis, Abhinav Khare, Anjali Khatwani, Sunitha Mamidi, Saima Mobeen Noor, Mark Ranford, Mohamed Thomson, Dr. Roger Vreugdenhil, Jabir Walji and Moataz Yousif.

James Creelman

1 Continuous Turbulent Times: The Case for Risk-Based Performance Management

To future economic historians, the Credit Crunch might be the defining moment that separates the industrial age from the networked, digitized (or whatever name that they assign to it) era we moved into in the early part of the 21st century.

The early 21st-century revolution

A revolution is taking place in how organizations are structured, do work and go to market, and how they are regulated and scrutinized and secure sustainable competitive advantage. The competitive, regulatory and business landscape that senior managers will be expected to make sense of, manage and master in, say, 2020, will bear little, if any, resemblance to the organizational world that that they entered in 1990 – when most took their fledgling career steps as junior managers. Along the way they have witnessed (and largely successfully internalized into their thinking and working practices) unparalleled and breathtaking change: a technology-fuelled social, economic, political and competitive upheaval that has been simply staggering in its size, scope and impact.

As one quite humorous illustration, in the early 1990s one of the authors of this book interviewed a manager from a hi-tech organization that was a pioneer user of email. The poor manager complained that on some days he received almost 20 emails and that, as a result, managing his time was becoming increasingly difficult. We wish!

Fast forward to December 2010 and a tragic illustration of how this simple exchange of a few emails served as the foundation stone for unimaginable developments in digital technologies that would connect and redefine the world. A desperate, frustrated young man burnt himself to death in Tunisia because of his inability to find work and in despair at his treatment by the local authorities. What a few years earlier would have been noticed by just a few people (and quickly forgotten about by all but his family and friends) quickly served as a catalyst for the so-called Arab Spring, a series of protests and rebellions across the Middle East that brought down long-established governments and seriously destabilized others, and at the time of writing was still a long way from completion.

It was the global reach and influence of social media that led to this story being told to the world, and the galvanizing of others in Tunisia and quickly thereafter across the region to demand changes to their own circumstances. Who would have foreseen YouTube and Facebook back in 1990 and who would have foreseen the Arab Spring in early December 2010? And who can imagine what the world will look like in 2020, still less in 2030, as a result of further developments in digital technologies?

And switching our attention to the world of business, who can imagine the day-to-day challenges and realities that senior managers will grapple with in 2030? Most extrapolations that we make today will be far removed from reality. What we can predict with certainty is that senior managers will be leading organizations and making decisions in what can best be described as "continuous turbulent times". We know this for a fact because they already are.

The Credit Crunch and ensuing recession, the Eurozone crisis and the US debt issue, as well as the Arab Spring, have proven beyond reasonable doubt the veracity of that statement. And such sudden and unexpected destabilizing events are likely little more than tasters of things to come as technological advances continue apace. To use the beginning of the cinema industry as a comparison: looking just a few decades ahead, the ICT capabilities then available for organizations and society generally might make today's technology appear as primitive as the technology required to make single reel movies in the early decades of the 20th century appears to today's cinematographers. The implications for individuals, society and economies are impossible to estimate with any reasonable expectation of accuracy.

New models for managing organizations: Introducing Risk-Based Performance Management

For business leaders, therefore, what are required are new models for managing organizations in this new economic landscape. Approaches are needed that enable the risks of doing business and prosecuting strategies in globalized and fully networked digital markets to be understood, managed and controlled, yet are simultaneously designed to exploit and gain competitive advantage from the myriad opportunities that this new world will offer and effectively manage the inherent risks in attempting to do so.

In this book we introduce Risk-Based Performance Management (RBPM) (Figure 1.1). RBPM represents a pioneering and powerful framework and methodology for enabling senior management teams to compete and survive in continuous turbulent times. RBPM embeds risk management into strategic and operational decision-making and positions risk appetite – the amount of risk that an organization is willing to take in pursuit of its strategic and operational objectives – as a central management and control tool. RBPM represents a practical results-focused methodology that enables executive teams to manage their organizations while operating within risk appetite.

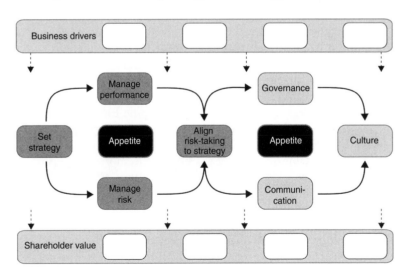

Figure 1.1 **The RBPM framework**

The RBPM framework describes a process from the capturing of the business drivers (the fundamental drivers of value of the particularly industry and organization) to the delivery of shareholder value.

Sequencing from the identification of the drivers of value to the delivery of shareholder value is through seven disciplines: Setting Strategy, Managing Performance, Managing Risk, Aligning Risk to Strategy, Governance, Culture and Communication; and an eighth (appetite) which serves as the glue that binds the others together into a unified strategy/risk management approach for these "continuous turbulent times". We do not label appetite a discipline as its influence weaves through the seven identified disciplines.

The RBPM disciplines are described within two interrelated circles.

The circle to the left (Figure 1.2) is about defining and then executing strategy (by managing performance and managing risk). Appetite sits at the heart of both circles. Aligning risk-taking to strategy is a core discipline of this circle but also serves as the linkage to the circle to the right.

The circle to the right (Figure 1.3) considers the "softer" disciplines of RBPM: Governance, Culture and Communication. By "softer" we mean there is a lack of established mechanisms/processes for managing these disciplines, which is not the case for the other four disciplines. Moreover, although supposedly softer, they are no less important. Indeed, failure of governance and communications and, perhaps more

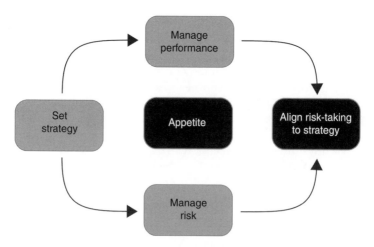

Figure 1.2 **The circle to the left of the RBPM framework**

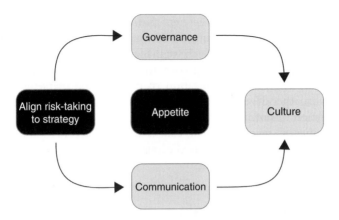

Figure 1.3   **The circle to the right of the RBPM framework**

importantly, culture is more likely than anything else to lead to the ignoring of risk appetite, the subsequent failure of risk management, and as a result, failure of the strategy. The RBPM framework delivers stronger governance at both the strategic (i.e., better tools and structures with which to manage the business) and cascaded levels through the RACI (responsible, accountable, consult, inform) model.

Chapter 2 is dedicated to fully describing the framework and methodology, Chapter 3 to explaining how it evolved from existing strategy and risk management frameworks, such as the Balanced Scorecard and the integrated Enterprise Risk Management Framework by the Committee of Sponsoring Organizations (COSO) of the Treadway Commission. The subsequent chapters explain how RBPM works in practice: describing how risk, and specifically risk appetite, is woven into the strategy formulation, execution and governance processes and how in applying the RBPM methodology, "softer areas" of culture and communication are powerful mechanisms to ensure that managers and staff are simultaneously strategy-focused and risk-aware, and so in the right shape to drive sustainable execution.

Learning from the past: The industrial revolution

But before we delve deeply into the disciplines of the RBPM approach, we should pause to reflect on how we got here. Doing so will provide insights into why strategy management is more important than it has ever been before and how the risks that organizations face today are also measurably more pressing – and therefore why we must rethink the central frameworks by which we manage organizations.

We will begin by stepping back to the late 18th century when, within the UK, the mechanization of parts of the textile industries along with other developments such as iron-making techniques and the introduction of canals and other transportation enhancements ushered in the industrial revolution. This catalysed the transformation from the 10,000-year-old agriculture-based economy toward one dominated by machine-based manufacturing.

The impact of Taylorism

However, the term "revolution" is something of a misnomer. What began in about 1775 was still unfolding in the early years of the 20th century, when a new work "revolutionized" approaches to working in industrial-age economies. The work was Fredrick W. Taylor's 1911 monograph *Principles of Scientific Management*,[1] which applied standard approaches to work methods along with detailed instructions for completing the required tasks and output-based incentives for workers.

Although Taylor's approach to work proved enormously successful, as demonstrated by enthusiastic adopters such as the Ford Motor Company, the rigidity of the approach meant that workers were explicitly proscribed from contributing ideas on how to improve the performance of their processes, in particular or the organization more generally. Managers had brains, workers did not. As a result factory floor workers found their work monotonous and skill-reducing and they became emotionally dissociated from the organizations for which they toiled. There's a compelling case for arguing that the shocking state of industrial relations in the West during the 1960s and 1970s can be laid at the door of *Principles of Scientific Management*, despite the undoubted benefits it brought to the efficiency of production. Taylor's principles (or Taylorism) remained the standard approach to management and production for most (in the West at least) for the duration of the 20th century. But for the bulk of the time Taylor's principles were deployed by organizations that operated in an economic landscape where competitors were few (even in industries significantly more mature than the manufacture of automobiles) and where customers were identifiable, local and generally loyal. Compare that environment with the one experienced by most organizations today.

Total quality management

In the latter part of the last century a new approach to running organizations emerged that had a profound effect on the management of manufacturing and other production processes, and later those that are more service related: Total Quality Management (TQM) and most notably the theories of the TQM "Gurus" Dr. Joseph M. Juran and Dr. W. Edwards Deming; although Deming, for one, never used the term "TQM".

Both Juran and Deming made their names by helping to rebuild the industrial capabilities in the economically devastated post-Second World War Japan. Juran (who died in 2008, aged 104) was one of the first to think about the cost of poor quality. This was illustrated by his "Juran trilogy", an approach to cross-functional management, which is composed of three managerial processes: quality planning, quality control and quality improvement. Without change, he claimed, there will be constant waste; during change there will be increased costs, but after the improvement, margins will be higher and the increased costs get recouped.

The theories of Deming (who himself lived to 93, dying in 1993) were encapsulated in his 14 points of management that, from one angle, went a long way to righting some of the more negative effects of *Principles of Scientific Management.*

Deming's points differed sharply from Taylor's principles in many ways. For starters, while Taylor put so much faith in the abilities of managers, Deming proclaimed that more than 90% of work problems were the fault of management, as did Juran. Whereas Taylor reduced the workers' role to completing routine, standardized and often mind-numbingly boring tasks, Deming urged the removal of barriers that prevented workers from taking pride in their workmanship. Where Taylor urged strict silo-working, Deming called for the breaking down of barriers between departments. Even more challenging to the Taylor school, Deming called for the elimination of numerical quotas or work standards. "Quotas take into account only numbers, not quality or methods. They are usually a guarantee of inefficiency and high cost," his points stated. Deming also argued against widespread usage of incentive compensation, and appraisals for that matter, on the grounds that there were too many variables in an individual's performance to make any measurement statistically reliable.

In the next section we discuss the knowledge age. Note the prediction of Deming in one of his points, Encourage Education: "Institute a vigorous program of education, and encourage self-improvement for everyone. What an organization needs is not just good people; it needs people that are improving with education. Advances in competitive position will have their roots in knowledge." In his own final years, Deming began to align his theories with the new challenges of the "knowledge age". This was appropriate, as a central Deming teaching was focused on "profound knowledge", which comprises four interrelated components: appreciation of a system; knowledge about variation; theory of knowledge; and knowledge about the psychology of change, all of which are still relevant today (and perhaps more so than ever).

Finally, the very first of Deming's points resonates with some of the key challenges we will have in competing in the 21st century. This point is Constancy of Purpose: "Create constancy of purpose for continual improvement of products and service to society, allocating resources to provide for long range needs rather than only short term profitability, with a plan to become competitive, to stay in business, and to provide jobs."[2]

To an extent, the theories of Juran and Deming led to a fundamental reshaping of the global competitive landscape. In the late 1970s and throughout the 1980s, organizations in the US eagerly grabbed hold of the promise of TQM for one simple reason: as a consequence of the successful penetration of their markets by Japanese suppliers, they were facing market extinction. The Japanese, of course, were armed with the principles of Juran, Deming and others. Famously, in the late 1970s the giant Xerox Corporation was shocked to discover that a Japanese competitor could sell photocopiers more cheaply than it cost them to manufacture. Xerox became an early adopter and champion of TQM. Just as famously, Deming said that "Change is not necessary. Survival is optional." So to survive, Xerox and other Western organizations chose to change. The popularity of TQM led to the creation of the Malcolm Baldrige model in the US (launched in 1987) and the European Foundation for Quality Management (EFQM) Excellence model (1992) as mechanisms to instil TQM into Western organizations and share best practices. As with the Balanced Scorecard – which we discuss in detail within this book as a primary influence in the RBPM approach – the models' premise is that success against non-financial enablers leads to successful non-financial and financial results. The Malcolm Baldrige model is shown in Figure 1.4, while the EFQM model is shown in Figure 1.5.

It might be argued that TQM was a solution to the challenges facing Western organization in the dying years of the industrial age. This was

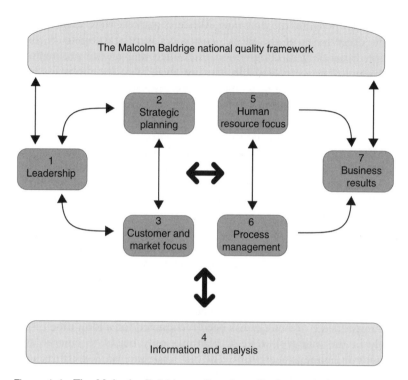

Figure 1.4 **The Malcolm Baldrige national quality framework**

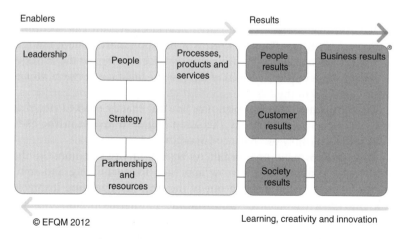

Figure 1.5 **The EFQM excellence model**

a period when, for the first time, Western markets were under attack from other parts of the globe, customers were starting to become more demanding as competition intensified and choice proliferated, and employees were gradually moving away from the "jobs for life" mentality and beginning to move more regularly between organizations, either for betterment of salary, career development or because they simply were no longer willing to work for an organization they did not respect and that treated them in ways encouraged by Taylorism.

Although a greater risk profile than that faced by companies earlier in the century, it was still nothing like what organizations face today. Although there were international companies, few if any in the 1980s and 1990s could be truly called global and, of course, the technology that would connect and network the world was still in its infancy; we were just beginning to witness sharing of information, data and insights through floppy disks, for instance, followed by the extraordinary phenomena of 20 emails in a day!

Throughout the 20th century and the golden years of Taylor, Deming and Juran, how strategy management and risk management were viewed and positioned was very different from today. Although the importance of strategy has been recognized for a long time (especially in the military) strategic planning only began to emerge as a serious discipline in the 1960s. The first strategic planning efforts were very much in keeping with industrial-age thinking, explained Professor Henry Mintzberg in a 1994 *Harvard Business Review* article:

> the scientific management pioneered by Frederick Taylor...separated thinking from doing and [created] a new function staffed by specialists, Strategic Planners. Planning systems were expected to produce the best strategies as well as step-by-step instructions for carrying out the strategies so that the doers, the managers of the business could not get them wrong.

He went on to say that planning has not exactly worked out that way.[3] Frameworks for strategy execution began to appear in the early 1990s, most notably the Balanced Scorecard.

Risk management first began to appear in organizations in the 1940s and 1950s with a narrow approach to quantifying and mitigating financial risks, evolving out of the work in managing insurable risk. Enterprise risk management, which includes risks in other business areas such as legal, operational and strategic, only began to properly emerge in the first decade of this century, largely as a consequence of large corporate scandals (see Chapter 3).

The knowledge or digital age

The final years of the "TQM era" took place during the early years of the knowledge age. If the agricultural age lasted for around 10,000 years and the industrial age about 200, the knowledge age has been with us for little more than 20. And during these two decades, the concepts of strategy and risk have taken on a completely new meaning.

Earlier in the chapter we spoke of the digital world in which we now live – where at the click of a button, and at the speed of light, information and potentially market-moving insights can be shared with as many people you wish within as many countries as you wish, and where networked collaboration is a working norm. Capturing and codifying such knowledge exchange is a challenge and not doing so a risk; keeping the brightest and best staff is a challenge and a risk in a global marketplace that is rapaciously seeking talent and where high performers are generally very visible on online groups such as LinkedIn and other such networked communities; and where sudden market movement, as a consequence of this knowledge exchange, is a challenge to organizational survival and therefore a risk that simply must be recognized and closely managed. Of course this knowledge exchange is occurring in a global landscape, which brings with it many risks – and therefore threats and/or opportunities.

Globalization

Globalized working has massive implications for how organizations compete and go to market and has already greatly changed the economic and competitive landscape. The 2009 report *The Finance Function: Achieving Global Excellence in a Global Economy*, written by one of the authors of this book, explored how globalization was transforming the work and structure of finance functions, but also analysed the implications for organizations more generally. The author noted:

> [The] shift in globalization from a relatively narrow manufacturing focus to new ways of thinking about where virtually every kind of work can be done ... has been enabled by the rapid development in the capabilities of information and communications technologies (in particular web-based), integrated Enterprise Resource Planning applications and workflow technologies. This has opened the way for a wide range of information work

to be carried out anywhere there is access to a suitable communications network. The age of location-independent working has arrived.

Interviewed for the report, and in response to a question regarding the negative reputation globalization has with many in the West, especially the offshoring of support function processes, Michel Janssen, Chief Research Officer at the US-headquartered benchmarking specialist, The Hackett Group, stated bluntly: "How many times have we changed the economy over the last few hundred years? Moving from an agrarian to an industrial economy caused big change and resistance from those that were affected by the upheaval." There's nothing different now, he says. "The economy is changing. It is becoming a global marketplace. Technology can move work 10,000 miles away – companies and individuals have to think global and not local."[4]

Janssen's comments are supported by figures in the 2008 report *Globalization and the Changing UN Economy* by the UK's Department for Business Enterprise and Regulatory Reform. The report noted that there has been a more than threefold increase in the world's stock of inward Foreign Direct Investment (FDI), from $3,083,106 million to $11,998,838 million between 1996 and 2006.

The report explained that not only has the total stock of inward FDI increased greatly, the direction and nature of FDI have also changed in the recent past, with developing and emerging economies now far more important in terms of FDI inflows than they were previously, with significant amounts of capital flowing from capital-abundant industrialized countries to a few developing countries, helping build up the latter's production and trade capabilities.

> These figures ... have partly been driven by the relatively recent emergence of global value chains – whereby firms locate different parts of the production process in different countries according to relative cost structures. The development of global value chains has been facilitated by technological progress which has made it easier to supply services remotely, to modularize production activities and manage them remotely and has resulted in a massive increase in cross-border trade in intermediates and business services.

> The emergence of global value chains is, in turn, associated with offshoring, which involves firms selecting and holding on to the stages in the value chain that they consider to be 'core', while relocating the firm's 'non-core' activities to foreign countries or to third parties in foreign countries.[5]

But note: China, and this also holds true for India, has not simply sat back to offer rich pickings for overseas companies. Rather, each has used incoming expertise and money to build powerful indigenous businesses that have then gone out to compete in Western markets. For instance, consider China. In the 2011 Financial Times Global 500 Index, three of the seven biggest companies in the world according to market capitalization were from China: PetroChina (2nd), Industrial and Commercial Bank of China (6th) and China Construction Group (7th). As an indication of what this means, US-headquartered global giants Microsoft came in just 10th and General Electric 11th, both behind the 5th place Brazilian company Petrobras. For reference, ExxonMobil ranked first. It is also notable that 19 of the 53 new entries to the Global 500 came from Asia.[6]

The 2010 report *The New Economic World Order* by BDO expanded on this story of the switch in power:

> A change is indeed happening that has profound implications for the economic influence of the wealthiest countries. As the capabilities of countries such as China and India grow to match their capacities, they are beginning to develop much more economic muscle in relation to the United States, Europe and other traditional centres of economic influence.

The numbers noted by the report are startling and of concern to the West when added to the cited FT figures. For instance, China sat on foreign exchange reserves of $2.4 trillion at the end of 2009, a gain of $453 billion in just one year. By comparison the total foreign exchange reserve of the 27 countries of the European Union was just $648 billion. The increase in China's reserves across the year was higher than the total reserves of all but one nation, Japan ($1.074 trillion). The reserves of the US, the world's erstwhile supreme economic superpower, came in at $84.4 billion.

The report went on to say that by 2020 China's nominal GDP will likely surpass that of the US, thereby ending over a century of US economic hegemony. Also noted was a report by the consultancy McKinsey & Co., which stated that India's manufacturing exports will increase to $300 billion by 2015, creating 25–30 million new jobs in the manufacturing domain and adding 1% to India's annual GDP growth rate. Table 1.1 illustrates the changing nature of national power up to 2030.

The New Economic World Order report concluded that:

> If the old world order was a hegemony led by the United States, the new world order will not best be described as hegemony at all. Rather it will be an order characterized by balance between an increasing number of centres

Table 1.1 The global GDP share of the big four economies (at purchasing power parities)

% of world GDP	2000	2010	2020	2030
US	23	20	17	16
EU	25	21	18	15
China	7	13	18	19
India	3	5	7	9
Total (big 4)	58	59	60	59

Source: The World Bank.

of influence. Sustainable success will be achieved by those able to recognize and adjust to a new world order with many centres of influence. The new world order means change for all of us, economically, socially, politically. Success will come soonest to those who change the quickest.[7]

"Change the quickest", yes. But just imagine the strategic agility and excellence in risk management required to take full advantage of the opportunities and negate the threats as organizations from old and new economies collide in highly competitive global marketplaces. If we can argue that to succeed requires new ways to manage performance and that this is about integrating strategy and risk, the story that we now unfold makes an even stronger case.

The Credit Crunch

So far in this overview of how working and economic dynamics are transforming to cope with a new global reality, we have not touched on the Credit Crunch and the ensuing economic meltdown, the long-term consequences of which are still uncertain. The BDO report *Insights into the Post Recession Business Environment* painted a picture of the future which certainly resonates with our argument that we live in "continuous turbulent times". "The forces driving change will continue well beyond the technical end of the recession and the consequences will be permanent and far reaching," the report predicted. "The recession will mark a series of transitions from the industrial structures and models of the past to the digital, networked age of the future. We are living through a dramatic period of creative destruction as a result of which many organizations will either transform or disappear."[8]

This is an interesting comment. To future economic historians, the Credit Crunch might be the defining moment that separates the industrial age from the networked, digitized (or whatever name they assign to it) era we moved into in the early part of the 21st century. And there is also a veritable avalanche of lessons we can learn from the global catastrophe called the Credit Crunch.

So what lessons can we learn? On one level the lessons are still unfolding. Despite the billions of words already published in books, journals and newspapers on the causes of the Credit Crunch and even more expended on blogs and other such information-sharing mechanisms, we might need billions more again before we get a definitive and generally accepted answer – if we ever achieve such a thing.

That said, on a simple level the Credit Crunch causes are easy to explain. It was a consequence of the collapse of the sub-prime lending market in the US, most influentially sub-prime mortgages.

The impact of sub-prime lending

Sub-prime lending became popular in the US in the mid-1990s, with outstanding personal debt increasing from $33 billion in 1993 to $332 billion in 2003. As of December 2007, there was an estimated $1.3 trillion in sub-prime mortgages outstanding. Of all mortgages that originated in 2006, 20% were considered to be sub-prime. A high percentage of these sub-prime mortgages, over 90% in 2006 for example, were adjustable-rate mortgages, through which the initial interest rate is normally fixed for a period of time after which it is reset periodically (often monthly) according to various benchmarks. The original rate is often much lower than the eventual rate that will be paid.

Overall, US households had become increasingly indebted, with the ratio of debt to disposable personal income rising from 77% in 1990 to 127% at the end of 2007, much of this increase mortgage related.

Now the banks were largely unconcerned about the substantially increased risk of default. Lenders realized that they could make hefty profits from origination fees, bundling mortgages into securities and selling these securities to investors. These structures produced bonds that yielded higher than other available investment opportunities, thus making them attractive. They also carried strong credit ratings from "reputable" credit ratings agencies.

The general belief was that securitizing allowed banks to simultaneously sell on the risk and replenish their capital. Ultimately, the mortgage-backed securities industry provided lenders with more cash to make more mortgage loans. This steady supply of mortgage funds kept mortgage rates competitive and mortgages readily available. Other loans to the sub-prime market were financed through similar security-backed systems. This "water-tight" protection was seemingly reinforced by fast rising house prices: if a mortgage holder defaulted, all the banks had to do was repossess and resell – simple. Everything seemed in control and many in the financial services made a great deal of money in the process, apparently with minimal risk. The champagne flowed.

Then the unimaginable happened. US house prices began to decline in 2006. As many borrowers realized that the value of their homes was less than the amount they owed they began to default on their loans, especially when the low-interest fixed term rates expired and reverted to rates they could not afford. This destroyed the value of mortgage-backed securities, forcing companies to take write-downs and write-offs; a downward cycle that led to the complete meltdown of the market, with an avalanche of unsaleable houses entering the market.

With investors deciding to invest in more stable assets such as Treasury securities, the collapse led to a massive reduction on the money available to banks to lend.

To compound an already bad situation, as banks began to post huge losses they became nervous about lending to each other (interbank lending in the US and Europe was critical for keeping the flow of credit circulating amongst banks, and hence among almost all economic agents in a market system). The world's major interbank lending markets froze. Some banks were basing the funding of their loan portfolio – overdrafts and commercial loans – on sourcing funds from these money markets as opposed to more stable sources such as retail deposits (savings and current accounts). Banks that were overly reliant on the interbank market started failing. This is what happened to the UK bank Northern Rock, which failed in September 2007 and was thus an early casualty of the Credit Crunch (it is now owned by Virgin Money). The UK's Royal Bank of Scotland was an even bigger casualty, as we explain in Chapter 4.

The lack of trust in the financial sector was so acute as to almost completely seize up credit flows and threaten the stability of the world financial system.

On a more complex level, we argue that there was a direct relationship between the Credit Crunch and the failures of financial service organizations to manage strategy and risk – and in particular the understanding of and proper management of risk appetite. Too many organizations were content with a "follow me" strategy; that is, follow the dominant industry model/approach and the ingrained discipline of focusing only on the next quarterly results, rather than think about strategic differentials such as positioning and building competitive advantage. And as we stress throughout this book, they essentially failed to understand the risks that they were taking with the dominant business model, which was essentially based on sub-prime lending. It has also been argued by many that organizational boards of directors, as well as regulators, were negligent in their oversight/governance roles – this is something that we shall return to later in the book.

Avoiding a great depression

To avert the first great depression since the 1930s – and given the networked nature of the world, perhaps a much worse one, with unthinkable social, economic and political consequences – coordinated action by large numbers of central banks and countries was carried out to regain a semblance of stability. This involved giving widespread promises of state protection to depositors, large injections of capital to banks, vast liquidity supplies to financial markets and increasing guarantees of short term bond issues. By as early as October 2008 the US had committed $1.5 trillion in loans and investments to its banking sector. It had also guaranteed another $3.6 trillion investments and deposits, not including $620 billion in currency swaps with other central banks. As of 2009, the IMF estimated that the global Credit Crunch had cost governments more than $10 trillion.[9]

And the story is still unfolding. The massive European Union bailout of countries such as Ireland, Portugal and Greece is proving a massive drain on central purses. As of August 2012 the combined lending ceiling for bailout funds stood at €940 billion.

The "psychology of denial"

In reviewing the basic causes of the Credit Crunch, it seems somewhat astonishing that nobody saw it coming. It appears such a blindingly obvious failure of basic risk management. Indeed, during a visit to the prestigious London School of Economics (LSE) in late 2008, the UK's Queen Elizabeth II asked LSE Professor Luis Garicano a simple question about the Credit Crunch and ensuing recession. "How come nobody could foresee it?" Her Majesty apparently asked. A group of eminent economists and historians then got together to ponder the question. Later, in a three-page missive, they provided their explanation to the Queen.

The letter told of the "psychology of denial" that gripped the financial and political world in the run-up to the crisis. The letter explained that as low interest rates made borrowing cheap, the "feel good factor" masked how out-of-kilter the world economy had become beneath the surface, with some countries, such as the US, running up enormous debts by borrowing from others, including China and the oil-rich Middle Eastern states, that were sitting on vast piles of cash.

Despite these yawning imbalances, they say, "financial wizards" managed to convince themselves and the world's politicians that they had found clever ways to spread risk throughout financial markets. But, the authors continued: "It is difficult to recall a greater example of wishful thinking combined with hubris."

The signatories went on to say that "everyone seemed to be doing their own job properly on its own merit. And according to standard measures of success, they were often doing it well", but, they added, "The failure was to see how collectively this added up to a series of interconnected imbalances over which no single authority had jurisdiction."

"In summary, Your Majesty," they concluded,

> the failure to foresee the timing, extent and severity of the crisis and to head it off, while it had many causes, was principally a failure of the collective imagination of many bright people, both in this country and internationally, to understand the risks to the system as a whole.[10]

The failure of risk management

So let's consider in more detail this failure of risk management: failures that the RBPM approach sets out to overcome.

Firstly, it should be noted that many of the financial institutions that collapsed as a consequence of the Credit Crunch firmly believed that they had robust risk management systems in their organizations: much of the pioneering and so-called best practice work in risk management before the Credit Crunch was taking place within the financial services sector. Indeed, note that the Economist Intelligence Unit's (a highly esteemed research body) 2007 report *Best Practice in Risk*

Management: A Function Comes of Age stated that respondents to their Risk Barometer (which tracked change in corporate attitudes to risk management) considered credit risk and foreign-exchange risk to be very low on their list of priorities due to the continuing innovation that had taken place in financial risk management. It stated that there had been "significant development in the tools to manage these more quantifiable risks, with many companies adopting hedging strategies to protect against risks such as credit defaults or swings in currency rates".[11]

Risk management, in particular financial risk management, was to all extent and purposes "sorted". It's difficult to think of another belief that was so far from the truth. Then again, the IMF Global Financial Stability Report in April 2006 comes pretty close:

> There is growing recognition that the dispersion of credit risk by banks to a broader and more diverse group of investors, rather than warehousing such risk on their balance sheets, has helped make the banking and overall financial system more resilient.
>
> The improved resilience may be seen in fewer bank failures and more consistent credit provision. Consequently the commercial banks may be less vulnerable today to credit or economic shocks.[12]

So how did a respected publication and a body as eminent as the IMF, no less, get things so wrong? What did they miss?

One early analysis of the causes of the Credit Crunch was provided in 2008 by the US Association of Chartered Certified Accountants (ACCA) in their policy paper *Climbing Out of the Credit Crunch*. They maintained that the principal causes could be distilled into five key areas:

▷ Corporate governance
▷ Remuneration and incentives
▷ Risk identification and management
▷ Accounting and financial reporting
▷ Regulation

The ACCA recommended that practices in all these areas had to change to avoid future failures. They claimed that a systematic failure by boards to provide strategic oversight and direction, to ensure a strong control environment and to challenge the executive appeared to have been inadequately discharged. Moreover, remuneration and incentive packages encouraged short-term thinking. "We need to ask what inhibited banks' boards from asking the right questions and understanding the risks that were being run by their managements," the report's authors stated.

The report concluded that "The financial industry and all involved in it needs to learn the hard lessons from the past year and be bold enough to make the changes needed to climb out of the Credit Crunch – and make sure the mistakes we have made are not repeated."[13]

Poor understanding of risk appetite and risk profiles

As a further analysis of the causes of the Credit Crunch, the 2009 white paper *Risk Management is Dead . . . Long Live Risk Management*, the Business Continuity Institute (BCI) made the useful observation that lessons from the Credit Crunch did not just apply to financial services:

> Although the catalyst to re-examine Risk Management practices has been the financial crisis, similar problems have been seen at other companies in different sectors. Moreover given the finance sector forms a part of any market economy's critical national infrastructure, any financial crisis will have an impact on organizations in other sectors manifesting itself in the form of the withdrawal of insurance for credit lines or reduced access to capital to fund the business. Loss of access to funding and insurance, arguably akin to a supply chain failure, can now be added to the threat register alongside the loss of IT, facilities and people.

Risk and business strategy

There is one statement within the BCI report – by Lord Turner, Chairman of the UK's Financial Services Authority – that we not only agree with, but have made central to the arguments that we make and the solutions that we outline within this book: "The failure to properly evaluate and challenge risk of overall business strategies was probably the biggest intellectual failure of boards, regulators and shareholders."[14]

In the same vein, recent developments within the UK Corporate Governance Code 2010, which is the primary set of corporate governance principles applicable to listed companies in the UK, are noteworthy. Responsibility for the oversight of the Code lies with the Financial Reporting Council (FRC).

In 2010, the FRC noted that there had previously been a gap in the requirement for boards to report on business strategy. Therefore, companies are now required to explain in their annual report the basis on which the company generates or preserves value over the longer term (the business model) and the strategy for delivering the objectives of the company.

The FRC has said that, with hindsight, it believes that the absence of a provision allocating the management of risk from the previous Code was a significant omission. As such, the Code now contains a provision that the board is responsible for determining the nature and extent of the significant risks (its risk appetite) that it is willing to take in achieving its strategic objectives. In managing risk, the board should maintain sound risk management and internal control systems, the FRC noted.[15]

Conclusion: Integrating strategy and risk

The above statement underpins a core message of this book. Given that organizations today compete and go to market in continuously unstable markets (as befitting continuous turbulent times) risk can no longer be divorced from strategy. No matter how well thought out a corporate strategy might be, it can be not just derailed but rendered completely worthless if the multitude of risks inherent in the pursuit of those strategic goals are not fully captured and mitigated, be they financial, reputational, political or geographic, the management of global supply chains or due to sudden changes in markets or customer offerings, or any of the many other risk dimensions that might be applicable.

It is safe to claim that underlying all of the myriad contributing factors, the main reason for the Credit Crunch was a failure by financial services organizations to develop and execute sustainable strategies that fully considered their risk environment, and their failure to embed risk management at the heart of their strategic and operational processes. The Royal Bank of Scotland case study in Chapter 4 makes this point well: a seemingly hugely successful strategy was found to be fatally flawed as a result of a failure to integrate risk into the organization's strategic and operational processes, and more fundamentally perhaps, a complete disregard for risk appetite.

Risk appetite – which we define as "the amount and type of risk that an organization is willing to accept, and must take, to achieve their strategic objectives and therefore create value for shareholders and other stakeholders" – is placed at the centre of the RBPM framework; a model that fully integrates risk management with strategy management and so goes a long way to fulfilling the recommendations of the various reports and thought leaders quoted above and throughout this book.

In essence we explain that in these continuous turbulent times it is no longer appropriate to focus on performance and risk in isolation from each other. As broadly described in the RBPM framework and methodology in the following chapter, and then elaborated on throughout the rest of the book, to drive sustainable strategic and operational execution organizations must integrate performance and risk management through the lens of risk appetite. For many organizational leaders this requires nothing less a paradigm shift in how they view and manage their organizations. What that paradigm shift looks like, we now begin to explain.

2 Risk-Based Performance Management: An Explanation of This New Strategic Paradigm

The Risk-Based Performance Management framework and methodology provides organizations with an integrated strategy and risk management approach which places risk, and specifically risk appetite, at the core of strategy execution.

Shifting paradigms

Many lessons have emerged from the Credit Crunch and ensuing economic crisis; at the time of writing they are still emerging, and are likely to do so for many years to come. There are lessons for governments, regulators, organizations and indeed citizens (let us not forget that irresponsible lending could only take place if there was an equal appetite for irresponsible borrowing). To what extent these unfolding lessons will be heeded has yet to be seen.

It is not within the scope of this book to proffer solutions to governments, regulators or citizens, although we will touch on the responsibilities of the first two. Our focus is almost wholly on assisting organizations to make sense of, and compete effectively within, a globalized 21st-century landscape that is very different to that of the previous century. As we stated in Chapter 1, to future economic historians the Credit Crunch might be the defining moment that separated the industrial age from the networked, digitized (or whatever name they assign to it) era we moved into in the early part of the 21st century: an era that can certainly be described as "continuous turbulent times".

Restructuring the relationship with risk management

Of the multitude of lessons that organizations must heed and integrate, none is more important than the need to be substantially better than they have ever been before in risk management, simply because the management of risk is much more strategically important than it has ever been before. But this is not just a matter of putting in place more robust risk management capabilities, however important that might be. It could be reasonably argued that prior to the Credit Crunch many organizations, in particular those from the financial services sector, had already put in place such capabilities – however incomplete and inadequate they subsequently proved to be.

What is required is a fundamental restructuring of an organization's relationship with risk management and how risk is positioned within their strategic management processes and their day-to-day operational actions. Risk must be fully understood within a strategic context; a link that historically has been made tenuously, or not at all in most cases. What is required is nothing short of a paradigm shift in how organizations are managed.

This might be easier said than done, particularly for the financial services sector that bore the brunt of the Credit Crunch and then, as we are all acutely aware, passed on that pain to many other industries, sectors, governments and citizens of many parts of the world. To explain, in May 2012 JP Morgan Chase reported a $2 billion trading loss through irresponsible derivative trading (total losses would eventually be reported at around $6 billion). According to Chief Executive Officer Jamie Dimon this was the result of a "terrible, egregious mistake" in a unit that managed risk, adding that "in hindsight, we took far too much risk. The strategy we had was badly vetted. It was badly monitored. It should never have happened." Dimon had told analysts just a month earlier that all was fine within that unit.[1]

What is particularly alarming is that JP Morgan Chase was seen by many as a beacon of good risk management practices. After all, they emerged virtually unscathed from the Credit Crunch, mostly because of their apparent excellence in risk management, or so we were led to believe. If an organization such as JP Morgan Chase can fall victim to poor risk management in this post-Credit Crunch, risk-sensitive world, it doesn't bode well for the rest of the sector. And it doesn't imbue weary governments and citizens with a sense that we have learnt any lessons from the Credit Crunch and that such an event is unlikely to happen again.

RBPM: Integrating strategy and risk for the 21st century

The RBPM framework and methodology provides organizations with an integrated strategy and risk management approach which places risk, and specifically risk appetite, at the core of strategy execution (Figure 2.1).

It is the emphasis on risk appetite that makes RBPM particularly appropriate for managing in "continuous turbulent times" and ensuring the lessons of the Credit Crunch are heeded. Bringing strategy and risk closer together is right and proper and fundamentally important, but it is working within the parameters of appetite – the amount and type of risk that an organization is willing to take in pursuit of its strategic objectives – that will enable organizations to both establish the controls and inculcate the agility that are required in today's markets.

Although risk appetite is the central pivot of the RBPM framework and methodology, the approach is essentially a strategic management methodology, *not* a risk management solution. The RBPM methodology begins with formulation of strategy, and in execution enables organizations to align risk-taking to strategy to drive sustainable strategic execution.

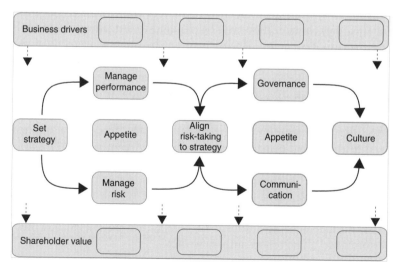

Figure 2.1   **The RBPM framework**

UK financial services study

The RBPM approach developed as a result of a series of performance and risk management related projects completed by Andrew Smart – the architect of RBPM – with UK-based clients of his consultancy Manigent, particularly within the financial services industry. Influential in the development of the methodology was a year-long academic research project involving 21 financial services organizations in the city of London during 2006–2007 (and so preceding the Credit Crunch – just). The study was predicated on one question: how can UK financial services organizations integrate and align their corporate performance management and operational risk management processes to enhance strategic execution?

During the study, primary data were collected using semi-structured interviews with influential managers within these 21 organizations and was complemented by a comprehensive literature review of current and best practices. To answer the study's guiding question, the analysis considered six performance dimensions. These are listed in Table 2.1, which includes a flavour of the key findings.[2]

So the pre-Credit Crunch Manigent study strongly suggested a need to rethink risk management and, especially, its integration into strategy, although ensuring we don't face a major Credit Crunch again – at least one of the size and intensity of 2008–2009 – will require multiple interventions, from governments, regulators and organizations alike. For their part, organizations will be required to fundamentally restructure their understanding of what is meant by the management of risk in these early decades of the 21st century.

The emergence of the Risk Master

What that restructuring is starting to look like was neatly summarized in the global management consultancy Accenture's *2011 Global Risk Management Study,* a quantitative survey of 397 C-level executives with risk management responsibilities, for which it gave the insightful subtitle (as it points to the upside of risk management as well as the downside, which is something we strongly recommend), "Risk management as a source of competitive advantage and high performance". The report authors wrote:

At its best, risk management is a matter of balance – the balance between company's appetite for risks and its ability to manage them.

Table 2.1 Performance dimensions of Manigent Financial Services study

Dimension	Sample key findings
Structure	• Silo processes existed. • There was a lack of clarify as to the right focus for risk management and Compliance functions.
Strategy	• Improvement efforts were largely reactive and driven by individual regulatory requirements. • Organizations were not taking a strategic view.
Systems	• There was a lack of use of the Balanced Scorecard. • A tactical indicator-driven approach dominated.
Shared values	• A significant challenge existed in embedding operational risk into the culture and the day-to-day decision-making processes.
Style	• A lack of maturity surrounded Corporate Performance Management (CPM) and Organizational Risk Management (ORM). • Organizations were suffering from data, data and more data (what we would now call the Big Data issue).
Staff	• Linking compensation to CPM and/or ORM indicators was a significant challenge.

An advanced risk management capability includes the ability to understand and manage ... "risk-bearing capacity" – a company's capacity to take on new opportunities (which by definition will include a share of risk), as well as its ability to withstand the economic shocks should those risks become issues. Neither too cautious nor too reckless, the best companies use their risk management capabilities to adjust either their capacity or their appetite to make more prudent – and ultimately successful – investment decisions.

In line with the thinking that informed the development of the RBPM approach, this statement places risk appetite at the centre of an organization's approach to competition and its success. Aligning with another core argument of RBPM, the Accenture authors also noted the critical important of integrating risk with strategy: "risk management at the top-performing companies is now more closely integrated with strategic planning and is conducted proactively, with an eye on how such capabilities might help a company move into new markets faster or pursue other evolving growth strategies."

Based on survey findings, Accenture described the characteristics of what they called "Risk Masters" (representing about 10% of their surveyed universe).

Look to create shareholder value from risk management

Risk Managers are adept at creating processes and mechanisms that link risk to business performance, Accenture noted. Almost two-thirds of Risk Masters (64%) indicate that their risk management capabilities provide competitive advantage to a great extent, compared with only 42% of the peer group (those not classified as Risk Masters).

Involve the risk organization in key decision-making processes

Risk Masters make sure that the risk function is included in activities such as strategic planning, objective setting and incentives, financing decisions and performance management processes. As one example, 79% of Risk Masters say their risk function is involved to a great extent in strategic planning, compared with only 46% of non-Risk Masters.

Improve the sophistication of measurement, modelling and analytics to anticipate risks in an increasingly complex environment

Risk Masters go beyond a compliance mindset of risk management to deliver more complete business solutions that drive competitive differentiation. As examples, 90% of Risk Masters measure strategic risks, compared with just 63% of peers; 95% measure business risks, compared with 70% of non-Risk Masters.

Integrate risk management capabilities across business units and organizational structures

Risk Masters excel at the integration required for effective risk management, something that requires a commitment to evolving organizational capabilities over a multi-year programme of change. For example, whereas 63% of Risk Masters state that strategic risks are highly integrated into the decision-making process, this falls to just 37% for the peer group.

Establish a dedicated, C-level risk executive with oversight and visibility across the business

Top performers separate themselves from the pack by having in place a dedicated risk executive with sufficient visibility and leverage to influence risk management capabilities across the entire organization. Risk Masters are more likely to have risk management owned by a Chief Risk Officer (CRO) – 55% compared to 43% among the peer group. Risk Masters are also more likely to have a risk executive with the CRO title (81% versus 62%).

Infuse risk awareness across the organizational culture

Risk Masters put in place mechanisms to create and distribute more broadly across the organization an awareness of risk exposure, detailed training and the means to mitigate risks. Whereas 69% of Risk Masters are actively infusing a risk culture into the organization, this falls to 36% for the peer group.

Invest in continuous improvement

Risk Masters recognize that risk management is an ongoing, evolving capability; that the world changes rapidly and so companies must be nimble in terms of staying ahead of the curve when it comes to meeting the risks and challenges ahead and, of course, capitalizing on emerging opportunities. For example, 64% of Risk Masters are at work on better analytics and risk modelling capabilities, while only 47% of non-Risk Masters have such plans.

Risk Masters – summary

The authors summarize Risk Masters this way:

> They apply risk management capabilities across the enterprise effectively to mitigate risk and also to drive competitive advantage. The Risk Masters include risk in the decision-making processes of the organization across strategy, capital planning and performance management. In doing so, these companies fully integrate their risk organization into business operations, establishing risk policies based on their appetite for risk, and they delineate processes for managing risks which are communicated across the

enterprise. These activities are underpinned with robust analytic capabilities that support efficient compliance processes and provide strategic insight.[3]

Critical capabilities – The experts' consensus

The Accenture findings are similar to a number of other useful studies that have been published since the Credit Crunch, many of which we refer to within this book. Although each of these puts a slightly different spin on the story, what is compellingly evident from an analysis across these works is that there is near unanimity in identifying the critical capabilities that organizations must master as they evolve their risk management solutions: consensus as to what it takes to be a Risk Master, if you will.

1   Organizations must fully understand their appetite for risk: that is, how much risk they have to, or are willing to take in pursuit of their strategic goals.
2   Risk management has to be fully integrated into, and supportive of, the strategy management process; from planning, through execution to learning.
3   Risk management has to be fully integrated into the operations of the organization.
4   Risk management is as much about capitalizing on opportunities as it is about avoiding minor or major disasters. Getting this balance right is critical.
5   Succeeding with risk management interventions is more a cultural challenge than it is technological, process or structural, although the latter three dimensions are certainly important.

What has been lacking thus far is a framework that integrates these and other emerging concepts. Each of the listed capabilities is captured within the RBPM framework and methodology.

RBPM: An integrated approach

We will now provide a summary of the RBPM disciplines, each of which will be fully described in subsequent chapters. But note that although for ease of explanation and reference the RBPM framework is here described according to sequential steps, in application it has to be understood holistically, with added clarity around the interdependencies between the disciplines. As examples:

– Appetite serves as an overarching determinant through the framework and methodology
– Managing Performance and Risk happen simultaneously and indeed work in unison with both involving an interrelated set of indicators
– the outcomes from the Aligning Risk-Taking with Strategy step directly inform earlier steps
– the Governance, Communication and Culture piece ensures that any excellent work in aligning risk, and in particular that of risk appetite, with strategy management is not underdone by inappropriate behaviours.

Business drivers

We start from the left of the RBPM framework with business drivers (see Chapter 4). These are the vital few factors that disproportionately influence the success or otherwise of the business or industry. For example, access to capital at a competitive price might be a key determent of success of a bank; therefore capital may be defined as one of the bank's business drivers. As part of the strategy formulation process, subjective statements such as "we are a low risk organization" are translated into tangible values based on the identified business drivers. This enables a common understanding of risk to emerge at the board and executive level. With a common definition of potential levels of risk-taking, the board is then in a position to set the boundaries within which it expects organizations to operate while they go about the business of strategy execution.

RBPM: Two connected halves

The seven disciples of the RBPM framework and methodology are described through two interconnected halves (left and right) both of which we will now describe.

Left Circle

The left Circle comprises four disciplines: Setting Strategy, Managing Performance, Managing Risk and Aligning Risk-Taking to Strategy, as well as appetite, and is shown in Figure 2.2.

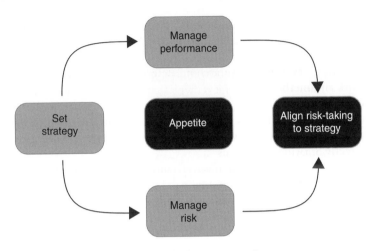

Figure 2.2   **The left cirlce of the RBPM framework**

Appetite

The most important element of the RBPM approach is that of Appetite (see Chapter 4). This is about defining the organization's appetite for risk within the context of strategy and then executing accordingly. By defining a clear statement of risk appetite, the board and executive can establish clear boundaries within which the organization can execute the strategy and manage risk. It also provides the foundation for cascading the strategy and risk management disciplines through the organization, thus shaping the organization culture. For these reasons, the Appetite discipline appears in both the left and right halves of the RBPM framework.

The efficacious management of appetite, from shaping an Appetite Statement at the board level, through to communicating with and putting in place effective controls at the front-line, is the golden thread of RBPM and serves as a central commentary throughout the book.

Set strategy

Strategy formulation is described fully in Chapter 4. In the context of RBPM, Strategy Management is about developing a clear sense of direction as to where the organization is going, how much risk it is willing or required to accept to get there, and what the key opportunities and threats are along the way.

During the strategy formulation stage an organization develops or reviews a set of broad, often long-term business goals, and a series of strategic options for their achievement. Traditional SWOT or PESTEL tools are used here, along with an analysis of business drivers as well as a review of the business model and any business model innovations that might alter (slightly or massively) the way that value is delivered to the customer. At the formulation stage, risk appetite plays a central role in that it broadly defines the risk boundaries for the subsequent execution phase. Risk appetite should play a key role in strategic options evaluation and the decision-making processes around which option(s) the organization will pursue.

Managing performance

In Chapter 6 we look at the Managing Performance discipline (although we also consider the Key Performance Indicator (KPI) element in Chapter 5). For this discipline, RBPM draws from many influential thinkers and much useful work, but we draw mainly from the excellent work done by Harvard Business Professor Dr. Robert Kaplan and consultant Dr. David Norton in developing and evolving the Balanced Scorecard strategy execution framework since they first introduced the concept in a seminar Harvard Business Review article in 1992.[4] Since that time they have published numerous articles on the Balanced Scorecard, as well as five books that have plotted its evolution from a simple measurement system to a broader strategy execution framework.[5]

A Balanced Scorecard framework comprises a Strategy Map and a scorecard. The Strategy Map describes how value is created through cause-and-effect relationships between objectives. Key benefits of creating such a map are that it provides a roadmap for strategy execution and creates clarity and agreement within the senior team as to the primary performance levers that drive the strategy. An example Strategy Map is shown in Figure 2.3.

Supporting the Strategy Map is a scorecard of KPIs, targets and strategic initiatives. The KPIs are used to track progress to the objectives, targets are set over the lifetime of the strategic plan and initiatives are launched to close targeted performance gaps. An example scorecard schematic is shown in Figure 2.4. Note that it is a conventional

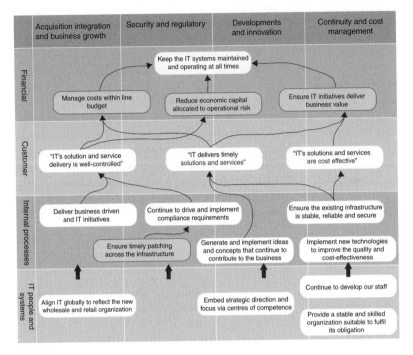

Figure 2.3 **An example of a Strategy Map**

Balanced Scorecard. Within the RBPM approach we have made some alterations to how performance is reported.

The Strategy Map and scorecard are collocated according to four perspectives (although the exact number and even titles are not mandated) that are described hierarchically, with shareholder (or financial) at the apex and then flowing down through customer, internal processes and learning and growth. A slightly different hierarchy is typically used in the public sector.

As part of the objectives definition process, the organization should develop an Appetite Statement with clear, measureable expressions of the organizational appetite for risk-taking. This allows for an appetite to be expressed for the overall strategy. Defining risk appetite as part of the objectives definition process creates the opportunity for organizations to iterate their strategy multiple times until a point is reached when the board and executive are comfortable with the level of strategic ambition expressed in the strategy and how much risk is required to effectively deliver this strategy.

Vision and strategy							
To succeed financially, how should we appear to our shareholders?				To achieve our vision, how should we appear to our shareholders?			
Financial perspective				Customer perspective			
Objectives	Measures	Targets	Initiatives	Objectives	Measures	Targets	Initiatives
To satisfy our shareholders and customers, what business processes must we excel at?				To achieve our vision, how will we sustain our ability to change and improve?			
Internal process perspective				Learning and growing perspective			
Objectives	Measures	Targets	Initiatives	Objectives	Measures	Targets	Initiatives

Figure 2.4   **An example of a conventional Balanced Scorecard schematic**

Undertaking this iterative process also means that the key risks related to the strategy are defined and refined based on the decisions around what strategy is to be pursued and which specific objectives will be sought.

Part of this process is plotting the key risks on a four perspectives risk map (Figure 2.5) and understanding how the choice of objectives relates to key risks and how making a decision to not pursue an objective(s) or to reduce targets around an objective(s) relates to the key risk profile.

Once the organization has gone through the iterative process of defining a set of objectives, testing those objectives against the defined risk appetite and consolidating all the potential risks into an agreed set of key risks, it has established the foundation for sustainability in executing the strategy.

At the measurement level, the RBPM methodology brings clarity through the use of three types of indicators, KPIs, Key Risk Indicators (KRIs) and Key Control Indicators (KCIs). KPIs form part of the Managing Performance discipline of RBPM, while KRIs and KCIs fall within Managing Risk. Each of these indicator types provides different yet complementary data to support management conversations and decision making.

▷ KPIs are used to enable the organization to monitor if they are on track to achieve their strategic objectives.
▷ KRIs are used to enable the organization to monitor changes in its level of risk-taking and risk profile.
▷ KCIs are used to enable the organization to monitor changes in the effectiveness of its controls.

So in simple terms, strategy execution is about doing what we do well, day-to-day, managing the process performance via KPIs, KRIs and KCIs. The latter two play a key role in the Managing Risk discipline of the RBPM approach.

Key indicators serve as important tools for performance evaluation and communication but also for the identification of any performance gaps.

As performance gaps are identified, initiatives are used to change the business and to drive both strategic and operational performance. The extent of change will vary depending on the level of deviation from expected performance. Typically, initiatives improve the business (deliver small changes to correct relatively minor performance deviations), change the business (deliver major changes to the way we do things) or transform the business (the most radical type of change, involving changing how we do things and often changing what we do completely). That said, it is also true that when new initiatives are launched, potential new risks are introduced that must be managed appropriately.

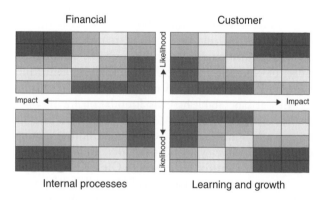

Figure 2.5   **A Four Perspective Risk Map**

Managing risk

The Managing Risk discipline is explored in Chapter 7. In the context of RBPM, risk management is all about understanding the risks the organization faces in pursuit of its objectives, and the continuous monitoring and management of those risks. It is also about understanding that risks can present opportunities as well as threats.

As with objectives, a broad set of risks are identified as part of the strategy management process and therefore within the Set Strategy RBPM discipline. These are then the basis for the executive team to define a set of key risks, which are monitored and managed to increase the probability that the objectives of the organization will be achieved. The set of key risks should be regularly reviewed with a level of challenge to ensure that they really are the "key" risks. Additionally, as the strategy is executed other risks are likely to emerge which also need to be monitored and managed, and "Key" risks may then become non-key.

A key part of the risk management process is regularly assessing risk to understand the level of risk that the organization is taking. Typically this is done on the basis of a Likelihood × Impact assessment, which provides an "at risk" value, and can be used as one of the steers to identify where risk mitigation interventions are required.

One of the main ways that risks are managed is via an effective controls environment. Controls are the processes, policies, practices or other devices or actions designed to affect control over the risk. Key controls should be defined for each risk identified and the effectiveness of those controls regularly assessed. The key controls can be either preventive, that is, designed to reduce the likelihood of the risk materializing, or detective, that is, controls that are designed to detect when a risk has materialized.

By paying close attention to, and integrating, the RBPM disciplines of Managing Performance and Managing Risk, organizations gain significant clarity over and above that provided by a suite of objectives and a suite of risks that have been defined in isolation from each other. The end result is a much more focused and clearly defined strategic framework made up of a "vital few" objectives, risks and controls, supported by a clear but more detailed operational framework made up of processes, initiatives, systems or people with each having their own set of specific risks and controls. Another important benefit is the contribution toward the fashioning of a strategy-focused, risk-aware culture that results from the process and conversations that are a critical part of integrating strategy and risk into a single management framework. Box 2.2 describes how Manigent client HML has integrated risk management with strategy management and the creation of Strategy Maps.

Aligning risk-taking with strategy

Chapter 8 is where we explain how to align risk-taking with strategy. A key component of "operating within appetite" is what we call appetite alignment: the process of continuously aligning current risk exposure to the defined risk appetite. To translate into simple terms, it is about understanding if an organization's current risk-taking is aligned to its chosen business strategy, that is, are we operating within appetite?

The RBPM methodology introduces a new and innovative tool for managing and assessing appetite, the Appetite Alignment Matrix, which assesses an organization's exposure to risk against its agreed appetite levels (Figure 2.6). It is our field observations that by deploying this tool, organizations sometimes find that they are under-exposed to risk; that is, they are not taking enough risk in the prosecution of their strategies. One of the key benefits of paying close attention to appetite and one that is rarely recognized is that doing so sometimes leads organizations to take on more risk, because in doing so they are still "operating within appetite". This brings us back to the core message that managing risk is about exploiting opportunities as well as minimizing threats.

Organizations should also make good use of scenario planning for the completing of analyses of the various ways that markets,

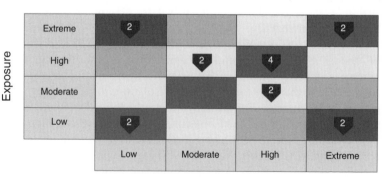

Figure 2.6 **The Appetite Alignment Matrix**

competitors, geographies, etc. might alter at various junctures in the future, put in place possible mitigation plans if the likelihood of a negative risk event happening increases and plan to rapidly take advantage of opportunities (positive risk).

Indeed, given that we now live in continuous turbulent times, scenario planning is becoming increasingly important; hence the use by senior management of tools such as tail-risk meetings, where the executive discuss the consequences of unlikely external events occurring (they are called tail-risk meetings because the likelihood of the events is in the "tail" of the probability distribution). The group assesses the ramifications of the event, the impact on the company's strategy, and what might be done to avoid or mitigate the adverse consequences should it occur. Figure 2.7 provides an implementation roadmap for the left circle of the RBPM approach.

Aligning Risk-Taking with Strategy is a discipline within the left circle of the RBPM framework, but also serves as a linkage to the right circle, as ensuring this takes places takes us into the disciplines of Governance, Communication and Culture.

Right Circle

The right circle of the RBPM framework comprises Aligning Strategy, Governance, Culture and Communication, as well as Appetite and is shown in Figure 2.8.

Governance

It is generally agreed that a failure of corporate governance was a major contributor to the Credit Crunch. Such failure was somewhat surprising as corporate governance is hardly new, and was believed to be essentially in good shape, that is, robust and effective – as was risk management.

The first version of the UK Code of Corporate Governance, produced in 1992,[6] provided what has become regarded as a classic definition of corporate governance: "Corporate governance is the system by which companies are directed and controlled."

The focus of standards such the UK Corporate Governance Code 2010 has generally been on the obligations of the board in respect to governance. Governance is embedded into the RBPM approach, supporting the corporate level obligations and enabling

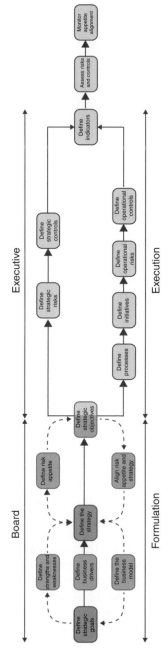

Figure 2.7 **An implementation roadmap for the left circle of the RBPM approach**

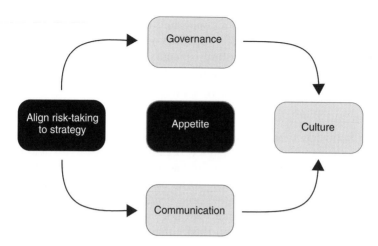

Figure 2.8   **The right circle of the RBPM framework**

those commitments to be cascaded through the organization. We discuss this in Chapter 9, where we explore why corporate governance was found wanting at the outset of the Credit Crunch and explain what needs to be done to drive more consistent and effective corporate governance into organizations. A greater focus by the board on demanding the parameterizing of risk appetite and then supervising how executives execute strategy within those boundaries is now a critical governance role, and has been stressed in many reports by regulatory and expert bodies.

However, as part of the RBPM approach, governance also has a more operational, day-to-day role to play within an organization. This approach to governance is based on the RACI framework which has been widely used within the programme and project management world. RACI is an acronym for Responsible, Accountable, Consult and Inform, and is used to clarify individual roles in the achievement of objectives and management of risks.

Using the RACI framework within the RBPM approach ensures that each individual has a high level of clarify regarding their role and responsibilities in relation to the delivery of the strategy and the management of risks which goes beyond the traditional "objective owner" or "risk owner" that is so often used with organizations today. It provides clarity in the decision-making process and creates focus in management meetings. Additionally, embedding governance using the RACI framework clarifies communications around strategy and risk management, and plays an important role in shaping an organizational culture that instinctively "operates within appetite". Culture and communication are both critical elements of RBPM and are covered together in Chapter 10, as they are so closely interwoven.

Culture

The importance of getting the culture right is often overlooked in major change efforts. Although few organizational leaders would publicly state that culture is less important than process, structure or technology, the fact is that due to its being so nebulous, and so difficult to define and to equate a precise financial figure to its effective management, it is more often than not "dealt with" through a nice-sounding value statement and then either forgotten about or handed over to the HR function to manage. Many organizations live to regret this oversight. And this is particularly true in the execution of strategy, for as the management guru Peter Drucker once said, "culture eats strategy for breakfast".[7]

In implementing a management approach that integrates strategy and risk, success or failure certainly relies heavily on getting the culture right. Implementation of the RBPM approach is a significant undertaking and will present any organization with a number of challenges, of which the behavioural aspect is almost certainly the most daunting.

It is clear that dysfunctional and inappropriate behaviour and cultural underpinnings were a significant cause of the Credit Crunch. Indeed, banking hiccoughs since (such as the JP Morgan Chase example mentioned earlier in this chapter) appear to have been at least partly the result of an inappropriate culture being allowed to flourish. After all, that one of the key people at the heart of the JP Morgan Chase failure went by the name of the London Whale, or Lord Voldemort (after the evil character in the Harry Potter books) due to the size of the bets he made hardly points to a culture that encouraged the deployment of a sensible and sustainable risk appetite. Moreover, an article in the *New York Times* stated that "individuals amassing huge trading positions were not effectively challenged, there were regular shouting matches and difficult personality issues".[8]

The importance of getting the culture right cannot and should not be underestimated. Culture is, quite simply, a showstopper. Indeed an August 2012 article in the *Financial Times* reported a survey of risk managers that found that 62% of major risk events were the result of culture, leadership or behaviour.[9] If culture eats strategy for breakfast, it eats risk for lunch! The moniker "London Whale" certainly suggests a culture that eats risk for lunch.

However, it is important to recognize that a culture that encourages an organization to operate within appetite must be designed and created; it does not simply happen.

We use the term "strategy-focused, risk-aware culture" to describe the type of culture which has the dexterity to simultaneously remain focused on delivering a clear set of objectives while scanning broadly to identify threats and opportunities which may help or hinder the achievement of those objectives.

There are seven key characteristics of the strategy-focused, risk-aware culture, which we describe fully in Chapter 10.

1   Driven by a compelling vision
2   Live by a clear set of values
3   Led with integrity
4   Align risk-taking to strategy
5   Established clear accountabilities
6   Engage in high quality conversations
7   Incentives are aligned to appetite

Culture is perhaps the ultimate strategy and risk management tool: get the culture right and objectives will more likely be achieved and risk managed. Get the culture wrong and failure will be just about inevitable; even though ultimate failure might well be preceded by a period of stunning financial success, as we have seen with many organizations that suffered catastrophic failure. An aligned and appropriate culture is a prerequisite for a strategy that is successful and sustainable.

We strongly argue that culture should be treated as an organizational asset, as important as any other. Many CEOs who fail – most notably of course those who recently ran major financial services organizations which collapsed – might well have surveyed their corporate wreckage and thought to themselves, "I wish I'd paid more attention to culture". More specifically we would argue that the thought should be "I wish I'd paid more attention to creating a culture that operated with a clearly defined and communicated appetite for risk that was aligned to our corporate strategy."

Communication

Communication is an important aspect of getting the culture right. It is a key management discipline in any circumstance, and especially when large-scale change is taking place. Communication is critical when an organization is setting out to take an integrated approach to strategy and risk management and so has been included as a discipline within the RBPM approach – most notably in getting the appetite message across and in driving the correct behaviours.

We would stress, however, that communication should be an ongoing process, rather than a one-off exercise repeated on an ad hoc basis. Messaging must be a constant part of reinforcing the dos and don'ts around strategy, risk and risk appetite and the importance of balancing risk and reward. If this is not done, there is a pressing danger that decision-makers and indeed all employees might revert to inappropriate behaviours. The mantra "communicate, communicate, communicate" is commonly heard, but less often acted upon.

During the implementation of the RBPM approach, and after the approach has been operationalized, we believe that an effective communications programme should be based on these five C's: clarity, credibility, concision, context, consistency. These are fully fleshed out in Chapter 10.

Shareholder value

The final part of the RBPM framework is shareholder value. Simply, the purpose of implementing the RBPM approach is to deliver value to shareholders. Shareholder value is included here to ensure that the central purpose of a commercial organization's existence (to deliver a reasonable return to owners) is kept front-of-mind of decision-makers. That said, the rigor provided through the seven RBPM disciplines might go a long way toward ensuring that the value delivered is sustainable over the longer term; that the pursuit of profit and the delivery of short-term and superior returns to shareholders is not at the expense of long-term value, or even continued survival.

Conclusion

This chapter has introduced the RBPM framework and methodology. For a more complete understanding of how the RBPM framework and methodology developed, the next chapter provides an explanation of how the approach was influenced by and evolved from existing and proven strategy execution models – most notably the Balanced Scorecard and risk management frameworks and standards – most notably COSO's Enterprise *Risk Management: An Integrated Framework* and ISO31000 – that influenced the development and evolution of RBPM. This will provide greater granularity as to how RBPM fully integrates the best from the worlds of strategy and risk management and the background for the fuller explanation of the seven RBPM disciplines in the subsequent chapters. Box 2.1 describes seven RBPM tools that used in the implementation of these disciplines.

Box 2.1   Seven key RBPM tools

Core to the delivery of RBPM methodology are seven tools that are designed to answer specific management questions, inform a better quality management conversation and lead to better quality decision-making at all levels of the organization. The dashboards, shown in Table 2.2, are aligned to key disciplines within the left circle of the RBPM framework but also serve as key tools to align the disciplines within the right circle. The dashboards are configured to work together to provide a comprehensive overview of risk-based performance.

Table 2.2   Key dashboards and management questions

RBPM discipline(s)	Dashboards	Management questions
Setting Strategy/ Managing Performance	Strategy Map	• What is the "story" of our strategy? • What are our objectives and are we on track to deliver our strategy? • What are the causal relationships within our strategy? • Is the strategy working?
Managing Risk/ Managing Performance	Four Perspective Risk Map	• What is the level of our risk-taking against our strategic objectives? • What risks are we taking within specific strategic perspectives and what are the relationships between risks across perspectives? • Where are our main exposures? • Are our risks clustering together?

Table 2.2   (Continued)

RBPM discipline(s)	Dashboards	Management questions
Aligning Risk-taking with Strategy	Appetite Alignment Matrix	• Is our risk-taking aligned to our strategy? • Are we operating within appetite? • Where are we taking an inappropriate amount of risk? • What opportunities are provided through not taking enough risk?
Managing Risk	Risk Scorecard	• Are we managing our risks to enable the organization to deliver its objectives? • Are our risks within prescribed tolerance levels? • Over time, are the risk management-related trends going in the right direction? • What are the risk management exceptions we need to review and investigate?
Managing Performance	Performance Scorecard	• Are we achieving the right level of performance within our organization? • Over time, are we improving our performance? • How are we progressing against key performance improvement initiatives? • What are the performance exceptions we need to review and investigate?
Managing Risk	Control Scorecards	• Is our controls environment effective in enabling us to mitigate and manage risk? • Are we meeting our compliance and regulatory obligations? • Over time, are the control effectiveness trends going in the right direction? • What are the control effectiveness exceptions we need to review and investigate?
Managing Risk	Control Map	• Are our controls effective? • What does our controls environment look like? • How aligned are our controls to appetite levels? • How aligned are our controls to exposure levels?

The Strategy Map, Four Perspective Risk Map and the Appetite Alignment Matrix together provide a powerful summation for the senior team as to how the organization is progressing towards its strategy and whether it is operating within appetite. They enable focused conversations on the solutions required to rectify performance shortcomings or exploit emerging opportunities.

Supporting Performance, Risk and Control Scorecards provide greater granularity around how the organization is managing performance and risk and whether this is within the appetite boundaries set by the board. Collectively, the scorecards serve as powerful day-to-day RBPM steers for operational managers and staff.

Box 2.2   HML case study

With about 1,200 employees, financial outsourcing specialist HML is a wholly owned subsidiary of the UK's Skipton Building Society. Working for more than 30 UK- and Ireland-based financial institutions, HML manages more than 45,000 financial products and assets of approximately £45 billion.

In January 2008 HML appointed a new Chief Executive Officer who set out to transform the business – in particular, the role of risk management. In March that year Gillian Weatherill also joined HML, as Head of Operational Risk. Soon afterwards, efforts began to make risk management central to strategic and operational decision making. "Our goal was to enhance profitability, lower operational losses, and reduce the economic capital held against the business," she says. Pivotal to this was laying the foundation for state-of-the-art, next-generation risk management capabilities, which support the needs of all staff and clients.

Weatherill's appointment coincided with the onset of the Credit Crunch. "Because of the Credit Crunch the prime mortgage market was disappearing and there was no new lending, so the focus of the business was turning to credit management and getting the arrears position down and monies in," she explains.

As the business model changed, recognition was that HML needed to control operational losses, improve their effectiveness and efficiencies, redesign processes and better assign responsibility and ownership. "Money wasn't coming in and times were getting harder and the cracks were starting to show."

Early in her tenure, Weatherill completed a risk management effectiveness review which consists of a series of interviews at several staff levels and a review of existing risk reports. "HML did have risk management in place but it was very much an old-fashioned risk management silo-based approach where people reported key failures and where reports were almost exclusively financial in nature," she explains. "Risk was very much seen as task-focused and about ticking boxes." Consequently, risk management wasn't viewed as especially useful and was completely disconnected from planning and strategy.

Later in 2008 the UK regulator, the Financial Services Authority (FSA), visited HML. It recognized that although HML was not a well-known organization, its collapse would have a disproportionate impact on the mortgage market. "The FSA realised that we were quite a threat to their objectives to maintain financial stability in the UK and therefore they became significantly more interested in what we were doing and how we were organized and managed," says Weatherill. "The FSA gave HML actions, such as put in place a risk mitigation plan (RMP) and a 12 month timeframe for compliance, but they largely approved the plans that were already being put in place."

With the goal of integrating risk management with strategy, HML partnered with Manigent and its sister company StratexSystems. Manigent provided the strategy and risk consulting advice and StratexSystems provided StatexPoint, a software solution that has been designed to support the RBPM framework – see Chapter 11 for a description of StatexPoint.

With Manigent's support, HML created an Operational Risk Maturity Model (ORMM) to inculcate better operational risk processes and to understand organizational maturity in relation to risk management, as well as a Strategy Map and Balanced Scorecard.

The ORMM determines maturity from two dimensions: (1) process enabler and (2) organizational capability, and sets out to then align these performance requirements.

HML's process enablers are design, performance/risk champions, owners, infrastructure and indicators, whereas organizational capability enablers are leadership, culture, expertise and governance.

Both are assessed against five levels: initial, competent, proficient, expert and exemplary. Through ORMM, HML identified risk champions in each department, identified "as is" states for enablers, organizational capability and their maturity levels and implemented risk management processes and frameworks within each department. In managing and monitoring the implementation HML has made much use of Risk Management Maturity Dashboards throughout the organization, such as at corporate and business service levels, through which they track previous, current and desired levels.

The dashboards support the Strategy Map and Balanced Scorecard for Operational Risk. Figure 2.9 shows a conceptual Strategy Map and Figure 2.10 the scorecard indicators for the process perspective.

In using the Balanced Scorecard, HML has been careful to ensure that strategic objectives are supported by "key" indicators and not a mass of metrics that makes an understanding on performance and risk impossible. "Through past experiences I have seen organizations with about 400 indicators that they are tracking and the world ends up as amber against the red, amber, green colour coding system – so it's just about shuffling things around so the world looked a little bit better than it should," Weatherill says, adding that with such a vast array of indicators it was very difficult to understand what needed to be done.

Within HML the focus is on the word "key." "So, for every entity we look for a maximum of 16 Key Performance Indicators aligned to the objectives within the four perspectives of the Balanced Scorecard."

Although indicators are important, in terms of understanding risks, Weatherill believes that risk appetite is much more useful in getting people to focus on what really matters. "We went down the risk appetite route rather than using lots of indicators as we were more interested in getting people to talk about what their appetite for loss and sales might be and where they think they currently are," she says. "It's about understanding risk in the context of the business rather than seeking precision."

Aligned with the RBPM approach, HML has paid close attention to inculcating a "risk-aware" culture. HML has put the appropriate structure, procedures and systems in place (for example, following a complete review of the business structure HML created a risk committee with sub-committees to focus on specific topics, such as critical suppliers); however, the senior team recognizes that successfully managing risk and strategy only works if the culture is right. "One of our CEO's favourite expressions is that 'when strategy and culture clashes, culture always wins' " says Weatherill, emphasizing that this means that the conversations are the most important things.

"For a risk-aware culture to be embedded, the tone must be set by the senior team, and most importantly the CEO," Weatherill stresses. "Having the buy-in from the very top and their asking the questions and challenges brings the right attitudes to the organization," she explains. "As one example, we do quarterly control self -assessments and our CEO sits down with all of our directors and challenges them over the control effectiveness views that have been put forward from their division. This brings a lot of focus."

Effective communication has also been central to creating a risk-aware culture. "It's all about talking it through with people," says Weatherill. "We spent a lot of time in workshops and other forums explaining risk, the relationship with strategy and why it's important to the organization. Basically it's about making sure everybody is on the same journey and that they're not at a different bus stop. It's just engaging and talking."

Training was also used extensively. This included innovative training initiatives which people hugely enjoyed. For example, as a team development activity HML conducted a "The Weakest Link" risk management exercise

50

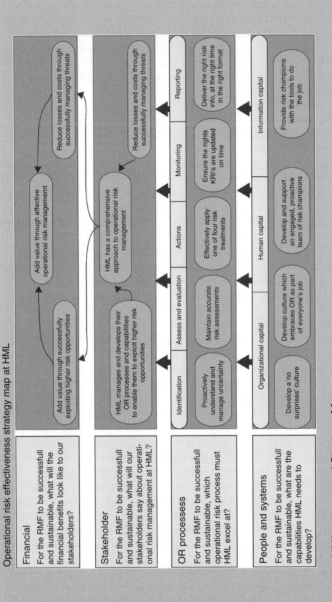

Figure 2.9 **HML conceptual Strategy Map**

Operational risk process perspective		
For the RMF to be successfull and sustainable, which operational risk processes must HML excel at?		
Objective	Leading indicator(s)	Lagging indicator(s)
Proactively understand and manage uncertainty	Attendance rate by key people to key meetings	% of cross-sell and up sell sales opportunities in the sales pipeline ORMM level vs. target level
Maintain accurate risk assessments	Average age of risk assessments (months)	Average losses vs. forecast/budget
Effectively apply 1 of 4 risk treatments	% Risks without treatment (explicitly) applied	% YTD reduction in the number of realised risk events
Ensure the right KPI's are updated on time	% KRI's automated	% KRI's failed to be updated
Deliver the right risk information, at the right time, in the right format	% Key risk reports/dashboards not generated via RMRS % Key risk reports/dashboards not delivered on-time	ORMM level vs. target level

Figure 2.10   **HML scorecard indicators for the process perspective**

(based on the popular TV show) as well as something similar on the equally popular show "Who wants to be a Millionaire". "We had lots of training initiatives like that so people could realize that this could be fun as well as important to the business," says Weatherhill.

Technology, via the StatexPoint solution, has also proved critical in effectively managing strategy and risk. Weatherill confesses that she is not a "technophile" and so wanted a practical tool via which everyone could quickly access their own data and information and that they could update easily.

The key thing I needed from any technology solution was something that was web-based and so people from across the whole organization can go in and view performance, although within set permissions.

Weatherill states that being web-based has an impact on behaviour.

People know their information is easily available online and they know that their manager and their manager's manager can look at it as well, so there's a lot more interest in trying to keep something that's so visible up to date and relevant. This brings a different set of behaviours to how people look and manage the information.

"Also, being on SharePoint, employees can better manage improvement plans, e.g., around the risks and controls or they can put in initiatives and use the tool to track progress and performance", Weatherill comments.

As a result of implementing an RBPM approach HML has managed to significantly reduce its economic capital – the amount held against risk necessary to survive in a worst-case scenario; direct operational losses have fallen significantly and risk compliance targets are being met. But in conclusion Weatherill stresses that sustaining successes requires constant focus and attention, especially around the people side. "Never assume that everybody's with you," she says. "Keep talking to them and let them see the connections between their objectives and what the organization is trying to achieve."

Note: HML does not wish to disclose exact economic capital or operational loss-related figures in this case study.

3 RBPM: Integrating Risk Frameworks and Standards with the Balanced Scorecard

Each discipline within the RBPM framework and methodology has been constructed from both Balanced Scorecard and Risk Management viewpoints. In essence, it allows organizations to "manage with one eye on performance and one eye on risk".

Introduction

As a key message throughout this book, we argue that compartmentalizing strategy management and risk management within separate organizational silos is inappropriate – we go as far as to say "dangerous" – given the economic, competitive and other pressures faced in these "continuous turbulent times". If silo thinking is inappropriate, then it is safe to also argue that managing organizations according to separate Strategy and Risk Management frameworks is equally unsuitable and, in these times, unsustainable. The Credit Crunch made this fact abundantly clear.

The RBPM approach is designed to meld strategy and risk management into a single, unified framework, thereby rectifying the shortcomings of managing both strategy and risk in isolation. Shortcomings include failing to articulate, and therefore manage, the key risks associated with the delivery of specific strategic goals, and more profoundly, not aligning the organization's appetite for, and exposure to, risk with those goals.

But this is not to imply that in designing the RBPM approach the advances made in recent years in formulating and evolving

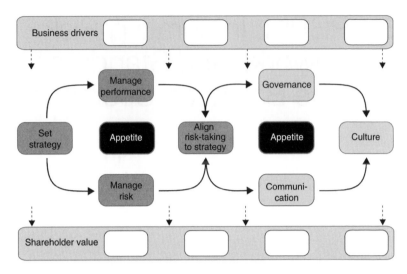

Figure 3.1 **The RBPM framework**

strategy management frameworks and Risk Management standards and frameworks have been ignored or dismissed. On the contrary, the RBPM framework and methodology were deliberately designed to build on existing Strategy and Risk Management frameworks and best practices, drawing on the best from both. RBPM pulls together into a holistic approach the best of leading-edge strategy management practices – most notably the Balanced Scorecard – and Enterprise Risk Management frameworks – most notably the COSO framework and the ISO31000 Risk Management standard. Therefore, RBPM enables organizations to evolve their existing approaches into an integrated offering, rather than having to deconstruct what they already have (Figure 3.1).

The Balanced Scorecard framework explained

Introduced by Harvard business professor Dr Robert Kaplan and consultant Dr David Norton in a seminar Harvard Business Review article in 1992[1] and since evolved through numerous articles, as well as five books,[2] a Balanced Scorecard framework comprises two key components: a Strategy Map and a scorecard.

The Strategy Map

The Strategy Map describes through causal relationships between strategic objectives how value is created by the enterprise. A central goal of creating such a map is that it provides a roadmap for implementing strategy (and the Balanced Scorecard is a strategy implementation framework *not* a formulation model). A Strategy Map can be described as a "Plan on a Page", and indeed many organizations call it just that to avoid the connotations that the term scorecard has with measurement. An example Strategy Map is shown in Figure 3.2.

The Strategy Map is collocated according to four perspectives (although the exact number and even titles are not mandated) that are

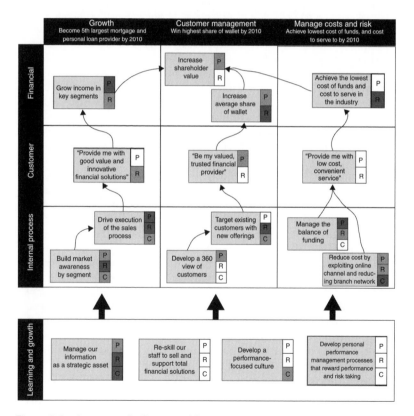

Figure 3.2 **An example Strategy Map**

described hierarchically, with shareholder (or financial) at the apex and then flowing down through customer, internal processes and learning and growth. A slightly different hierarchy is used in the public sector. This is shown in the case study in this chapter on Ashghal, the Public Works' Authority of Qatar, which replaces the shareholder and customer perspectives with national outcomes and stakeholder outcomes, and learning and growth with enablers – see Box 3.1.

Box 3.1   Ashghal case study

The following case study explains how one organization is looking to incorporate risk management into the Balanced Scorecard process. Although it doesn't follow all of the steps of the RBPM approach, it does provide some insights into identifying and managing risk at the strategic objective level, which is a key element of RBPM. It is also useful as it shows how the integration of strategy and risk management is of growing importance in the government or public sector.

The State of Qatar, located in the Persian Gulf, is experiencing an infrastructural transformation that is unparalleled anywhere in the world. Indeed it can be argued that the scale of the work within this nation of just 1.8 million people might only be compared with the industrial revolution in the UK. The timescales, though, are incomparable: from 2011 to 2016 Qatar will expend about $41 billion in infrastructure expenditure (excluding the bulk of the spending required for the FIFA 2022 World Cup, which Qatar will host).

Ashghal, the Public Works Authority, is accountable for about two-thirds of this investment, and is responsible for the construction and maintenance of the nation's roads and drainage networks as well as the construction of public buildings. Infrastructural transformation is integral to Qatar's National Vision 2030 of being an advanced nation, globally recognized for its excellence in human, social, economic and environmental development.

To deliver to its demanding obligations, and led by Ashghal's President Nasser Ali Al Mawlawi with the full support of his senior management team, in 2009 a new strategy was formulated, at the heart of which beats the following vision: "In 2016 Ashghal will be a dynamic, responsive and customer centric organization that creates shared value for all stakeholders through outsourcing and partnership with the world's best."

In turn, this vision represents a set of deliverables toward the achievement of Ashghal's mission: "To deliver and manage state-of-the-art, sustainable world class buildings and infrastructure that fulfil the Qatar National Vision 2030."

Ashghal has formulated three strategic themes that collectively describe the core deliverables of this strategy: the main theme is outsourcing and delivery, which triggers the fundamental refocusing of Ashghal from being an organization that manages programmes of projects to one that assumes a governance role. A network of world-leading Program Management Companies (PMCs) and Management Contractors, supported by General Engineering Companies (GECs) have been engaged and mobilized and are working as strategic partners with Ashghal in Qatar's infrastructure transformation. These partners were chosen following an exhaustive global search amongst the best in their field.

The other two themes comprise transforming the organization into one that is (1) customer-centric, and (2) dynamic and responsive.

To execute the strategy each of the three themes was distilled into several strategic objectives. Together the objectives deliver a theme, but importantly the objectives and themes work together in the delivery of the strategy. The themes are component objectives as described through a Corporate Strategy Map (Figure 3.3) which has an aligned scorecard of KPIs and targets, as well as strategic initiatives, described through 12 major transformational programmes, that are about transforming how Ashghal is managed and operates and not the delivery of the capital programmes.

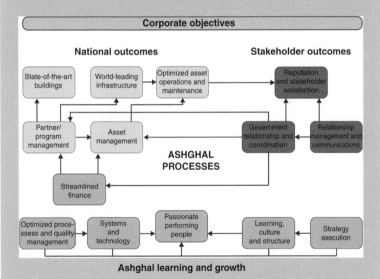

Figure 3.3 Ashghal Corporate Strategy Map 2012

The 12 programmes are actively driving up the performance of Ashghal to deliver the strategic objectives and serve as Ashghal's strategy implementation roadmap. Collectively these programmes include more than 60 separate initiatives: as examples, "define standards for world leading infrastructure" is an initiative within the world-leading infrastructure transformation programme and "establish risk and contingency management practices" appears in the asset management programme. Through a customer service and communications programme Ashghal is also leading the effort to create a true customer-centric organization that will include a dedicated customer contact centre, a state-of-the-art customer relationship management system and a dedicated customer web portal, amongst other offerings. Other programmes focus on driving Ashghal's IT and HR capabilities to world-class levels and transforming the organization's processes.

Three core values have been identified to help drive delivery of the corporate objectives and to shape the culture of Ashghal. Each value has supporting descriptions that capture behavioural expectations: We Lead with inspiration and integrity: behaviours include "we are trustworthy, honest, open and transparent" and "we do not compromise our ethics and integrity"; We Deliver with passion and commitment: behaviours include "we care deeply about outcomes, performance and sustainability" and "we empower and manage partners to deliver the right outcomes"; We Care with empathy and respect: behaviours include "we look to create shared value for all our customers and stakeholders" and "we take pride in our work, credibility and the corporate reputation".

Crucially, risk management is also intrinsic to the Strategy Management framework. The approach essentially focuses on integrating the Balanced Scorecard with the ISO31000 standard. Strategy Advisor Mark Ranford explains the rationale: "The management of risk should focus the organization around achieving its strategic objectives by best recognizing and even undertaking risks that might be deemed necessary to achieve the objectives, while also avoiding risks that are considered unacceptable to the organization, its mission, vision, values and strategic objectives."

He continues that Ashghal has adopted "Effect of Uncertainly on Events" (from the ISO Standard) as the definition of risk for the organization. "This definition clearly relates risk to the things that affect the achievement of Ashghal's strategic objectives and hence puts strategy at the centre of risk management," he says.

Within Ashghal risks have been identified for each strategic objective on the Corporate Strategy Map. For example, poor supply chain coordination is an identified risk for the Partner/Programme management objective within the internal processes perspective. Controls are in place to track this and other risks and ensure that actions are in place to safeguard Ashghal from the risk materializing. Overseen by a dedicated risk team within Ashghal's Office of Strategy Management (called the Corporate Planning and Development Department) the recommended ISO3100 process for managing risk is deployed (shown in Figure 3.9).

Establish the context

This considers the strategic, organizational and risk context and analyses external and internal threats and opportunities at the perspective level. So, as examples, the threats and opportunities regarding reputation will be considered within the stakeholder outcomes perspective and issues with suppliers, contractors and raw materials within the internal processes perspective.

Risk assessment

Based on a review of strategic objectives and KPIs, risks are brainstormed, identified and agreed: validated risks are recorded in the risk register.

Identified risks to an objective are then plotted onto a Risk Heat Map (which are created for each objective), using the consequence versus likelihood calculation to determine the level of risk. Those risks that appear in the top right hand quarter of the map are typically those where immediate action is required to reduce the risks. Ashghal has set the appetite bar at the point where risks move into the "act now" space. That said, conversations are held as to whether the appetite and tolerance levels should be modified for the pursuance of the strategic objective. Consequently, a higher or lower appetite level might be applied for specific objectives.

Treat risks

Within Ashghal, risk treatment essentially focuses on reducing the likelihood or changing the consequences; although risk avoidance through risk sharing – such as insurance – or not accepting a risk and therefore terminating an activity might also be appropriate at times.

Risk treatment is normally achieved through a mitigating initiative, which serves the same purpose as a strategic initiative in a conventional Balanced Scorecard approach. In both cases, initiatives are captured on an initiative sheet with full description, milestones and assessments of risk/difficulty in implementation, benefits and strategic alignment, as shown in Figure 3.4.

Risk is managed and reported through the same governance cycle as strategy management (including formal strategic reviews with the President and the senior management team); therefore the Risk Maps are updated at the same time as the overall Balanced Scorecard. Any identified issues through these reviews are signalled for action and progress is reported at the following review.

Finally, the Corporate Strategy Map and scorecard have been cascaded to Ashghal's six business units (including Infrastructure Affairs, Asset Affairs and

Initiative details

Initiative name	
Initiative owner/sponsor	
Project manager	

Initiative description

Timelines

Major tasks/milestones	FY2009				FY2010				FY2011				FY2012			
	Q1	Q2	Q3	Q4	Q1	Q2	Q3	Q4	Q1	Q2	Q3	Q4	Q1	Q2	Q3	Q4
1. Initiation																
2. Planning																
3. Implementation																
4. Phase 1																
5. Phase 2																
6. Phase 3																
7. Phase 4																
8. Testing																
9. Monitoring and control																
10. Closeout																

Assessment of risk/difficulty to implement

	FY2009	FY2010	FY2011	FY2012
FT staff hours rqd	2.5	2	1.5	
$ Capital costs rqd	200,000			
$ Other costs rqd	30,000	30,000	30,000	
Total cost	M	H/M/L assessment of the above costs in total (for this business plan period)		
Duration	M	H/M/L assessment for this business plan		
Tech complexity	M	H/M/L assessment		
Org. complexity	M	H/M/L assessment		

Assessment of benefits

$ Return (saved/made)	M	H/M/L assessment
Intangible benefits	M	H/M/L assessment

Assessment of strategic alignment

Level of alignment	M	H/M/L assessment
% Strategic impact	M	H/M/L assessment

Figure 3.4 **Initiative sheet used by Ashghal**

Building Affairs, as examples). To drive enterprise strategic alignment each devolved Strategy Map has a number of strategic objectives that are identical to those at the corporate level, examples being the learning and growth objectives "business-focused systems and technology" and "knowledge transfer and learning", which are capabilities that must be built and shared Ashghal-wide. Furthermore, there are a number of other objectives that are identical across the business unit. For instance "External Customers" Satisfaction and "Internal Departments' Satisfaction", both of which are important for infusing a customer centric mindset within Ashghal and which support the corporate objective "Reputation and Stakeholder Satisfaction".

Each business unit has also identified an aligned set of risks; therefore a strategic management framework that incorporates risk is how Ashghal will deliver its part of the ambitious goals of transforming a nation.

Although hierarchically moving from financial down to learning and growth (financial outcomes must be described first, and then how these are achieved through the customer and other perspectives), cause and effect is described from the base up, showing how creating capabilities at the learning and growth level enables the delivery of the strategic processes, which in turn delivers customer value and in turn improved financial performance.

Commonly, a further performance lens is used within a Strategy Map – Strategic Themes. These are used to arrange a group of objectives that deliver a specific component of the strategy and will typically cross over perspectives. Note, for example, Ashghal's three themes of outsourcing and delivery, customer-centric, and dynamic and responsive.

The Strategy Map itself is a distillation of the organization's vision and mission statements and a representation of the rest of the work completed during the strategic formulation phase, which we discuss in detail within the next chapter.

The scorecard

Supporting the Strategy Map is a scorecard – which is arranged according to the same perspectives – of Key Performance Indicators (KPIs), targets and strategic initiatives. The KPIs are used to track progress to the objectives, targets are set over the lifetime of the strategic plan (plotting improvement to that target over that timeframe) and strategic

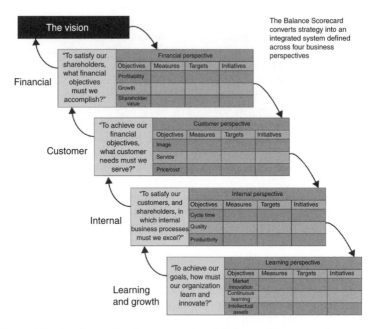

Figure 3.5   **A schematic of a conventional Balanced Scorecard**

initiatives are launched to close targeted performance gaps (that is, the value gap between where the organization is presently and the KPI target – the gap is set to decrease over the lifetime of the strategy). An example of a schematic of a conventional scorecard is shown in Figure 3.5.

From first to second generation Balanced Scorecards

As cited, the Balanced Scorecard has continued to evolve since its launch in 1992 as a balanced performance measurement system that was based on a simple proposition: that the financial model of business alone as the primary means of managing performance was inadequate for work in the knowledge era. The financial model was useful, argued Kaplan and Norton in their 1992 Harvard Business Review Article, for providing detail on what happened yesterday, but was of little use in managing the future development of the business.[3] Figure 3.5 above, essentially serves as a schematic for a first generation Balanced Scorecard. It is called "first generation" because at this time the idea of a Strategy Map had yet to emerge.

The emergence of the Strategy Map came about because although early adopters gained substantial value from the first generation Balanced Scorecard, some of the most successful early users, such as Cigna Property & Casualty, Mobil Oil's North American business and Saatchi & Saatchi Worldwide, found that the Balanced Scorecard worked best not when used simply as an extension of the financial measurement system, but when it was hardwired to strategy and deployed as a strategic implementation framework. By the early 1990s strategy implementation had come to be recognized as a significant challenge for organizations, in spite of established strategic planning functions, with findings that just one out of ten strategies were successfully executed.[4] The problem was not strategy formulation, but execution.

These pioneering scorecard organizations found it useful to separate out the objective dimension of the Balanced Scorecard framework and lay out a cause-and-effect relationship between, and within, the strategic objectives housed within the four perspectives. Thus was born the idea of Strategy Maps, which were originally referred to as Linkage Maps, and what might be called the second generation Balanced Scorecard.

The strategy-focused organization

With the Balance Scorecard being gradually repositioned during the 1990s as strategy – as opposed to measurement-focused – Kaplan and Norton's second scorecard book, published in 2001, set out a step-by-step process for creating a strategy-focused organization.

The authors specified five principles for creating a strategy-focused organization (Figure 3.6). These principles were not arbitrarily chosen. Rather they emerged from the authors' observation of the interventions deployed by the most successful scorecard adopters of the 1990s.

Principle 1: Translate the strategy into operational terms

This principle comprises two sub-components: Strategy Maps and Balanced Scorecards that together describe the strategy and its implementation. It is by translating strategy into the logical architecture of a Strategy Map and a Balanced Scorecard that organizations create a common, understandable point of reference for everyone.

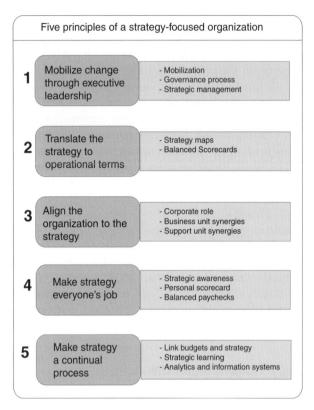

Figure 3.6 **The five principles of the strategy-focused organization**

Principle 2: Align the organization to the strategy

Synergy is the overarching goal of organization design. Organizations consist of numerous sectors, business units and specialized departments, each with its own strategy. For organizational performance to become more than the sum of its parts, individual strategies must be linked and integrated. The corporation defines the linkages expected to create synergy and ensures that those linkages actually occur.

Principle 3: Make strategy everyone's everyday job

Moving strategy out of the boardroom into the office and on to the shop floor and making it "everyone's everyday job" is the pre-eminent challenge for organizations and this principle considers personal scorecards and balanced pay-cheques. It is essentially about measuring, and rewarding, employees against the strategy.

Principle 4: Make strategy a continual process

Putting the Balanced Scorecard at the heart of the organization's management system involves creating links from strategy to budgets and also calls for a robust learning process. An important sub-component of this principle is "analytics and information systems" (see Chapter 11 for an RBPM software solution that is architected according to the Balanced Scorecard framework but also integrates best risk management practices).

Principle 5: Mobilize change through executive leadership

Kaplan and Norton emphasize the make-or-break influence of top management: "If those at the top are not energetic leaders of the process, change will not take place." Simply, if the CEO does not want the scorecard then don't try to do it: the scorecard effort will fail. Field observations of the authors of this book would testify to the accuracy of this advice.[5]

The Execution Premium

In their most recent book: *The Execution Premium: Linking Strategy to Operations for Competitive Advantage*, Kaplan and Norton evolved the Balanced Scorecard methodology further by introducing the six-step "Execution Premium" model to align operational performance with strategy management. Through this model, Strategy Maps and the Balanced Scorecard are central components of the overall strategy management process. Shown in Figure 3.7, these steps are:

Stage 1: Develop the strategy

At this stage organizational leaders address three questions.

1   *What business are we in and why (clarify mission, values and vision – MVV)?*
     The MVV statements establish guidelines for formulating and executing the strategy.

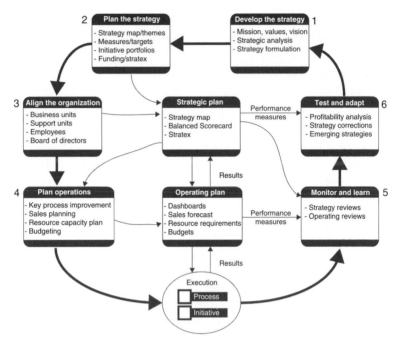

Figure 3.7 **The six steps of the "Execution Premium" model**

2   *What are the key issues (conduct strategic analysis)?* Managers review the situation on their competitive and operating environments since they last crafted their strategy.

3   *How can we best compete (formulate the strategy)?* This considers areas such as the customer value proposition, key processes required to create the differentiation in the strategy, and human capital and technological requirements to enable the delivery of the strategy.

Stage 2: Plan the strategy

In this stage, managers plan the strategy by developing strategic objectives, measures, targets, initiatives and budgets that guide action and resource allocation. Questions addressed at this stage include:

1   *How do we describe our strategy (create Strategy Maps)?* This describes the objectives required to deliver to the strategy.

2   *How do we measure our plan (select measures and targets)?* Here, managers convert the objectives defined in the Strategy Map into a Balanced Scorecard.
3   *What action programmes does our strategy need (choosing strategic initiatives)?* The initiatives and action programmes aimed at achieving targeted performance for the Strategy Map objectives.

Stage 3: Align the organization with the strategy

At this stage, managers ask three key questions:

1   *How do we ensure that all organizational units are on the same page?* This is about devolving the scorecard to lower level business units.
2   *How do we align support units with business unit and corporate strategies?* This is about creating Strategy Maps and scorecards for support units such as HR and finance, as two examples.
3   *How do we motivate employees to help execute the strategy?* Essentially this is about proper communication and the linking of personal objectives and (more common in the commercial sector) incentive compensation to the scorecard.

Stage 4: Plan operations

Companies need to align process improvement activities with strategic priorities. At this stage managers focus on two key questions.

1   *What business process improvements are most critical for executing the strategy?* Companies might focus on Six Sigma, reengineering and/or other efforts on improving performance to a strategic objective.
2   *How do we link strategy with operating plans and budgets?* The process improvement plans and the high level strategic measures and targets on the Balanced Scorecard must be converted into an operating plan for the year.

Stage 5: Monitor and learn

This is where the organization monitors the execution of its strategic and operating plans and learns from experience. To do this they hold two meetings: an operational review meeting and a strategy review meeting, which answer two questions.

1 *Are our operations under control (operational review meeting)?* Companies hold these meetings to review short-term performance and respond to recently identified problems that need immediate attention.
2 *Are we executing our strategy well (strategy review meeting)?* These meetings review the progress of the strategy, identify problems and order remedial action.

Step 6: Test and adapt the strategy

This is where organizations question whether their fundamental strategic assumptions remain valid. Collectively the senior leadership team asks one question:

1 *Is our strategy working (hold a strategy testing and adapting meeting)?* Periodically, the senior team meets to question and challenge the strategy and, if necessary, to adapt it.[6]

As well as the structure, the role of the Balanced Scorecard in an organization has come a long way in the two decades since its launch. The right to be positioned as an organization's central management framework has largely been earned because throughout its various evolutions, the Balanced Scorecard has remained a hugely popular tool.

The enduring popularity of the Balanced Scorecard

As a measure of this popularity, the global consultancy Bain & Company has since 1993 tracked usage of and satisfaction with a range of popular management tools such as strategic planning, benchmarking, business process reengineering, etc. Throughout the intervening years, the Balanced Scorecards has consistently been a top-performer against both usage and satisfaction dimensions. At the time of writing this book, the most recent Bain survey *Management Tools & Trends 2011* considered usage of the 25 most popular management tools with 1,230 organizations from a broad range of industries, sectors and countries. The Balanced Scorecard was found to be the sixth most used tool across the globe: the top three were benchmarking, strategic planning and mission and vision statements. It also ranked sixth in satisfaction (the top three being strategic planning, mission and vision statements and customer segmentation).

Interestingly, expected usage of the Balanced Scorecard was set to grow by 16% from 2010 to 2011 (from 47% to 63%). Also, Enterprise Risk Management was due to rise from 30% to 57%.

As we can see, both the Balanced Scorecard and Risk Management disciplines are growing in importance. Clearly, strategy management and risk management are hot topics across the globe, driving greater urgency for their integration.[7]

The financial benefits of scorecard usage

It is also notable that there is much research evidence that points to the financial benefits of deploying the Balanced Scorecard. For example, in the article "The Effects of Adopting the Balanced Scorecard on Shareholder Returns", which appeared in the June 2008 edition of *Advances in Accounting*, authors Aaron Crabtree and Gerald DeBusk reported the findings from research on the financial impact of the Balanced Scorecard. Based on a sample size of 164 publicly traded companies, their findings are compelling, showing that adoption has a positive impact on shareholder returns, as shown in Table 3.1.[8]

Successful deployment of the Balanced Scorecard is also extensively captured in many case studies, books and articles (a number of which have been written by one of the authors of this book).[9]

The shortcomings of scorecard usage

But despite the reported successes of the Balanced Scorecard, note an important caveat. During the years running up to the Credit Crunch many financial services organizations reported great benefits from using

Table 3.1 Research into the financial impact of using the Balanced Scorecard

Description	Balanced Scorecard firms (%)	Control group (%)
Market value to equity	50.72	27.12
Book to market	39.14	8.9
Net assets	41.05	13.47

the Balanced Scorecard, and the sector was one of the earliest and biggest users.

However, the financial crisis found the scorecard somewhat wanting as a predictor of future financial performance (one of its key selling points) and it seemingly offered little protection against the economic hurricane that hit these companies. Soon after the onset of the Credit Crunch Kaplan stated: "The high level objective in a Balanced Scorecard's financial perspective is growing and sustaining shareholder value: revenue growth and productivity improvements. The third method for sustaining shareholder value, missing in many companies' strategies, should be risk management."[10]

As the Credit Crunch played out Kaplan turned his attention to figuring out how best to integrate risk management into the Balanced Scorecard and publish these findings, which we will discuss in the later section on approaches to integrating the Balanced Scorecard and Risk Management.

First though, we will provide an overview of the Risk Management frameworks and standards that, alongside the Balanced Scorecard, greatly influenced the development of the RBPM framework and methodology.

Risk Management frameworks

While the Balanced Scorecard framework and methodology were evolving, separate work was progressing on Risk Management frameworks and standards. Note that whereas the Balanced Scorecard developed firstly to overcome the shortcomings of relying on financial measures alone to assess the health of the enterprise and then to grapple with the equally vexing challenge of organizations' continued failure to execute even the best thought out and most logical strategies, risk management solutions were being sought to deal with another set of issues. The early 1990s saw increasingly regular corporate scandals and failures in which investors, employees and other stakeholders were suffering greatly. This led to calls for greater corporate governance and more systematic risk management.

Corporate failures and scandals

Some of these corporate failures and scandals were particularly large, beginning with the uncovering of widespread accounting irregularities with Enron Corporation in late 2001, which led to its eventual bankruptcy (at $64 billion in assets the biggest ever US bankruptcy at that time) and also the collapse of its auditor Arthur Andersen (then one of the "big 5" accounting firms). As an aside it's worth mentioning that prior to its demise Enron was one of America's Most Admired Companies and that Arthur Andersen's competitive advantage was largely based on its reputation – which was destroyed in a matter of days. Arthur Andersen would have been wise to closely manage the risk to their reputation and their appetite for that risk: if they had done so their demise would have been significantly less likely.

Right on the heels of Enron, in 2002 there was the WorldCom scandal, and the uncovering of systematic fraud that had inflated the organization's assets by about $11 billion. The organization filed for bankruptcy in 2003 and emerged from this in 2004 as part of the new MCI Corporation. Tyco International was another large organization to suffer a serious accounting scandal in the first years of this century. And there were others.

Sarbanes-Oxley

Such scandals inspired the Sarbanes-Oxley act in 2002, which set new standards for financial reporting and included areas such as accounting oversight, auditor independence and enhanced financial disclosures. Applicable to all organizations whose shares were traded in the US, the cost of complying with the act proved an onerous time and cost burden (on average a US publicly traded organization expended 15,000 man-hours in ensuring compliance).[11] But it was seen as time and money well spent, as it was supposed to guard against any future shocks emerging from questionable financial practices of large organizations. Before the decade was out, of course, we had the Credit Crunch and more collapses of large, venerable firms, government interventions to save many more and the near destruction of the reputation of others.

COSO: Enterprise Risk Management – Integrated Framework

A ground-breaking project was launched in 2001 when the Committee of Sponsoring Organizations of the Treadway Commission (COSO), a joint initiative of five organizations including the American Accounting Association and The Association of Accountants and Financial Professionals in Business, initiated a project to develop a framework that management could deploy to assess and improve their organizations' approaches to enterprise risk management. The global consultancy PricewaterhouseCoopers conducted this project.

COSO first published its *Enterprise Risk Management – Integrated Framework* in 2004.

In the foreword to the report that introduced the framework, the authors noted that "among the most critical challenges for managements is determining how much risk the entity is prepared to and does accept as it strives to create value". The concepts of appetite and exposure were firmly introduced.

In the report, COSO defined enterprise risk management as

> a process, effected by an enterprise's board of directors, management and other personnel, applied in strategy setting and across the enterprise, designed to identify potential events that might affect the entity, and manage risk to be within its risk appetite, to provide reasonable assurance regarding the achievement of entity objectives.

Building on this definition, the report also said that the underlying premise of enterprise risk management is that every entity exists to provide value for its stakeholders.

> All entities face uncertainty, and the challenge for management is to determine how much uncertainty to accept as it strives to grow stakeholder value. Uncertainty presents both risk and opportunity, with the potential to erode or enhance value. Enterprise risk management enables management to effectively deal with uncertainty and associated risk and opportunity, enhancing the capacity to build value.

Critically, the framework made the direct link between risk and strategy. Value, the authors argued, is maximized when management sets strategy and objectives to strike an optimal balance between growth and return goals and related risks, and efficiently and effectively deploys resources in pursuit of the entity's objectives. Enterprise risk management, they stated, encompasses

▷ *Aligning risk appetite and strategy* – Management considers the entity's risk appetite in evaluating strategic alternatives, setting related objectives and developing mechanisms to manage related risks.

▷ *Enhancing risk response decisions* – Enterprise risk management provides the rigor to identify and select among alternative risk responses: risk avoidance, reduction, sharing and acceptance.

▷ *Reducing operational surprises and losses* – Entities gain enhanced capability to identify potential events and establish responses, reducing surprises and associated costs or losses.

▷ *Identifying and managing multiple and cross-enterprise risks* – Every enterprise faces a myriad of risks affecting different parts of the organization, and enterprise risk management facilitates effective response to the interrelated impacts, and integrated responses to multiple risks.

▷ *Seizing opportunities* – By considering a full range of potential events, management is positioned to identify and proactively realize opportunities.

▷ *Improving deployment of capital* – Obtaining robust risk information allows management to effectively assess overall capital needs and enhance capital allocation.

These capabilities, the report argued, help management achieve the entity's performance and profitability targets and prevent loss of resources. "Enterprise risk management helps ensure effective reporting and compliance with laws and regulations, and helps avoid damage to the entity's reputation and associated consequences. In sum, enterprise risk management helps an entity get to where it wants to go and avoid pitfalls and surprises along the way."

The definition reflects certain fundamental concepts. Enterprise risk management is

▷ A process, ongoing and flowing through the entity
▷ Effected by people at every level of an organization
▷ Applied in strategy setting
▷ Applied across the enterprise, at every level and unit, and includes taking a an entity-level portfolio view of risk
▷ Designed to identify potential events that, if they occur, will affect the entity and to manage risk within its risk appetite
▷ Able to provide reasonable assurance to an entity's management and board of directors
▷ Geared toward achievement of objectives in one or more separate but overlapping categories: strategic, operational, reporting and compliance.[12]

COSO influenced the development of the RBPM approach in many ways – in particular the focus on managing within appetite and applying risk within a strategy setting. But all of the seven bullet points above are integrated into the RBPM offering, as we will show as we progress through this book.

The year the COSO framework was introduced also witnessed the publication of two further Risk Management works – which shows how serious an issue it had become in the scandal-hit early years of the first decade of this century.

The Australian and New Zealand Standards of Risk Management

First consider the *Australian and New Zealand Standards of Risk Management*: AS/NZ 4360:2004. This provided a useful risk management process, which is shown diagrammatically in Figure 3.8, and includes the following steps:

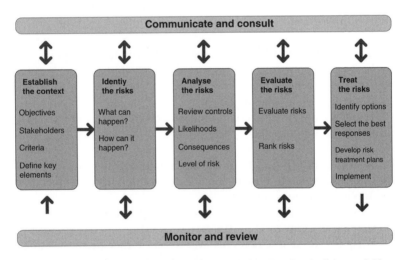

Figure 3.8 **A risk management process from the Australian and New Zealand Standards of Risk Management: AS/NZ 4360:2004**

▷ Establish the context: objectives; stakeholders; criteria; define key elements.
▷ Identify the risks: what can happen; how can it happen.

▷ Analyse the risks: review controls; likelihoods; consequences; level of risks.
▷ Treat the risks: identify options; select the best responses; develop risk treatments plans; implement.

Running through the process steps are requirements to "communicate and consult" and "monitor and review".[13]

The Orange Book: Management of Risks – Principles and Concepts

Second, consider *The Orange Book: Management of Risks – Principles and Concepts*, published in the UK by Her Majesty's Treasury. The 2004 *Orange Book* stated that

> It is a matter of definition that organizations exist for a purpose – perhaps to deliver a service, or to achieve particular outcomes. In the private sector the primary purpose of an organization is generally concerned with the enhancement of shareholder value; in the central government sector the purpose is generally concerned with the delivery of service or with the delivery of a beneficial outcome in the public interest. Whatever the purpose of the organization may be, the delivery of its objectives is surrounded by uncertainty which both poses threats to success and offers opportunity for increasing success.

They defined risk as this uncertainty of outcome, whether positive opportunity or negative threat, of actions and events. They argued that risk had to be assessed in regard to the combination of the likelihood of something happening, and the impact which arises if it does actually happen. Risk management includes identifying and assessing risks (the inherent risks) and then responding to them.

> The resources available for managing risk are finite and so the aim is to achieve an optimum response to risk, prioritized in accordance with an evaluation of the risks. Risk is unavoidable, and every organization needs to take action to manage risk in a way which it can justify to a level which is tolerable. The amount of risk which is judged to be tolerable and justifiable is the "risk appetite".

The 2004 *Orange Book* provided useful guidance on risk appetite, and we will fully explain these insights in Chapter 4. But here we will highlight that the guidelines understood that appetite and exposure must be understood from both the viewpoint of threats and opportunities.

> When considering threats the concept of risk appetite embraces the level of exposure which is considered tolerable and justifiable should it be realized. In this sense it is about comparing the cost, financial or otherwise, of constraining the risk with the cost of the exposure should the exposure become a reality and finding an acceptable balance.

> When considering opportunities the concept embraces consideration of how much one is prepared to actively put at risk in order to obtain the benefits of the opportunity. In this sense it is about comparing the value, financial or otherwise, of potential benefits with the losses which might be incurred (some losses may be incurred with or without realizing the benefits).

The report goes on to say that the management of risk at strategic, programme and operational levels needs to be integrated so that the levels of activity support each other. In this way, the report claims, the risk management strategy of the organization will be led from the top and embedded in the normal working routines and activities of the organization. "All staff should be aware of the relevance of risk to the achievement of their objectives and training to support staff in risk management should be available," the report noted.[14] The Culture discipline of the RBPM approach focuses on inculcating a "strategy-focused, risk-aware" culture in which all staff are aware of the relevance of risk and of working "within appetite".

ISO31000

The International Organization for Standardization (ISO), a worldwide federation of national standards bodies, brought further useful insights to risk management and its integration with strategy through the ISO31000:2009 standard *Risk Management Principles and Guidelines*. The ISO guidelines built on the good work from the three previously cited works.

The standard recommends that organizations develop, implement and continuously improve a framework whose purpose is to integrate the process for managing risk into the organization's overall governance, strategy and planning, management, reporting processes, policies, values and culture.

The ISO31000 standard defines risk as the "effect of uncertainty on objectives". Note an effect is a deviation from the expected – positive and/or negative – and that objectives can have different aspects, such as financial, health and safety, and environmental goals, and these can apply at different levels, such as strategic, organization-wide, project, product and process. The standard also provided a number of risk management principles, which are as follows:

▷ Risk management creates and protects value.
▷ Risk management contributes to the demonstrable achievement of objectives and improvement of performance in, for example, human health and safety, security, legal and regulatory compliance, public acceptance, environmental protection, product quality, project management, efficiency in operations, governance and reputation.
▷ Risk management is an integral part of all organizational processes.
▷ Risk management is not a stand-alone activity that is separate from the main activities and processes of the organization. Risk management is part of the responsibilities of management and an integral part of all organizational processes, including strategic planning and all project and change management processes.
▷ Risk management is part of decision making.
▷ Risk management helps decision-makers make informed choices, prioritize actions and distinguish among alternative courses of action.
▷ Risk management explicitly addresses uncertainty.
▷ Risk management explicitly takes account of uncertainty, the nature of that uncertainty, and how it can be addressed.
▷ Risk management is systematic, structured and timely.
▷ A systematic, timely and structured approach to risk management contributes to efficiency and to consistent, comparable and reliable results.
▷ Risk management is based on the best available information.
▷ The inputs to the process of managing risk are based on information sources such as historical data, experience, stakeholder feedback, observation, forecasts and expert judgement. However, decision-makers should inform themselves of, and should take into account,

any limitations of the data or modelling used or the possibility of divergence among experts.
▷ Risk management is tailored.
▷ Risk management is aligned with the organization's external and internal context and risk profile.
▷ Risk management takes human and cultural factors into account.
▷ Risk management recognizes the capabilities, perceptions and intentions of external and internal people that can facilitate or hinder achievement of the organization's objectives.
▷ Risk management is transparent and inclusive.
▷ Appropriate and timely involvement of stakeholders and, in particular, decision-makers at all levels of the organization, ensures that risk management remains relevant and up-to-date. Involvement also allows stakeholders to be properly represented and to have their views taken into account in determining risk criteria.
▷ Risk management is dynamic, iterative and responsive to change.
▷ Risk management continually senses and responds to change. As external and internal events occur, context and knowledge change, monitoring and review of risks take place, new risks emerge, some change and others disappear.
▷ Risk management facilitates continual improvement of the organization.
▷ Organizations should develop and implement strategies to improve their risk management maturity alongside all other aspects of their organization.

As with earlier approaches, the ISO3100 standard suggests a useful risk management process, which is shown in Figure 3.9 and includes establishing the context and risk assessment components. Note too, the importance ascribed to communication and consultation, and monitor and review.

The principles and guidelines make the important observation that:

Although this International Standard provides generic guidelines, it is not intended to promote uniformity of risk management across organizations. The design and implementation of risk management plans and frameworks will need to take into account the varying needs of a specific organization, its particular objectives, context, structure, operations, processes, functions, projects, products, services, or assets and specific practices employed.[15]

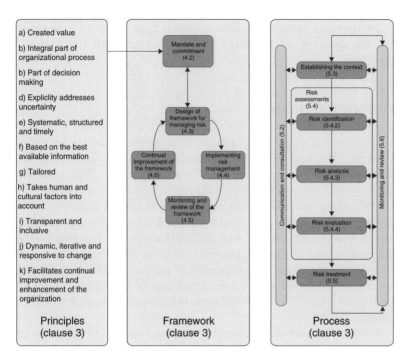

Figure 3.9   **ISO3100 risk management principles, framework and process**

Although we endorse the standard and recognize its importance in integrating strategy and risk management (the integration of ISO31000 with the Balanced Scorecard has become a hot topic within both Balanced Scorecard and Risk Management communities and integration is being actively pursued by a number of organizations; see the Ashghal case study in Box 3.1), there is one glaring omission from the standard. It makes no mention of risk appetite, although it does list "risk criteria", which has a slightly different meaning from appetite. Risk criteria are described in the standard as terms of reference against which the significance of a risk are evaluated. Risk criteria are based on organizational objectives, and external and internal context. Moreover, the criteria can be derived from standards, laws, policies and other requirements.[16] Still, in our view, not explicitly recognizing risk appetite seriously impacts the practical value of the standard and is clearly out of step with the advice from COSO and others. But the importance of ISO31000 should not be underestimated, nonetheless.

In the next section we discuss several approaches to integrating risk management with strategy management through the Balanced Scorecard.

Integration models

In retrospect it might seem strange that, as the Balanced Scorecard sequenced through its various evolutions and became widely adopted worldwide, risk management rarely warranted more than a cursory glance – until the onset of the Credit Crunch in 2008, of course.

It is strange because the financial sector was a heavy Balanced Scorecard user and was also perceived to be the leader in risk management; strange because frameworks such as COSO strongly recommended the alignment of risk to strategy; strange because as the Balanced Scorecard was positioned as *the* central management model that all others orbited, yet risk was one that wasn't considered part of the strategy management solar system, at least within the mainstream Balanced Scorecard community.

Neither, for that matter, was the Balanced Scorecard on the radar screen of risk professionals. In the consulting engagements of one of the authors of this book during the past decade or so, it has been rare indeed to find a risk professional who had even heard of the Balanced Scorecard – although they often liked the idea when it was presented to them.

Manigent's financial services study

The RBPM approach was evolving before the Credit Crunch, being developed as a result of a series of performance and risk management related projects completed by Andrew Smart, the architect of RBPM, with UK-based clients of his consultancy Manigent, particularly with the financial services industry, that began a year-long academic research project, undertaken as part of the completion of Smart's MBA, involving 21 financial services organizations in the city of London in 2006–2007. The value of creating a new approach that built on and evolved the best from the Balanced Scorecard and Risk Management frameworks was identified through this study.[17] See Chapter 2.

The integration approaches of Kaplan and Norton

As cited, with the Credit Crunch finding significant weaknesses in the Balanced Scorecards used by many organizations, Kaplan and Norton (but more extensively Kaplan) – finally turned their attention to considering how risk management and the Balanced Scorecard could work together. Kaplan first shared his developing ideas in a series of articles that appeared in the Balanced Scorecard Report, most notably in 2009.[18]

With the January 2012 article "The Future of the Balanced Scorecard", published in the US *CGMA Magazine*, Kaplan and Norton offered five ways that the methodology would likely evolve going forward: along with suggestions such as "use the Strategy Map as a central management tool" and "expand the role of analytics for strategy execution", the authors stated that organizations should "Use the Strategy Map as a jumping-off point for risk management, especially the identification and management of strategic risk", arguing that

> Much of risk management today is narrowly oriented around compliance and controls. While managing these risks is important, companies often neglect the inherent and unavoidable risks that arise from their strategies. For each strategic objective on their map, company managers should identify the risk events that could lead to failure to achieve the targeted performance. They can then quantify the likelihood and consequence from each identified risk event and develop key risk indicators and risk mitigation initiatives that serve to reduce the likelihood and/or consequences of the most significant risk events.[19]

As we can see, Kaplan and Norton stress the importance of identifying risks at the level of the objective, which had been suggested in the ISO31000 guidelines and is central to the RBPM approach.

In the June 2012 edition of the *Harvard Business Review* Kaplan, along with Harvard Business School Assistant Professor Annette Mikes, published the article 'Managing Risks: A New Framework'.

Within the article Kaplan and Mikes identified three categories of risk (preventable, strategy and external) and provided guidance on risk mitigation objectives and control models for each. For strategy risks – defined as risk taken for superior returns – the risk mitigation objective was "reduce likelihood and impact cost effectively", while the control models were interactive discussions about risks to strategic objectives drawing on tools such as "maps of likelihood and impact of identified risks; Key Risk Indicator scorecards; and resource allocation to mitigate critical risk events".

Volkswagen Do Brazil case example

A case illustration on Volkswagen (VW) Do Brazil, a subsidiary of the German carmaker, illustrated good practice. VW's risk unit, the article explained, used the company's Strategy Map for a discussion on risk. The unit identified the risks that could derail the objective and generated a risk event card for each objective on the map, listing the practical effects of the event on operations, the probability of occurrence, leading indicators and potential mitigation actions. It also identified who had primary responsibility for managing the risk. The risk event card included the following components:

▷ Strategic objective (guarantee reliable supplier-to-manufacturing process)
▷ Risk event (interruption of deliveries)
▷ Outcomes (such production losses and quality problems)
▷ Risk indicators (such as later deliveries and incoming defects)
▷ Likelihood/consequence (using a likelihood/consequence heat map)
▷ Management controls (such as hold daily meetings with logistics, purchasing and quality assurance)
▷ Accountable manager (Director of Manufacturing Logistics)

A summary of strategic risks was presented to the senior team in the form of a "risk report card", which listed assessed and critical risks against each strategic objective.

The case of JP Morgan Chase

This article showcased JP Morgan Chase as an organization that exemplifies excellent risk management, stating that JP Morgan Chase weathered the financial crisis well because it had a strong internal risk management function and leadership team that understood and managed the company's multiple risk exposures. Barry Zubrow, then chief risk officer, was quoted in the article as saying "I may hold the title but [CEO] Jamie Dimon is the chief risk officer of the company."[20]

The article appeared at the time the multi-billion dollar JP Morgan Chase risk management failure was front-page news. Bad timing, to say the least!

Interestingly, and somewhat perversely, an article that appeared in the June 3, 2012 edition of the *New York Times* suggested that JP Morgan Chase's risk management successes during the Credit Crunch might be partly to blame for the subsequent trading loss. The bank, the article reported, had dismissed warning a year earlier from the CtW Investment Group, who had cautioned bank officials that the company had fallen behind the risk management practices of its peers and had become complacent with regard to risk management. The article stated that "having successfully navigated the financial crisis in 2008, JPMorgan's risk officers became complacent about the danger posed by the chief investment office's increasingly aggressive bets. In addition, while the office was profitable throughout the financial crisis, the chief risk officer was focused on problems elsewhere, including the bank's money-losing mortgage business. That complacency also caused JPMorgan Chase to lose ground, even as large rivals overhauled their risk management operations as a result of the crisis," the article noted.[21]

Conclusion

The previous chapter described the RBPM concept: the framework, if you will, whereas the following chapters explain how the framework might be practically deployed – the methodology piece.

In this chapter we have described the Balanced Scorecard and Risk Management frameworks and standards, which provide much of the raw material for the RBPM approach. Each discipline within the RBPM framework and methodology has been constructed from both Balanced Scorecard and Risk Management viewpoints. It allows organizations to "manage with one eye on performance and one eye on risk".

Within the RBPM approach, risk appetite is the glue that binds together Strategy and Risk and that enables the full and proper integration of these two disciplines. Simply put, when strategy is executed without paying close attention to risk appetite, senior managers are managing their organizations with incomplete information. Yes, through the narrow lens of performance management everything might appear positive (perhaps even amounting to a scorecard full of green

KPIs). But the risks that the organization has taken to deliver that "green" performance and their appetite for that risk might be a time-bomb, ticking away and ready to blow the strategy to smithereens – as the Royal Bank of Scotland case example in the following chapter powerfully illustrates.

4 Defining Strategy: The Question of Appetite

The critical linkage between strategy execution and risk management is made at the objective setting stage, where a risk appetite level is set for each objective. This enables the board and executive to indicate the level of risk they believe to be acceptable for the pursuing of individual objectives.

Introduction

At its heart, the Risk-Based Performance Management (RBPM) approach is about sustainably delivering a set of strategic objectives by taking an acceptable (and known) amount of risk (Figure 4.1).

Through deploying the RBPM approach, organizations develop a deep understanding and appreciation of the risk associated with the strategic choices that it decides to take, and are able to monitor on an ongoing basis both the achievement of strategic targets and the alignment of risk-taking to appetite: by doing so the board can be assured that in working towards its strategic goals, the organization is taking an acceptable amount of risk – that is, it is "operating within appetite". But before explaining the RBPM approach further we should pause to define both strategy and risk appetite, as there is little unanimity on either in strategy and risk professional circles and literature.

Defining strategy

At the time of writing, a lively discussion thread was playing out on a LinkedIn site for strategy professionals. The debate was in response to this simple member post: "What is Strategy?" That this question triggered a huge response and heated debate pointed to one evident

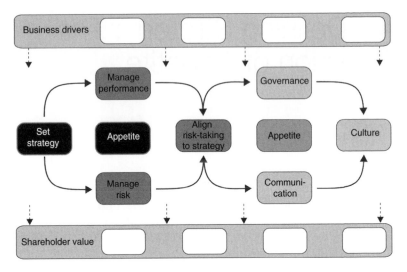

Figure 4.1 **The RBPM framework**

truth – there is no general agreement as to what is meant by strategy, even amongst strategy professionals.

The lack of definitional clarity is a concern, given that the senior executive team of any organization is primarily charged with delivering to a strategy. As an interesting anecdote, a couple of years back one of the authors of this book interviewed a Chief Executive Officer (CEO) of a large organization that had recently completed a Balanced Scorecard implementation and asked him this question: "If you were to start the scorecard program again, what would you do differently?" He replied: "That's easy. I would have got the senior team together and agreed a definition of strategy upfront, because as we began to discuss strategy execution I found, and after several difficult sessions, that we were all talking about completely different things."

Sun Tsu – *The Art of War*

People have been talking about, and debating the meaning of strategy for a very long time. Even today, one of the most oft-quoted strategy experts is the Chinese army general Sun Tsu, who lived about 500 BC. His seminal work *The Art of War*, a philosophy of war for managing conflicts and winning battles, is accepted as a masterpiece on strategy. Long used by military leaders (etymologically "strategy" is derived from the Greek *strategia*, meaning generalship) it has influenced the thinking of many leaders from a diverse range of industries and sectors. Sun Tsu's comment "Strategy without tactics is the slowest route to victory. Tactics without strategy is the noise before defeat" is a regularly used opening PowerPoint slide in strategy presentations and is routinely used by one of the authors of this book.

In introducing his work, Sun Tsu noted that the art of war (or strategy) had by then become so important that it could no longer be ignored.[1] Fast forward 2,500 years and various research studies strongly suggest that Sun Tsu's advice is still not being heeded. One study by the leading management thinkers Professors Gary Hamel and C.K. Prahalad found that less than 3–5% of executive time was devoted to looking outwards and developing foresight – they recommended 20–30%.[2] A further study by Professor Robert Kaplan and Dr David Norton, the co-creators of the Balanced Scorecard, revealed that 80% of executives spend less than one hour a month discussing strategy: remarkably, 50% spend no time at all.[3]

An operational focus

A primary reason why most organizations fail to properly consider strategy is that they continue to be operationally rather than strategically driven. To an extent this is unsurprising. Operations are where organizations make products and then deliver to customers. From a simplistic viewpoint this is logical, as the value chain might be described as: make the product, sell it at a profit and therefore make money for shareholders and/or other owners. Also, most senior leaders rise through the ranks as a consequence of their operational excellence.

Therefore, many organizations have become overly obsessed with improving operations to the virtual exclusion of everything else. This can prove disastrous – the noise before defeat!

Consider the US-headquartered multinational telecommunications company Motorola as a case in point. In the 1980s Motorola pioneered the Six Sigma approach to performance improvement. A Western spin on Total Quality Management, Six Sigma is both a metric and a methodology. As a metric a Sigma measures the capability of the process to perform to a given defect level. A defect is anything that results in customer dissatisfaction: Six Sigma is defined as 3.4 defects per million opportunities. As a methodology Six Sigma represents a set of tools that enable continuous improvement from defining the customer requirements through fixing or preventing problems to keeping the process on the new course.

Six Sigma is extremely process focused. Motorola achieved mouth-watering cost savings as a result of adoption, and there are other organizations that have also gained outstanding results. Motorola reduced manufacturing costs by $1.4 billion from 1987 to 1994 and reportedly saved $15 billion over a period of about a decade. But viewed from another perspective we are presented with a very different performance story. Motorola continually underperformed financially throughout the first decade of this century. And after having lost $4.3 billion from 2007 to 2009, the company was divided into two independent public companies, Motorola Mobility and Motorola Solutions on January 4, 2011. In August 2011 Google acquired Motorola Mobility for $12.5 billion. The noise turned into defeat.

We would argue that Motorola was overly focused on using Six Sigma to identify cost saving opportunities rather than as a tool to continuously improve performance against strategic goals. What they missed is that adeptness in strategy management (from formulation through to – and perhaps more importantly – execution) is more important that process improvement. We are not saying that the latter is not important; of course it is, but it *must* be conducted in the context of strategic goals. To reiterate a key message behind the creation of the RBPM approach – *everything* flows from strategy. Note the comment from revered strategy guru Professor Michael Porter in his 2006 *Harvard Business Review* article, "What is Strategy?"

> Improving operational effectiveness is a necessary part of management. But it is *not* strategy...

> Managers must clearly distinguish operational effectiveness from strategy. Both are essential but the two agendas are different.

> The operational agenda involves continual improvement everywhere, there are no tradeoffs... the strategic agenda [defines] a unique position, making clear trade-offs and tightening fit.

Michael Porter's definition of strategy

Porter defines strategy as about being different. "It means deliberately choosing a different set of activities to deliver a unique mix of value." Porter argues that strategy is about assuming a competitive position, about differentiating yourself in the eyes of the customer, about adding value through a mix of activities different from those used by competitors. To Porter, the essence of strategy "is choosing what not to do".[4]

Michael Treacy and Fred Wiersema's three "value-disciplines"

In their 1993 *Harvard Business Review* article, "Customer Intimacy and Other Value Disciplines", Michael Treacy and Fred Wiersema identified three "value-disciplines" that can serve as the basis for strategy: operational excellence, customer intimacy and product leadership. The authors maintained that only one of these value-disciplines can serve as the basis for strategy.

Operational excellence

The authors state that

> The term Operational Excellence describes a specific strategic approach to the production and delivery of products and services. The objective of the company following this strategy is to lead its industry in price and convenience. Companies pursuing operational excellence are indefatigable in ways to minimize overhead costs, to eliminate intermediate production steps to reduce transaction and other "friction" costs and to optimize business processes across functional and organizational boundaries.

The authors highlighted firms such as Dell and Wal-Mart as exemplary implementers of such a strategy.

Customer intimacy

The authors argue that those organizations following a customer intimacy strategy continually tailor and shape products and services to fit an increasingly fine definition of the customer.

> This can be expensive but customer intimate companies are willing to spend now to build customer loyalty for the long term. They typically look at the customer's lifetime value to the firm and not the value of a single transaction. This is why the employees in these companies will do almost anything – with little regard to initial cost – to make sure that each customer gets exactly what he or she really wants.

Nordstrom and Home Depot were cited as organizations that were successfully prosecuting such a strategy.

Product leadership

"Companies that pursue product leadership focus on producing a continuous stream of state-of-the-art products or services," the authors explain. "Such organizations are creative, can commercialize their new ideas quickly and their processes are engineered for speed.... most important, product leaders relentlessly pursue new solutions to the problems that their own latest products or services has just solved. If anyone is going to render their technology obsolete, they prefer to do it themselves." Johnson & Johnson was one company cited by the authors as particularly adept at implementing a product leadership strategy.[5]

Blue ocean strategy

More recently, W. Chan Kin and Renee Mauborgne introduced the concept of blue ocean strategy. In their book *Blue Ocean Strategy: How to Create Uncontested Market Space and Make the Competition Irrelevant*, the authors differentiated between competitive spaces known as red ocean and blue ocean. Red oceans represent all the industries in existence today or the known market space. "In red oceans industry boundaries and defined and accepted. Here companies try to outperform their rivals in order to grab a greater share of demand."

Blue oceans denote all the industries *not* in existence today or the unknown market space. In blue oceans "demand is created rather than fought over". The authors explain that there are two ways to create blue oceans. "In a few cases, companies can give rise to completely new industries, as eBay did with the online auction industry. But in most cases a blue ocean is created from within a red ocean when a company alters the boundary of an existing industry."[6]

Defining strategy for both commercial and non-profit organizations

The approaches to strategy above describe how to compete strategically. As a useful definition of strategy management, consider this from Ukerto Moti in his work, *Aligning Human Capital to Execute Corporate Strategy for Public Sector Growth*:

Corporate strategy is defined as the art, science and craft of formulating and implementing cross-functional decisions that will enable an organization to achieve its long-term objectives. It is the process of specifying the organization's mission, vision and objectives, developing policies and plans, often in terms of projects and programs, which are designed to achieve these objectives and then allocating resources to implement the policies and plans, projects and programs.[7]

As we can see, Moti's definition speaks of strategy implementation as well as formulation. Strategy is as much about what is done as what is intended. But many would argue that this definition is still incomplete, as strategic learning should also be included in a complete definition. Learning, and inculcating the agility capabilities to change track when needed, is a critical capability for competing in these "continuous turbulent times".

Risk – The missing component in definitions

Also missing from the cited descriptions of strategy is any mention of risk: another tell-tale sign that historically strategy and risk have been formulated, implemented and managed in isolation. A June 2012 working paper on risk culture, published by the Institute of Risk Management, illustrated the folly of doing so in the following way:

In the 1990s capital was cheap and freely available; therefore many firms based their strategies on "geographic flag planting" in order to chase profit growth regardless of the risks and capital requirements. In recent years, many business failures (e.g., Kodak, AIG) have occurred as a result of failure to inextricably link risk and strategy as part of the same process and to have a clear understanding of the appetite and risk implications of one particular strategy.[8]

Authors' definition of strategy

We define strategy as "to develop a sustainable (and defendable) position which enables the organization to achieve its objectives while operating within defined risk appetite boundaries". For example:

We will be No. 1 or 2 in all markets within which we operate within three years of entering the market. In markets where we are already No. 1 or 2 we will adopt a low-risk posture, whereas in markets where we are targeting to becoming No.1 or 2 we will adopt a high-risk posture.

We believe that strategy can be distilled into three parts:

1   Objectives – the specific strategic objectives that the organization wishes to achieve
2   Appetite – given the stated strategy and specific objectives, the level and type of risk-taking that is acceptable and required
3   Activities (Processes and Initiatives) – the specific set of activities and initiatives that the organization needs to undertake to enable it to achieve its strategy, while operating within appetite

Central to strategy execution is the alignment of risk-taking: the exposure to risk appetite which expresses the amount of risk required to execute strategy.

RBPM: From formulation to execution

Although RBPM is essentially a strategy execution framework and methodology, it also has an important function in the strategy formulation phase. Figure 4.2 shows the complete strategy management process, comprising formulation, setting and execution phases and the role that risk and risk appetite play. As described, appetite is central to each phase.

Strategy formulation

▷ Define the business context.
▷ Review the business model.
▷ Given the business context and business model, what is the risk appetite required to achieve the business goals?
▷ What are the business drivers?

Setting

▷ Develop specific business objectives based on the high-level strategies.
▷ Define specific business objectives and appetite for specific entities.
▷ Allocate scarce resources by entity, risk category, product lines, etc.

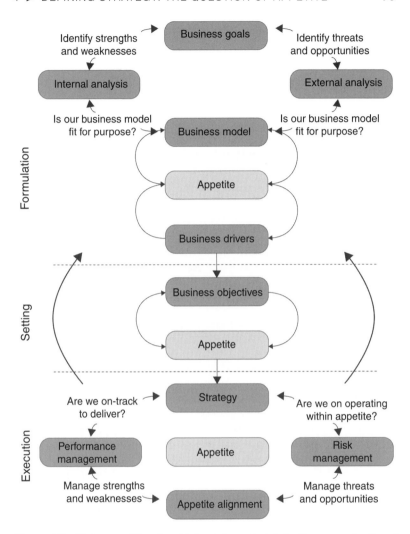

Figure 4.2 **Risk appetite should be integrated into the organizational strategic framework**

Execution

▷ Continually monitor whether the organization is on track to achieve its business objectives.

▷ Ensure that in pursuit of these objectives the organization is operating within appetite – not taking too much or not enough risk.
▷ Align the change agenda to the strategic agenda.
▷ Execute process – the day-to-day execution of strategy – at an operational level.

The strategic importance of appetite

As we can see, appetite is central to the RBPM strategy mindset, and for one simple reason. Organizational failure to fully comprehend and operationalize risk appetite in the prosecution of their strategies is a significant contributor to corporate failure. Without question, a lack of proper rigor around appetite management was a significant influencer of the Credit Crunch, as the Royal Bank of Scotland (RBS) case study in this chapter amply demonstrates (Box 4.1).

Box 4.1   The failure of RBS: Strategy and risk appetite

In March 2000, RBS acquired the UK bank NatWest in a £21 billion deal that was then the largest takeover in British banking history. The acquisition was considered at the time to be a masterstroke of strategy and execution. Thus began a "golden period" in RBS's near 300-year history. RBS embarked on an ambitious strategy to transition from a regional to global financial services firm and one that drove aggressive revenue growth. RBS's stock price grew and performed well in the early years of the 2000s and by 2007 the now global financial player was viewed by most analysts as a highly successful bank. For instance:

- From 1997 to 2007 Earnings per share (EPS) had grown from about 50p to close to 250p.
- In 2007 RBS reported a record group operating profit of £10.3 billion (£7.7 billion after tax).
- RBS increased its assets by a multiple of 29 between 1998 and 2008 (assets grew by an average of 41% per year).
- It moved from outside the top 20 global banks by market capitalization prior to its acquisition of NatWest to ninth in the world by 2007.

Then came the Credit Crunch and disaster: RBS essentially failed in October 2008. To prevent collapse the UK Government injected £45.5 billion of equity capital (worth only about £20 billion as of December 2011) and RBS was part nationalized. Overall its stock price dropped from a high of over 700p in early 2007 to around 20p in late 2011.

The failure of RBS is one of the most notorious banking collapses precipitated by the Credit Crunch. Not only did it lead to a one-time darling of the stock market becoming part nationalized, it also led to a catastrophic collapse in reputation. A 2011 study by the Reputation Institute found that the bottom ranked of 260 listed companies in terms of reputation, and by some distance, was RBS.[9] Financial, market and reputational recovery will be a long, brutal road for RBS.

But what went wrong?

The UK Financial Services Authority's (FSA) December 2011 report *The Failure of the Royal Bank of Scotland* answers this question in great detail (running to 435 pages). The immediate cause of RBS's failure was a liquidity run and although, as we summarize, poor decision-making, especially in relation to risk, was a key driver of failure, the report did point to broader reasons, most notably:

- The key prudential regulations being applied by the FSA, and by other regulatory authorities across the world, were dangerously inadequate; this increased the likelihood that a global financial crisis would occur at some time.
- The FSA had developed a philosophy and approach to the supervision of high impact firms and in particular major banks, which resulted in insufficient challenge to RBS's poor decisions. The supervisory approach entailed inadequate focus on the core prudential issues of capital, liquidity and asset quality, and insufficient willingness to challenge management judgements and risk assessments.
- The capital rules which the FSA was applying were in retrospect severely deficient: they allowed RBS to operate with dangerously high leverage. This was one of the most crucial drivers of RBS's failure.
- The erroneous belief that financial markets were inherently stable, and that the Basel II capital adequacy regime would itself ensure a sound banking system, drove the assumption that prudential risks were a low priority.

Nevertheless, the report described a whole raft of poor decisions by RBS management and board. Among the most striking was the decision to go ahead with the AB AMRO acquisition in 2007, which played a significant role in RBS's failure. The board decided to go ahead with the acquisition on the basis of due diligence which was clearly inadequate relative to the risks entailed.

With incredulity, the report stated that "Many readers of the Report will be startled to read that the information made available to RBS by ABN AMRO in April 2007 amounted to 'two lever arch folders and a CD' and that RBS was largely unsuccessful in its attempts to obtain further non-publicly available information."

The acquisition was a primary cause of failure for this reason: RBS entered the crisis with extensive reliance on wholesale funding. Its short-term wholesale funding gap was one of the largest in its peer group, and it was more reliant on overnight funding and unsecured funding than most of its peers. The acquisition of ABN AMRO increased its reliance on short-term wholesale funding.

By early 2007, RBS had accumulated significant exposures containing credit risk in its trading portfolio, following its strategic decision in mid-2006 to expand its structured credit business aggressively. The acquisition of ABN AMRO increased RBS's exposure to such assets just as credit trading activities were becoming less attractive. This increased the firm's vulnerability to market concerns.

Structured credit markets, of course, deteriorated from spring 2007 onwards. RBS, like many others, was by then holding positions which were bound to suffer some loss. The crucial determinant of how much loss was the extent to which a firm could distribute its existing positions, or was willing to take losses earlier by hedging or closing those positions out. RBS was among the less effective banks in managing its positions through the period of decline, according to the report.

It is evident that in pursuing its aggressive strategy RBS was exposed to a plethora of high risks. The FSA analysis raised serious questions about the effectiveness of the RBS board's role in relation to strategy. The report stated:

> Given the scale of RBS's ambitions for growth, in particular during 2006 and into 2007, it is reasonable to expect the Board to have assured itself that the growth strategy was accompanied by a very high degree of attention to the associated risks. In retrospect, this was not clearly and demonstrably the case.

This is a sample of the evidence cited in the report:

– The "Board, Remuneration Committee and Nominations Committee Performance Evaluation 2005" report said that a quarter of the board disagreed that the board's review and evaluation of strategic issues in relation to the group's present and future environment was satisfactory, that directors would like more time to consider and debate strategy, and that a number of them felt that there should be a formal report or discussion of risk appetite when the budget was reviewed. The 2006 report said that directors felt there was insufficient input to and review of risk appetite at board level, that the board needed to articulate its risk appetite and that a third of them did not appear to be satisfied with the board's role in defining and developing strategy.

- Strategy documentation provided to the Group Board for Global Banking and Markets (GBM) did not include detailed analysis of the relevant markets to support the aspirations for growth or of the key risks involved. The risk impact was typically summarized in a bullet point for each initiative, with no information as to how the various risks identified were to be addressed or mitigated. There was no evidence of any significant challenge by the risk function to the proposals.

- Feedback from an adviser who contributed to the RBS executive programme stated that RBS was unique among major banks in having many "hill climbers" but almost no "hill finders". The bank was seen as exceptionally strong in people who would reliably implement agreed strategy but relatively much weaker in its capacity for strategic thinking.

- The relevant risk functions within RBS were not heavily involved in the process of strategy formulation and they did not carry out a risk assessment until after the strategy had been presented to the RBS board. When the strategy was presented to the RBS board in June 2006, the key risks were identified as "Market risk from newly evolved products and model complexity". The FRS found no evidence to suggest that this brief description was expanded on to provide more detail as to the nature of the risk, how and when it would crystallize, and what steps would be taken to minimize it.

Overall, the report stated that within the RBS board and executive team there was a pattern of decisions that may reasonably be considered poor, suggesting the probability of underlying deficiencies in: the bank's management capabilities and style; governance arrangements; checks and balances; mechanisms for oversight and challenge; and culture, particularly its attitude to the balance between risk and growth.

The FRS highlighted to RBS the need for it to have best practice risk management systems including, in particular, to make improvements in stress-testing to show that it would be able to withstand a severe economic downturn; and for the RBS board specifically to consider and debate its risk appetite and establish appropriate limits.

Based on the above and other evidence, the RBS Group internal audit report, delivered to the Chairman in July 2008, said: "Based on our review and meetings with Board members, discussions of strategy could be expanded to include more analysis of strategic options and their associated risks. These discussions would also be supported by appraisals of current risk levels versus risk appetite" and "this should include the nature and scale of the risk that the Board is prepared to take".

Finally, risk and, in particular, risk appetite, had become an agenda item for the Board of RBS.

Note: This case study is based on the report *The Failure of the Royal Bank of Scotland* by the FSA, December 2011 and some additional materials.[10]

It is true that the financial services organizations that suffered catastrophic failure did so due to a complex web of reasons. However, their systematic failure to describe and parameterize the amount of risk that was prudent to accept and be exposed to in pursuit of their strategic goals was a crucial strand of that web.

The 2012 white paper, *Thought Leadership in Understanding and Communicating Risk Appetite* by the Committee of Sponsoring Organizations of the Treadway Commission (COSO) stated that "One major problem that led to the current financial crisis was that although objectives had been created, there was no articulation of risk appetite or identification of those responsible when risks were incurred," and went on to describe how an understanding of risk appetite might have helped avoid the economic (and it could be argued political and social) catastrophe that followed:

> History shows that when risk appetite is not considered (especially in compensation schemes), the organization often suffers from greater risks than anticipated. For example, had financial institutions clearly communicated a risk appetite for unsecured mortgage-backed financial instruments, their management and boards would have likely asked questions that would lead to better risk identification, such as the following:
>
> ▷ What if housing failures differ from the historical model?
> ▷ What if mortgages fail systematically and are highly correlated to an area we are investing in?
> ▷ Could decisions made by some of our operational personnel be creating risks that go beyond our risk appetite?[11] See also Box 4.2 for the role of management and boards in setting risk appetite.

This does not in itself imply a lack of appetite, just a recognition of its role in strategy and in articulation: indeed it is reasonable to argue that the appetite for risk within many of the banks that failed was huge – bordering on insatiable. However, managing, or parameterizing that risk

Box 4.2   COSO's overview of managing risk appetite

Within their white paper *Understanding and Communicating Risk Appetite*, COSO stressed that when determining risk appetite, the board and executive management should take three steps:

1 Develop risk appetite
2 Communicate risk appetite
3 Monitor and update risk appetite

1. Develop risk appetite

Developing risk appetite does not mean the organization shuns risk as part of its strategic initiatives: quite the opposite. Just as organizations set different objectives, they will develop different risk appetites. There is no standard or universal risk appetite statement that applies to all organizations, nor is there a "right" risk appetite. Rather, management and the board must make choices in setting risk appetite, understanding the trade-offs involved in having higher or lower risk appetites.

2. Communicate risk appetite

Several common approaches are used to communicate risk appetite. The first is to create an overall risk appetite statement that is broad enough yet descriptive enough for organizational units to manage their risks consistently within it. The second is to communicate risk appetite for each major class of organizational objectives. The third is to communicate risk appetite for different categories of risk.

3. Monitor and update risk appetite

Once risk appetite is communicated, management, with board support, needs to revisit and reinforce it. Risk appetite cannot be set once and then left alone. Rather, it should be reviewed in relation to how the organization operates, especially if the entity's business model changes.

Management should monitor activities for consistency with risk appetite through a combination of ongoing monitoring and separate evaluations. Internal auditing can support management in this monitoring. In addition, organizations, when monitoring risk appetite, should focus on creating a culture that is risk-aware and that has organizational goals consistent with the board's.

Extracted from the white paper *Understanding and Communicating Risk Appetite*, Dr Larry Rittenberg and Frank Martens, the Committee of Sponsoring Organizations of the Treadway Commission, January 2012.[12]

appetite was not part of their thinking because they fundamentally failed to comprehend that that they were actually taking huge risks. In the run-up to the Credit Crunch the general belief was that securitizing mechanisms meant that it was possible to simultaneously sell on risk and replenish capital without any meaningful risk exposure. Indeed a report in 2007 by the *Economist Intelligence Unit* found that risk management (in particular financial risk) was no longer a front-of-mind concern for banking leaders. Risk management was, to all intent and purposes, "sorted".[13] If risk management was no longer an issue, then why even think about appetite, never mind enclose it in boundaries?

The events that swiftly followed the publication of that report exposed the almost incalculable deficiencies in – and arrogance of – this approach.

We explain the role that a failure of risk management, and in particular risk appetite, played in RBS's stunning fall from grace in Box 4.1. But note that as RBS pursued its high-risk actions it did so to deliver to an ambitious strategy launched in 2000 to transition from a regional to a global banking player. By 2007 it was one of the ten biggest banks in the world by capitalization. Moreover, RBS was simultaneously pursuing aggressive revenue growth, at which it also proved adept. All in all, it appeared that the strategy was being delivered, as demonstrated by RBS's soaring stock price and the many plaudits heaped upon the bank and its leaders. But it was an illusion. The Credit Crunch hurricane of 2008 had little trouble in blowing the bank away.

The RBS story is a powerful illustration of the pressing need for a new approach to strategy/risk integration such as the RBPM framework and methodology that we present. RBS is not a lone example.

Defining risk appetite

But what do we actually mean by risk appetite? Before looking at definitions, it should be understood that risk appetite is *not* a technique, or a consultancy inspired performance improvement intervention that organizations might choose or discard as they see fit. Risk appetite is a natural and everyday part of doing business.

Every decision a manager makes has a risk appetite component. They inherently recognize that there is the potential for both success and failure and therefore make a go/no-go choice based on the amount of risk to which they are willing to be exposed in their attempts to secure the desired strategic outcomes: this is risk appetite, whether the term is formally recognized and managed or not.

It should also be noted that some risk is unavoidable and not within the ability of the organization to manage to a tolerable level. As one example, many organizations have to accept that there is a risk arising from terrorist activity which they cannot control. In these cases the organization needs to make contingency plans to minimize the consequences of such an event.

COSO's definition of risk appetite

In defining risk appetite, we will first consider the definitions according to the risk frameworks and standards discussed mainly in Chapter 3, starting with the 2004 work, *Enterprise Risk Management: An Integrated Framework* by COSO.

COSO included risk appetite as a critical element of its general definition of enterprise risk management:

> Enterprise risk management is a process, effected by an entity's board of directors, management and other personnel, applied in strategy setting and across the enterprise, designed to identify potential events that may affect the entity, and manage risk *to be within its risk appetite* [authors' italics] to provide reasonable assurance regarding the achievement of entity objectives.

More specifically it defined risk appetite as the amount and type of risk that is acceptable to be taken by an organizational entity over a defined time period, to achieve the objectives of that strategy.[14]

The COSO definition is useful because it provides the "what, who, when and why" of risk appetite:

▷ What: the amount and type of risk
▷ Who: an organizational entity
▷ When: over a defined time horizon
▷ Why: to achieve the strategic objectives of the entity

COSO recommended that management should consider the entity's risk appetite in evaluating strategic alternatives, setting related objectives and developing mechanisms to manage related risks.

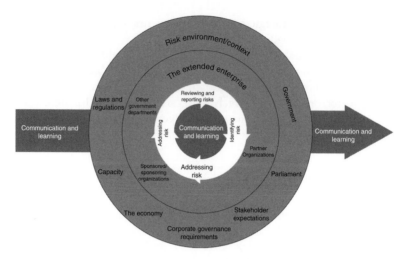

Figure 4.3 **The *Orange Book*: *Management of Risk – Principles and Concepts*: Overall risk management model**

The Orange Book definition of risk appetite

The Orange Book: Management of Risk – Principles and Concepts, published by the UK Government HM Treasury, also in 2004, makes even greater mention of risk appetite, dedicating one of its ten chapters exclusively to the issue. In describing its overall risk management model (Figure 4.3), the book stresses that

> the whole model has to function in an environment in which risk appetite has been defined. The concept of risk appetite ... regarded as an "overlay" across the whole of this model ... is key to achieving effective risk management and is essential to consider before moving on to consideration of how risks can be addressed.

As a definition, the book states that risk appetite

> can best be expressed as a series of boundaries, appropriately authorized by management, which give each level of the organization clear guidance on the limits of risk which they can take, whether their consideration is of a threat and the cost of control, or of an opportunity and the costs of trying to exploit it.

It adds that "an organization's risk appetite is not necessarily static; in particular the Board will have freedom to vary the amount of risk which it is prepared to take depending on the circumstances at the time."

As a short descriptor, the book defines risk appetite as "The amount of risk which is judged to be tolerable and justifiable."[15]

The Risk Management Code of Practice from the British Standards Institution's definition of risk appetite

The 2009 publication *ISO31000 Risk Management – Principles and Guidelines* makes no mention of risk appetite, which many observers (and naturally the authors of this book) consider an erroneous and somewhat odd omission.[16] However, the *Risk Management Code of Practice* from the British Standards Institution, BS31100:2008, which informed the thinking that shaped ISO3100, does define risk appetite: "the amount and type of risk that an organization is prepared to seek, accept or tolerate". This standard also relates appetite to strategy and governance stating: "considering and setting a risk appetite enables an organization to increase its rewards by optimizing risk taking and accepting calculated risks within an appropriate level of authority".[17]

RBPM definition of risk appetite

Within the RBPM approach we believe that firms require a slightly broader definition than those proposed above. We describe risk appetite this way: "the amount and type of risk that an organization is willing to accept, and must take, to achieve their strategic objectives and therefore create value for shareholders and other stakeholders".

By adding "and must take", our definition expresses that taking risk is an inherent part of strategy execution and value creation. Risk is not just about avoiding potential losses, but also about exploiting the opportunities that must be seized if a winning strategy is to be executed.

Risk appetite and risk tolerance

We will also stress that risk appetite is not the same as risk tolerance, although the two are often confused; and to be honest, there's a lack of consensus among risk professionals regarding the difference.

In essence, risk appetite enables the board and executive to define how much risk they are willing to accept, and is a strategic decision. Risk tolerance is more operational and sets the thresholds around Key Risk Indicators (KRIs). We consider risk tolerance and its relationship to risk appetite in detail in Chapter 7. For now, we offer this useful definition, with which we fully agree, from COSO's *Thought Leadership in Understanding and Communicating Risk Appetite* white paper:

> Risk tolerance relates to risk appetite but differs in one fundamental way: risk tolerance represents the application of risk appetite to specific objectives. Risk tolerance is defined as: The acceptable level of variation relative to achievement of a specific objective, and often is best measured in the same units as those used to measure the related objective.
>
> In setting risk tolerance, management considers the relative importance of the related objective and aligns risk tolerances with risk appetite. Operating within risk tolerances helps ensure that the entity remains within its risk appetite and, in turn, that the entity will achieve its objectives.
>
> While risk appetite is broad, risk tolerance is tactical and operational.[18]

Our definition of risk tolerance

In the context of RBPM we define risk tolerance as "the acceptable level of variation of risk taking in the pursuit of strategic objectives".

Creating a risk appetite statement

Now we will outline the process for defining the risk appetite for the organization, and crucially how to ensure this is hardwired to the strategy. We will do this by explaining how to craft a risk appetite statement in seven steps, which clearly describes and parameterizes the amount of risk the organization is allowed to take in pursuit of its strategic goals. A risk appetite statement is also powerful in ensuring that in their day-to-day decisions and actions, employees demonstrate behaviours that are consistent with the organization's appetite for risk.

But note the advice from the COSO paper on risk appetite:

> There is no standard or universal risk appetite statement that applies to all organizations, nor is there a "right" risk appetite. Rather, management and

the board must make choices in setting risk appetite, understanding the trade-offs involved in having higher or lower risk appetites.[19]

Put another way, a risk appetite statement cannot be "plugged and played", but requires a rich and focused conversation by the board and executive team. Seven Steps to Creating a Risk Appetite Statement

1   Identify the key business drivers of your business
2   Define risk levels based on key business drivers
3   Define a set of strategic objectives
4   Define and assess a set of key risks
5   Align strategy and risk
6   Define the risk appetite statement
7   Monitor the alignment of risk-taking to appetite

Identify the key business drivers of your business

The first step in developing an effective risk appetite statement is for the board, in conjunction with the executive team, to identify the key business drivers that are most vital to the organization. This should be completed as part of the strategy formulation process.

Business drivers represent the fundamental drivers of value of the particular industry and organization. These drivers are used as a base for establishing the risk appetite and strategic objectives of the organization.

There is no one-size-fits-all set of business drivers, which vary across industries and sectors. The business drivers of success for a software provider will be rather different from those in retail clothing and again for a bank. Business drivers can be drawn from financial, legal, environmental, social, stakeholder and other areas. A bank, for example, might identify the following as business drivers: capital, income, reputation, regulatory uncertainty and technology innovation, as just some examples.

Key drivers

As the number of business drivers can be quite extensive, we propose distilling these into key drivers – the critical few (perhaps one to three) that have the greatest impact on the success of the organization and therefore need to be managed very closely. To do this we propose that

SWOT matrix organized by Balanced Scorecard perspectives

SWOT guidance			
Strengths	**Weaknesses**	**Opportunities**	**Threats**
Financial — Current financial performance strengths and weaknesses		Revenue growth and productivity improvement opportunities that can close the gap between current performance and the overarching financial objective	Threats to sustaining or improving financial performance; competitor threats that will influence our defence strategy and clarify the extent and velocity of improvement required
Customer — Existing strengths and weaknesses of our value proposition as perceived by customers, competitors and the market		Opportunities to expand the customer base, target new markets and improve the customer value proposition strategy-as perceived by customers and their requirements	Threats to customer and competitor issues
Internal — Strength in our internal processes where we excel	Weaknesses in our internal processes and value chain	Opportunities for internal process improvement to achieve opportunities outlined above	Threats posed by internal process weaknesses
Growth — People/culture, core competencies and strategic capabilities strengths and weaknesses		Opportunities to develop culture, competencies, capabilities to enble strategic priorities	Threats and risks to delivering on the strategy due to the shortfall in capabilities of our people, structure, competencies and culture

Figure 4.4 **A SWOT analysis organized by Balanced Scorecard perspectives**

organizations develop a long list of business drivers for their industry and then specifically for their organization (taking into account the organization's business model – see below – and output from SWOT and PESTEL type analyses. A SWOT analysis organized by Balanced Scorecard perspectives is shown in Figure 4.4, while Figure 4.5 shows the elements of a PESTEL analysis.

Once this long list is prepared, the senior management team should engage in a focused conversation to reach consensus as to which drivers are the most critical to their organization – the key drivers. These key drivers are used to frame a discussion around the alignment of

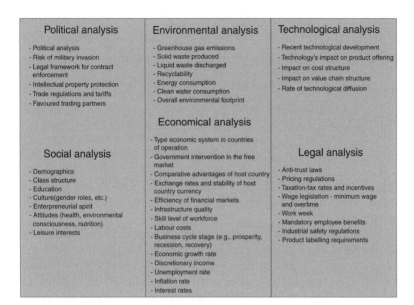

Figure 4.5 **Elements of a PESTEL analysis**

risk to strategy and to define the organization's risk appetite. The key drivers are then used to define levels of appetite using simple descriptors for each level; for example, low, moderate, high and extreme. The exact descriptors and number of levels can be adapted to suit organizational preferences, but the important point is that by defining multiple risk appetite levels which are tightly linked to strategy, the organization has the basis of a shared understanding of the risk-taking options that are available to the organization and the basis of a common language to express risk appetite and discuss risk in general.

Creating this common understanding and language is critical to enabling the board and the executive to effectively select the level of risk-taking – appetite – they are comfortable with and to effectively cascade and communicate the organizational risk appetite to lower levels in the organization, setting the "tone from the top" with regard to risk-taking and clearly establishing the boundaries for risk-taking.

It also becomes the basis for the risk assessment process because the same key drivers which are used to define appetite are used to define how risk will be assessed in the organization.

Tracking changes to business drivers

Organizations should assess whether the business drivers themselves are changing because of either external or internal factors and if so, take appropriate action.

As an example, prior to the Credit Crunch a number of UK retail banking organizations were reducing their reliance on their branch network as a channel to raise capital in the form of deposits to provide loans, mortgages, etc. Instead, many chose the wholesale money markets to raise capital. They had chosen this funding route because at that time there was an extremely competitive retail market and all participants were chasing growth while simultaneously seeking to carefully control costs.

While they may not have expressed it clearly, the organizations that accessed the wholesale markets were doing so because they were recognizing capital as one of their key drivers and adjusted their business model accordingly. This action also implies they had an appetite for the implied level of risk-taking associated with funding via wholesale markets – although subsequent events showed the folly in not parameterizing that appetite.

Post-Credit Crunch, with significantly lower risk appetites across the industry but capital still a key driver, many banks turned away from wholesale markets and once again focused on building their branch networks to generate funding.

Business models

Organizations should also be mindful of changes in the business model, which describe how an organization creates, delivers and captures value – economic, social and other forms. Business model innovation is becoming an increasingly important source of competitive advantage. Business model innovation may be driven from within the industry, whereby an existing player takes a different approach to creating, delivering and capturing value than its industry peers or it may come from outside the industry where a new entrant comes into the market via a different business model. Business model innovation is key to the blue ocean strategic approach cited above.

A powerful example of the market-changing impact of business model innovation is Apple's iPod/iTunes model. Into a world where music was typically purchased on Compact Discs (CDs) and where the consumer had to pay for the entire CD to get the one or two songs they actually wanted, Apple introduced the ability to download music via an integrated hardware and software platform and enable individual songs to be purchased. This was a radically different business model and it massively changed the economic dynamics of the music industry.

Globalization and technology are fundamentally altering how organizations compete in the "continuous turbulent times" of the 21st century. The impacts of both are dramatically impacting the business models within many industries and sectors. Organizations must be fully cognizant of this fact.

The Business Model Canvas

Manigent has found the Business Model Canvas (Figure 4.6) to be a useful tool for understanding the business model and to think about objectives and risk. To explain, the Business Model Canvas, initially proposed by Alexander Osterwalder, is a strategic management visual chart and template preformatted with the nine blocks of a business model, which allows an organization to develop and sketch out a new or existing business model. It assists firms in aligning their activities by illustrating potential trade-offs. This is described through a value chain

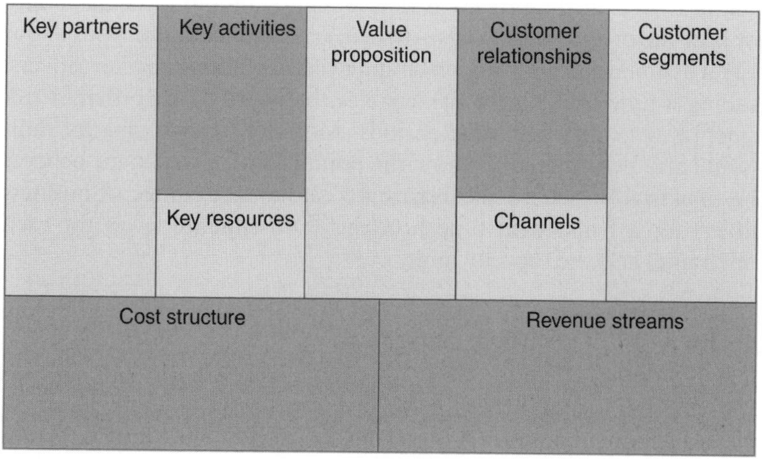

Key partners	Key activities	Value proposition	Customer relationships	Customer segments
	Key resources		Channels	
Cost structure			Revenue streams	

Figure 4.6 **The Business Model Canvas**

Defining levels of risk using key drivers

Risk dimension	Time horizon	No appetite	Low	Moderate	High	Extreme	Capacity limit
Capital	Overnight	No capital at risk	X% capital at risk	X% capital at risk	X% capital at risk	X% capital at risk	X above X£M
Capital	Annual		Upto X £M	X £M to Y £M	X £M to Y £M	X £M to Y £M	Above X£M
Reputation	Annual	No bad coverage	Up to X vol. bad coverage	Up to X vol. bad coverage	Up to X vol. bad coverage	Up to X vol. bad coverage	Up to X vol. bad coverage

Figure 4.7　**An example of business drivers for a bank, with time horizons (and appetite levels for each time frame) and the capacity limit**

comprising key processes; key activities; key resources; value proposition; customer relationships; channels and customer segment, and the underpinning cost structure and revenue streams.[20]

Brainstorming and agreeing the content of each of the nine components enables clarity around how the organization succeeds and can therefore be used to initiate a rich conversation about the business drivers of the organization and from that trigger discussions as to the strategic objectives that will ultimately house the corporate Strategy Map.

Define risk levels based on key value drivers

The next step in the process is developing a common understanding for how the organization will analyse, discuss and make decisions about risk. The framework for understanding risk is by using the key drivers. Adding a time horizon for risk enables the board to set different risk appetites over different time periods. Moreover, a risk capacity limit should also be included to show the point at which the board believes the organization would fail. Figure 4.7 shows an example of business drivers for a bank, with time horizons (and appetite levels for each timeframe) and the capacity limit.

Define a set of strategic objectives

The next step in the process is to determine a set of strategic objectives which the organization is seeking to achieve. The Strategy Map is a powerful framework for setting and communicating objectives. The Strategy Map is explained conceptually in Chapters 2 and 3, while

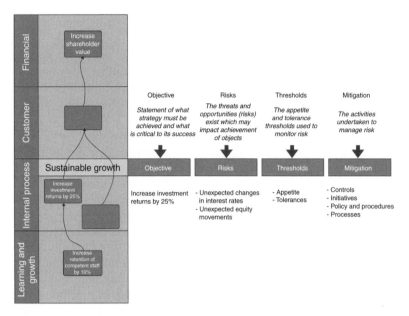

Figure 4.8 **The critical linkage between strategy execution and risk management is made at the objective setting stage**

in Chapter 6 we explain how to identify the component objectives. Example maps appear in each chapter.

The critical linkage between strategy execution and risk management is made at the objective setting stage, where a risk appetite level is set for each objective. This enables the board and executive to indicate the level of risk they believe to acceptable for the pursuing of individual objectives. For instance, a strategic objective within the internal process perspective of a Strategy Map might be to increase investment returns by 25%. An appetite level of "moderate" might be applied to this objective, which will guide the decisions made in pursuance of this goal, and will be supported by the risk tolerance levels assigned to the KRIs (Figure 4.8).

Defining and setting the risk appetite by objective is important for a number of reasons:

▷ Risk appetite can be formally embedded into the strategy management and monitoring process.
▷ The board/executive can be confident that the objective is achievable within the boundaries of the acceptable risk-taking. Risk

appetite can be rolled-up, to provide a view of risk-taking by theme, by perspective or by business unit.

▷ Any objectives and their associated initiatives, which are outside of appetite, can be immediately stopped, creating a more focused strategy and enabling costs to be cut in capital and operational budgets.

Another key value of assessing risk appetite at the objective level is that it furthers the goal of making risk appetite a business rather than technical focus. Indeed the problem of risk appetite is not the definition of what it is. It was well described some time ago within published works such as the COSO Integrated Risk Management Framework, etc., for some time. The real challenge is in the application of this concept – ensuring that risk appetite becomes a meaningful management tool.

Historically, risk appetite has been focused around risk and not objectives, therefore it has been a concept that has been owned by the risk management function, typically defined using technical risk management "tools" and models that can be somewhat abstract and not actionable, or even comprehensible, by the corporate board and executive. Moreover risk appetite (and risk management broadly) was not easy to devolve deep inside the organization, again for operational and language reasons, but also due to the complex mathematics about cascading and consolidating uncertainty. In short, how organizations were looking at risk appetite was not aiding the decision-making processes or the processes for effectively executing strategy in a sustainable way.

Define and assess a set of key risks

With strategic objectives defined, the organization is in a position to start the process of determining its key risks.

Key risks are those risks which are most significant to the organization – the biggest potential threats and/or opportunities – and should be defined based on the organization's objectives. One of the weaknesses with many enterprise risk management frameworks today is the lack of a clear articulation of the organizational objectives. Therefore, key risks are not defined within the context of strategy; rather they are defined based on other more subjective factors, such as gut feel or memory of the last major event to hit.

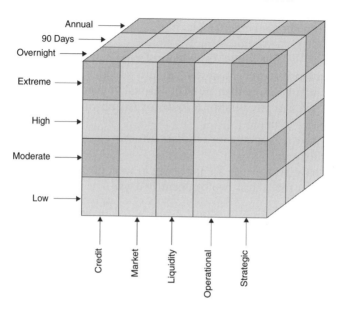

Figure 4.9 **Risk appetite is a multidimensional construct, which changes depending on the organizational entity and its objectives**

There are various techniques that can be used to develop a list of key risks. However, the general approach is to generate a long list of potential risks against risk categories, such as financial, legal, operational and reputation, and then conducting an assessment to understand which risks should be deemed to be key, non-key and emerging. The risk type will influence how the risk is managed. Key risks for the "increase investment returns by 25%" objective might be unexpected changes in interest rates and unexpected equity movement (chosen from the financial risk category).

Risk appetite is stated per risk, indicating the maximum level of potential adverse impact that can be tolerated by the business in order to execute the strategy defined in the third step.

Note too that risk appetite is a multidimensional construct. This will change depending on the organizational entity and its objectives (Figure 4.9). Again, there is no one-size-fits-all. For example, the amount of capital an organization is willing to put at risk overnight is generally very different from the amount to be put at risk for 90 days, one year, etc. Consider the following examples from different sectors.

Investment banking example

▷ We are willing to put £x million of capital at risk to trade on our own account over the next 12-month period.
▷ We hold no more than x% of our capital in overnight positions.
▷ We will accept operational losses of £x million per month. Water industry example.
▷ We have no appetite for causing customer illness by supplying poor quality water.
▷ We have no appetite for appearing in local press related to leaks or fines for more than two consecutive days.

Thinking about risk appetite as a multidimensional construct enables a more realistic, robust and stable approach to risk appetite. It increases visibility and transparency around risk-taking and around which risks are acceptable and which are not.

Align strategy and risk

Risk appetite can only be justified in order to deliver strategic objectives. Therefore, an essential feature of a risk appetite statement is its alignment with the strategy of the business.

An organization might choose to be more or less cautious on various aspects, ranging from credit risk to customer satisfaction, workplace safety, foreign exposure, data protection, legal and regulatory compliance and reputation risk. Priorities and preferences will vary according to the nature of the business, the legal and economic environment in which it operates and the individual inclinations of the board members.

During this stage in the process executive teams have to work hard to align their ambitions, as expressed by a set of strategic objectives, to the acceptable level of risk-taking as defined by the board via risk appetite. This alignment process is typically an iterative process and one that creates a strong, shared understanding of the strategy, acceptable level of risk-taking, agreed performance targets and key risks. Aligning risk appetite with business priorities is an essential step in building an effective risk appetite statement.

Define the risk appetite statement

In this step, the organization is able to produce a risk appetite statement that defines risk appetite while being aligned with strategic objectives.

There is no standard length of a risk appetite statement, or even format for its description. The following illustration of one part of a healthcare organization's risk appetite statement appeared in the COSO paper on understanding and communicating risk appetite. Importantly, the articulation of the statement was based on the firm's strategic objectives.

> The organization has specific objectives related to (1) quality of customer care, (2) attracting and retaining high-quality physicians and health researchers, and (3) building sustainable levels of profit to provide access to needed capital and to fund existing activities. The statement starts as follows:

> The Organization operates within a low overall risk range. The Organization's lowest risk appetite relates to safety and compliance objectives, including employee health and safety, with a marginally higher risk appetite toward its strategic, reporting, and operations objectives. This means that reducing to reasonably practicable levels the risks originating from various medical systems, products, equipment, and our work environment, and meeting our legal obligations will take priority over other business objectives.

> This risk appetite statement does three things effectively:

> ▷ Communicates, with sufficient precision, that the organization wants to sustain its business over a long period of time
> ▷ Expresses a low risk appetite in pursuing all the organization's objectives
> ▷ Expresses a very low appetite for risks associated with employee safety and compliance.[21]

Figure 4.10 shows a risk appetite statement summarized according to strategic perspectives, strategic themes and risk categories. This type of risk appetite statement has a powerful effect on the level of engagement and understanding of risk appetite, and risk management in general. Top level management relate to this simple, straightforward and business-orientated approach in defining risk appetite. This approach recognizes that strategy execution and risk management are surrounded by uncertainty and often lack the high-quality data required for optimal decision making. Therefore, the risk boundaries are expressed in ranges that can be translated into tolerance levels for key risk, control and performance indicators.

Risk appetite statement summarized using strategy map perspective

	Capital	Reputation	Appetite
Financial perspective	Up to X £M @ risk per year	Up to X points loss in NET promoter score	Low
Customer perspective	Up to X £M @ risk per year	Up to X points loss in NET promoter score	Moderate
Internal process perspective	Up to X £M @ risk per year	Up to X points loss in NET promoter score	Moderate
Learning and growth perspective	Up to X £M @ risk per year	Up to X points loss in NET promoter score	High

Risk appetite statement summarized using strategy themes

	Capital	Reputation	Appetite
Growth	Up to X £M @ risk per year	Up to X points loss in NET promoter score	Low
Innovation	Up to X £M @ risk per year	Up to X points loss in NET promoter score	Moderate
Manage cost	Up to X £M @ risk per year	Up to X points loss in NET promoter score	High

Risk appetite statement summarized risk catagories

		Capital	Reputation	Appetite
Financial perspective	Strategic	Up to X £M @ risk per year	Up to X points loss in NET promoter score	Low
	Credit	Up to X £M @ risk per year	Up to X points loss in NET promoter score	Moderate
	Market	Up to X £M @ risk per year	Up to X points loss in NET promoter score	Moderate
	Liquidity	Up to X £M @ risk per year	Up to X points loss in NET promoter score	Low
Customer perspective	Reputational	Up to X £M @ risk per year	Up to X points loss in NET promoter score	Moderate
Internal process perspective	Operational risk	Up to X £M @ risk per year	Up to X points loss in NET promoter score	High
Learning and growth perspective				

Figure 4.10   **A risk appetite statement summarized according to strategic perspectives, strategic themes and risk categories**

Measuring risk appetite

There are many ways by which risk appetite can be expressed and calculated and both quantitative and qualitative approaches can be used. Quantitative calculations include economic capital measures/balance sheet based expressions, profit and loss measures (e.g. tolerable level of annual loss), targets or thresholds for key indicators (e.g. +/− 5% variation in profit or 1–2½% variation in revenue). Qualitative expressions that are commonly used include: "we have no appetite for fraud/financial crime risk"; "we have a zero tolerance for regulatory breaches"; "will not take risks that affect the quality of customer service provided".

As stated in the 2009 report *Research into the Definition and Application of the Concept of Risk Appetite*:

> Such [qualitative expressions] can be very useful and they can help to fill the gaps of an organization's appetite for risk, by expressing certain attitudes or philosophies (e.g. an organization's wish to avoid regulatory sanction and

or reputation damage) that cannot be articulated numerically. Finally, they are often easy to understand and communicate across the organization and can even be integrated within an organization's policies, ethical statement or statement of values.[22]

Monitor the alignment of risk-taking to appetite

This final step embeds risk appetite and the thinking that was generated during the process outlined above into the continuous strategic and operational management processes, thus shifting the management culture from a "performance-only" one that is driven by "hitting their numbers" to one which is strategy-focused and risk-aware, driven by "operating within appetite".

A useful tool for monitoring the alignment between risk-taking and the strategy is the Appetite Alignment Matrix. This matrix provides a simple, visual way of understanding alignment between the current levels of risk-taking based on enterprise-wide risk assessments and the strategy as expressed by taking an aggregated view of the risk appetite levels assigned to each strategic objective. An appetite versus exposure result for the "increase investment returns by 25%" objective is shown in Figure 4.11.

Summary benefits of a risk appetite statement

To summarize, the benefits of creating a risk appetite statement include:

▷ Triggers a reflection on strategic objectives and the risks it implies
▷ Provokes discussions on risk capacity of the firm
▷ Raises risk awareness at board level and in the business
▷ Raises awareness on business value drivers
▷ Enables the board to establish clear boundaries within which the organization will operate
▷ Provides management with a policy document defining the amount of risk allowed in operations and new projects
▷ Constitutes a global decision criteria of "do or do not" when executing the strategy
▷ Reduces the number of ad hoc decisions on risk-taking
▷ Harmonizes risk-taking decisions aligned with strategy objectives

▷ Provokes reflection on risk assessment
▷ Influences the creation of a risk-aware culture

Cascading risk appetite

Although most companies define a single risk appetite statement at the corporate level there is a growing cadre of organizations that are beginning to cascade their statements to lower organizational levels, such as divisions or business units.

Such a cascade makes sense when scope and scale of the business units vary significantly and therefore are influenced by differing business drivers. For example, consider investment banking and retail banking (which have completely different drivers and inherent levels of risk). It would be logical to create a corporate risk appetite statement and then individual statements for the investment banking side and the retail side.

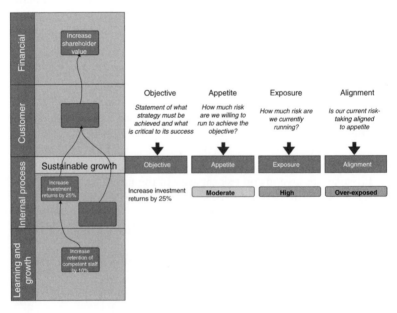

Figure 4.11 **An appetite versus exposure result for the "increase investment returns by 25%" objective**

The statement is not the end-goal

Although formulating an appetite statement is critically important, it is not an end-goal. As stated in the COSO paper of risk appetite:

> Remember the purposes of risk appetite are
>
> ▷ to provide effective communication throughout the organization in order to drive the implementation of enterprise risk management;
> ▷ to change discussions about risk so that they involve questioning of whether risks are properly identified and managed within the risk appetite; and
> ▷ to provide a basis for further discussion of risk appetite as strategies and objectives change.
>
> Developing risk appetite is about managing the organization. It is not about developing a statement to be filed in a report.[23]

Note too that the risk appetite statement sets limits within which a company is allowed to operate, so any breach of those limits during the execution of the strategy must be reported to the board. They will either allow an exception or revise the risk appetite based on due justification, or take appropriate actions to reduce to risk exposure and realign the exposure of the business within its appetite.

Conclusion

This chapter has explained the critical role of risk appetite in the strategy formulation process and described how to align risk appetite with strategy at the level of the strategic objectives. Risk appetite sets the boundaries by which strategy can be executed in a way that heightens the likelihood of sustainable (rather than short-term) strategic success. With strategy formulated and risk appetite agreed, and formalized through a risk appetite statement, the organization is in a good shape to safely begin the process of strategy execution, which we begin to focus on in the next chapter.

5 Understanding the Relationship between the Three Types of Indicators: KPIs, KRIs and KCIs

All indicators : Key Performance Indicators, Key Risk Indicators and Key Control Indicators – are equally important navigation instruments and are critical components of the overall strategic narrative... organizations require each of the indicator types to tell the story of strategy.

In the previous chapter we explained the key steps in formulating and clarifying an organizational strategy. We described how to shape the organization's appetite for risk and how it sets the investment and behavioural boundaries for the prosecution of that strategy (operating within appetite). The next step of course is the actual execution of that strategy – and this, alas, is where things often go wrong. In a 2006 interview, Harvard Business School Professor Robert Kaplan (the co-founder of the Balanced Scorecard) said, "There exists a persistent gap between the strategic goals that organizations set for themselves and the results they achieve."[1]

As we move deeper into these continuous turbulent times, where competition is increasingly global and often springs from unexpected sources, advantage is gained by being able to rapidly implement strategies, while also being able to modify strategic thrusts with equal speed.

But to do this, decision-makers need to receive good and reliable information. Key Performance Indicators (KPIs), Key Risk Indicators (KRIs) and Key Control Indicators (KCIs) are fundamental to that information supply, but are not the only source. As we discuss indicators, and the crucial role that they play, we should always anchor back to the remark from Albert Einstein that "Not everything that can be counted counts, and not everything that counts can be counted".[2]

The obsession with metrics

Indicators are hardly a new management concept. Organizations have long used indicators as a key input to their decision-making processes and as a way to monitor performance. This is right and proper, for although a somewhat hackneyed expression the maxim "what gets measured gets done"[3] is as relevant today as it has always been; as is the equally well-worn saying "if you can't measure it, you can't manage it".[4]

The trouble is that in recent decades, especially since the 1980s when Total Quality Management (TQM) became a dominant performance improvement philosophy, organizations have become obsessed with measurement. Many organizations, and this hold equally true for those in the commercial and public sector, have long since reached the point where they are literally drowning in metrics. Few organizational leaders will complain that they do not have enough metrics. One measurement expert has commented, "We used to have a saying in the US Army that went, 'if it moves measure it, if it doesn't paint it.'"[5] Humorous it might be, but the point he was making was that this mantra can be applied within most industries and sectors.

Measurement as an "end in itself"

Of all the visible misuses and misunderstandings of how indicators are used (and for most organizations this means KPIs), perhaps the most problematic is that they are too often seen as ends in themselves: that is, the primary (and often only) concern of the organization is to ensure that the indicators are reported. Consequently, a huge army of staff is deployed to collect the relevant data and pack it into bloated ring-bound reports. Such reports are rarely read and even more rarely used effectively for decision-making purposes. To use an analogy, organization managers have become akin to the gold prospectors of yore, who had to sift through masses of useless silt in order to find the few golden nuggets. Today, managers are often asked to sift through masses of useless metrics in order to find those few golden nuggets of valuable information.

Consider the following as a powerful marker of how inappropriately indicators are typically used within organizations.

In 2008, the UK-based Advanced Performance Institute (API) conducted a global survey of the performance management practices within over 1,100 public sector organizations across the world. Of the many worrying findings published within the subsequent white paper *Strategic Performance Management in Government and Public Sector Organizations,* perhaps none was more worrisome than the following two: firstly, that a mere 15% of respondents felt that all of their indicators were linked to the strategy of the organization; secondly, even fewer (6%) believed that all of their performance indicators were meaningful and relevant – a staggering 92% reported that many of the indicators were neither meaningful nor relevant.[6]

A later API study, *More with Less: 2011 Performance Challenges for the UK Public Sector* continued the damning indictment of performance management in the public sector with the shocking revelation that staff fabricate data to "look better" – a vast 66% of UK public sector leaders admitted that individuals in their organizations make up or fabricate performance data. Cheating, the study noted, is particularly likely in situations when staff don't see measures as relevant or insightful.

As a result, the study noted, systems can't be trusted and often provide invalid input into the decision-making process. This sometimes leads to wrong or counter-productive decisions and resource allocation, and ultimately the failure of the indicators to make any positive impact on performance. Indeed many might make a negative impact.[7] Although the cited studies come from the public sector, it is safe to assume that similar findings would emerge from an analysis of the commercial sector.

RBPM and the three sets of indicators

The Risk-Based Performance Management (RBPM) framework and methodology have been purposefully designed to ensure that when using indicators (be they KPIs, KRIs or KCIs) organizations can avoid the performance-sapping problems listed above (Figure 5.1).

For instance, in sequencing through the RBPM approach formulating and clarifying strategy precedes the identification of indicators. It is only through building a robust strategy proposition that indicators can be deployed as effective decision-support tools.

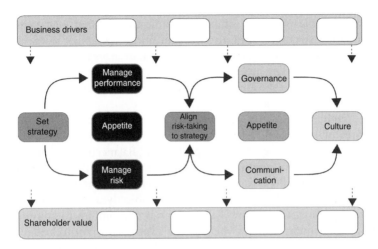

Figure 5.1 **RBPM framework**

Key indicators and a performance conversation

But note that once indicators (even the most robust and reliable) are selected and embedded and with targets identified, this must not be seen as "job done" or to the belief that all that is subsequently required is to collect data and report metric scores though the defined reporting processes.

We argue that as a decision-support tool, indicators are most useful not as absolute measures of performance but as the beginning of a conversation. Within the report *Reinventing Budgeting and Planning for the Adaptive Organization* (co-authored by one of the authors of this book) Bjarte Bogsnes, Senior Advisor in Performance Management Development with the Norwegian oil and gas giant Statoil (a long-term exemplary user of the Balanced Scorecard) made this insightful comment: "the problem is that we often forget what the 'I' stands for in KPI. It is only an indicator of whether or not we are moving forward toward our strategic objectives, not an end in itself." KPIs are, he states, "the beginning of a performance conversation". He also advises against searching for the perfect KPI. "It doesn't exist. I've spent [many] years looking for it. There are good KPIs and good combinations of KPIs, but there's no perfect KPI."[8]

We would add that organizations also forget about the "K". Rather than focusing on key indicators and really doing the work to figure out those key indicators, they simply add indicators to their management information structure, leading to organizations becoming overloaded with indicators, and "signals" from the key indicators becoming lost in the noise of non-key indicators. Forgetting about the "K" is perhaps more of an issue in the context of creating a focused set of KPIs within the RBPM framework.

A further valuable insight from Bogsnes, who has led the introduction of successful Balanced Scorecards within two organizations that have been inducted in the prestigious Balanced Scorecard Hall of Fame – an honour reserved for those organizations that can demonstrate breakthrough performance results from their strategy execution – is that KPIs must be aligned to strategic objectives. "I've seen a lot of scorecards that just show KPIs, which is not enough to communicate or implement strategy," he says. "It's very important to bridge the gap between strategy and KPIs with well formulated strategic objectives. This will help you communicate the strategy and select the right KPIs."[9]

KPIs have to be seen as an integral part of a broader performance story – the story of the strategy. KPIs are the vital navigation instruments used by managers to understand whether the organization is on a successful voyage or whether it is veering off course. Without the right KPIs managers are sailing blind.

We would take this a step further and state that all indicators – KPIs, KRIs and KCIs – are equally important navigation instruments and are critical components of the overall strategic narrative and should be viewed holistically. This is a critical point: organizations require each of the indicator types to tell the story of the strategy. KPIs are part of a "performance-only" framework. KRIs and KCIs provide much greater insight into the future, and promote much greater quality of management conversation than can be gained by simply using KPIs.

An integrated set of indicators

Unfortunately, it is our field observation that most organizations are indeed using indicators in isolation. KPIs are collected and reported that are not, or at best loosely, linked to strategic objectives.

Others might be using both KPIs and KRIs: although this is certainly an improvement on KPIs alone, they still tend to be managed separately by a performance management team and a risk management team, and feeding into different reporting and decision-making processes. As the KPIs and KRIs are not integrated they deliver a "siloed", and often competing, view of the organization and its performance. Therefore, the executive team does not have the appropriate data and information to inform the required high quality management conversations that provide a more complete view of progress toward the strategic objectives or enable the trade-off between risk and reward to be discussed, understood and acted upon.

We will now separately define each of these types of indicators. But note that KPIs, KRIs and KCIs are also discussed in subsequent chapters: KPIs in Chapter 6, in which we consider their role in inculcating the RBPM Managing Performance discipline; KRIs and KCIs in Chapter 7, in which we consider their roles in managing risk.

In this chapter we are primarily concerned with providing robust definitions of each indicator type and delineating clear descriptions of their roles. This will give the reader the level of understanding required to most appropriately deploy and integrate these indicators in the management of performance and risk, and ultimately use them effectively for the delivery of strategy.

Also, definitional clarity will remove much of the confusion that today exists concerning the meaning of these three indicator terms, which is widespread. As a measure of this confusion, Googling the terms "key performance indicators", "key risk indicators" and "key control indicators" in early 2013 accumulated an aggregate return of 63 million results (note: the same exercise in 2009 resulted in the substantially smaller figures of just over 2 million hits).

Clearly there is a huge amount of information available on these topics and this will grow exponentially; and note the burgeoning number of dedicated online KPI and KRI libraries. Yet it is our experience, both in client assignments and through myriad conversations with practitioners, consultants and academics alike that despite the mass of noise, confusion is still the prevailing sound. The gold prospectors' ears are beginning to hurt while they pan!

One cause of confusion is that many organizations that have existing indicators will be using the term "KPIs" for all the indicators: performance, risk or control. In our experience this leads to much misunderstanding during reviews and decision-making events as people interpret the data from a performance point of view, which often leads to a lot of time-wasting around discussing performance when they are actually discussing risk.

Additionally a similar raft of confusion arises when organizations use the terms "KRIs" and "KCIs". Often they mean different things in different functions within the organization or within different geographical locations. This also leads to no end of confusion and wasted time. As we now explain, the three types of indicators are not the same in meaning or deployment. Indeed it is through understanding the differences that it becomes possible to fully leverage the benefits that can be gained through their integration.

KPIs

KPIs enable an organization to do two things:

1   Monitor its progress towards achieving strategic objectives
2   Identify, and monitor progress towards, performance targets

In the broadest sense, a KPI can be defined as providing the most important performance information that enables organizations or their stakeholders to understand whether the organization is on track, and make timely interventions if not. By providing data and information on critical performance issues, KPIs are used to answer the question "Are we achieving our desired levels of performance?"

KRIs

KRIs are used to help define an organization's risk profile and monitor changes in that profile. KRIs are used to answer the question "How is our risk profile changing and is it within our desired tolerance levels?"

KRIs are used to support the risk assessment process in order to develop an understanding of the impact on the organization of identified risks materializing and the likelihood of their materializing. A simple likelihood multiplied by impact equation is often used to assess the level of risk the organization is taking. KRIs provide a base of data and trend information that informs the calculation of risk exposures and informs management conversations as to current level of risk-taking, changes in risk-taking and about how much risk needs to be taken to successfully deliver to the strategic or operational objectives.

KRIs are reported to help understand how the level of risk – the organization's risk profile – is changing over time.

The other function of KRIs is that they help translate risk appetite into operational risk tolerances (which are expressed as thresholds around the indicators). If the organization has a high/extreme appetite it would be expected that the threshold would be wider allowing for greater levels of variation away from the baseline; whereas a low risk organization is going to have tight thresholds to promote a higher level of control.

KCIs

KCIs are indicators that are used by an organization to help define its controls environment and monitor levels of control relative to desired tolerances. KCIs play an important role is managing the execution of strategy and management of risk as they enable the effectiveness of controls to be monitored and proactively managed. This in turn helps create an environment within which decisions can be effectively implemented. A robust controls environment also helps create a "no surprises" culture, thus enabling the organization to remain focused on delivering their objectives while "operating within appetite". KCIs are used to answer the question "Are our internal controls effective? Are we, as an organization 'in control'?"

By being very clear about the different types of indicators in use within the organization, being clear about their definitions, and being clear about the type of question that must be answered, it becomes possible to significantly improve the quality and clarity of the resulting management information and therefore the surrounding conversations.

Three indicator scorecards

Within the RBPM approach we use three "scorecards" to support decision-making – a Performance Scorecard (Figure 5.2), Risk Scorecard (Figure 5.3) and Control Scorecard (Figure 5.4) – which are the key tools for monitoring KPIs, KRIs and KCIs, respectively, and are discussed in the next two chapters. Each of the scorecards can be used by different audiences within the organization or to help focus these conversations.

In keeping with good scorecarding practice, these scorecards should only house the critical key indicators – as small a number as possible

Performance scorecard

Objective	Exposure	Appetite	Effectiveness	Accountable	Responsible	Perspective	Theme	KPIs	KRIs	KCIs
Increase shareholder value	■	■	□				●	●	○	
Grow income in key segments	■	■	□					●	○	○
Increase average share of wallet	■	▪	□					●		○
Lowest cost of funds and cost to serve	■	▪	□					○		
Good value and innovative solutions	■	▪	□							○
Valued, trusted financial provider	■	▪	□					●	○	
Low cost, convenient service	■	▪	□				○		○	○
Drive execution of the sales process	■	▪	□				○	●		
Build market awareness by segment	■	▪	□				○	●	○	
Develop a 360 view of customers	■	▪	□				○	●		○

Figure 5.2 **An example Performance Scorecard**

Risk Scorecard

Business drivers	Alignment	Appetite	Exposure	Accountable	Responsible	KRIs	KCIs
Failure to engage correctly with clients		■	■			○	○
Failure to manage CRM data over its lifecycle	▷	■	■			○	○
Failure to align our 360 profiles to market segments	▷	■	■			○	○
Failure to reduce branch network fast	▷	▪	▪			●	○
Outages due to cyber attacks	▲	■	■			●	○
Poor perception of our products	▲	■	▪			●	○
Access to securitization markets	▼	▪	■				○

Figure 5.3 **An example Risk Scorecard**

capable of providing the key performance insights. Just as earlier we stressed the importance of the "I" in KPI (which holds true for the other two indicator types) we should also note that the word "key" is just as important. What we need to capture are the indicators that provide the most insightful information that decision-makers most

Control Scorecards

Business drivers	Appetite	Account-able	Respon-sible	KCIs	Effective-ness
Compliance policy and process framework	■			●	▪
Four eye check	■			●	■
ATM outsourcing contract	■				▪
Online change control process					▪
Compliance policy and process framework	■			●	■
Product committee and exec challenge to take account of TCF outcomes	■			●	■
Copy of TandC scheme in place	■			●	▪
Liquidity and financial forecasting	■			●	■
Continous credit scoring process					■
Two-stage checking process				●	▪

Figure 5.4   **An example Control Scorecard**

need. When there are too many key indicators the word "key" is rendered meaningless. Furthermore, the key insights, some of which might be of mission-critical importance, are missed (the increasingly deaf prospectors also become more and more blind to the gold!).

As just one of many examples of where the word "key" had becomes meaningless, consider this example taken from the experiences of the authors of this book, gained while working with an organization that reported an extraordinary 400 KPIs on a monthly basis. Through a thorough strategy mapping and Balanced Scorecard exercise this was reduced to about 30. Simply, the organization completed an exercise that started with the question "What information do we *really* need to know to understand whether or not our strategic objectives are on track?" Not only was the number of KPIs dramatically reduced, but the senior team and other decision-makers commented loudly that they finally had information that they could do something with. Put another way, they could see how the KPIs played their part in telling the performance story and in navigating the organization toward its desired goals. The work "key" regained its meaning.

Note, however, that not all of the rejected "KPIs" were completely discarded, but were rather repositioned as measures (and therefore *not* key performance indicators) for which data was still collected, largely for external reporting purposes (it was a government organization). Importantly, however, they were no longer seen as strategic and did not fall like a heavy rock on the CEO's desk once a month.

HML case example

As Gillian Weatherill, Head of Operational Risk at HML, a case study in Chapter 2, describes why only key indicators should be identified: "Through past experiences I have seen organizations with about 400 indicators that they are tracking and the world ends up as amber against the red, amber, green colour coding system [see below] – so it's just about shuffling things around so the world looked a little bit better than it should," she says, adding that with such a vast array of indicators it was very difficult to understand what needed to be done. She says, "So, for every entity we look for a maximum of 16 key performance indicators that are aligned to the objectives within the four perspectives of the Balanced Scorecard."

Organizations should take the time to carefully consider their most important information requirements (based on their strategic objectives) and choose and design their vital few – or key – indicators accordingly.

How indicators work together

HML recognizes that securing the best results through reducing the number of indicators to those that are "key" also requires a better understanding of how all the key indicators work together, and this is confirmed through other Manigent assignments. In a client engagement with an investment bank, Manigent facilitated an exercise around combining indicators and reusing indicators for performance, risk and control purposes. As a result, the number of key indicators was reduced from 110 to 32. The subsequent quality of the performance conversation was markedly improved.

Leading and lagging indicators

To get the best from key indicators, it is important to outline the function of leading and lagging indicators.

The use of the terms "leading" and "lagging" has become a standard part of many companies' approach to indicator definition, particularly those that use the Kaplan and Norton Balanced Scorecard. It was in fact Kaplan and Norton who made the usage of leading and lagging indicators an accepted management practice when they first introduced the scorecard concept in a seminal *Harvard Business Review* article in 1992.[10] That said, the term "leading indicator" has been used in the field of economics since the early years of the 20th century.

The RBPM approach continues the use of leading and lagging indicators, as they are of great value in securing a more complete overview of past, present and likely future performance and therefore provide excellent trending data as well as a more granular understanding of causality (the relationship between objectives and indicators in the delivery of the strategy). They also provide useful insights that lead to the introduction of initiatives to mitigate likely performance or risk-based failures.

It should be noted that for all three indicator types, the meaning of leading and lagging are exactly the same. A *leading* indicator is one that is focused on those factors that are predictors of future results/outcomes, whereas a *lagging* indicator is focused on the result/outcome itself and whether the expected result was achieved or materialized. For example, customer satisfaction might be a leading indicator of customer loyalty or employee satisfaction might be a leading indicator of employee retention. However, for the sake of usefulness and clarity, there are slight differences in the definitions.

KPIs

▷ Leading – a predictive indicator which provides insight into the likelihood of achievement of an objective
▷ Lagging – an outcome indicator which provides insight into the actual achievement of an objective

KRIs

▷ Leading – a predictive indicator which provides insight into the likelihood of a risk materializing
▷ Lagging – an outcome indicator which provides insight into the actual frequency and impact of the risk materializing

KCIs

▷ Leading – a predictive indicator which provides insight into the likelihood of a control being effective
▷ Lagging – an outcome indicator which provides insight into the actual delivery of an effective control

Leading and lagging across indicator types

Although leading and lagging indicators are often viewed vertically within the individual indicator type, consider the following as a simple example of how leading and lagging indicators for KPIs and KRIs can be used together effectively. In a sales situation, a leading KPI might be ratio of connected calls vs. plan. This indicator tells us if the sales team is making enough outbound sales calls. A lagging KPI for sales might be ratio of year-to-date sales vs. quota. This tells us if the sales team is delivering the outcomes, that is, are they closing deals? Together these leading and lagging sales indicators provide useful information as to whether or not the sales team is performing to the standard required to achieve the corporate strategic target, which might, for instance, be growing sales by 10% in the current year and by 50% in the lifetime of the strategic plan. The ultimate strategic objective might be "Increase Revenue from Product Line X.," for example.

If the organization has identified a failure to correctly qualify a prospect early in the sales cycle as a major threat to success against the strategic objective, it might define a risk for the objective such as "failure to qualify the opportunity sufficiently in the first meeting". A leading KRI might be "% first meetings completed without qualified opportunity mutually agreed", and a lagging KRI could be "% opportunities lost during the sales process due to failure to qualify correctly". Together these KPIs and KRIs tell a good part of the story regarding the implementation of that sales strategic objective and so enrich the conversations of the senior team. With leading indicators providing powerful early warning signals of likely future problems, the senior team now has the information required to launch corrective actions – strategic initiatives or risk mitigations – which we discuss over the next two chapters.

On an ongoing basis, the correlation between the leading and lagging indicators of all types should be measured and monitored to create a powerful feedback loop and validate the indicator suite. This will also create a potent driver for continuous improvement of the quality of the indicator suite.

Indicators and behaviour

When using indicators, a critical watch-out is that measurement influences behaviours – inappropriate as well as appropriate. This holds true for all three sets of indicators. As one example, when one organization that we know first started doing risk assessments it didn't take very long for people to realize that if risks were assessed in the "high" and "extreme" zones they got attention. This was, of course, the point as risks assessed in these zones will likely require mitigation. However, the behaviour that quickly emerged was that people would purposely assess risks as high and extreme, then use this as evidence to get approval for capital projects – normally their pet projects!

Detecting such misbehaviour is one the reasons for using indicators beyond KPIs. The three types of indicators work together to help identify if the wrong behaviours are starting to emerge: they counterbalance each other.

For example, if a financial services organization sets an ambitious objective around growing their revenue from cross-selling, and to support this objective has set KPIs, with aggressive targets around PPI (Payment Protection Insurance), then this could encourage the mis-selling of PPI (which appears to have happened and has cost the UK banking industry something like £15 billion in fines and compensation to clients over the last few years).

Now had the organization defined some risks related to their cross-selling objective, such as the risk that they might sell inappropriate products to clients (for example, selling PPI to self-employed people although the terms and conditions clearly stated that self-employed people were not covered by the policy) then a KRI should have helped identify the emerging issue. For example, a KRI might have been as simple as "% of quote achievement by non-core product sales" – when this was consistently over 100% the sales team was either doing an excellent job or taking some short cuts. A KCI in this instance could have related to a random sampling of sales to ensure that the right products were being sold to the right clients.

Identifying inappropriate behaviour is one purpose of the colour code that we use to report indicator performance, as we now explain.

RAGAR colour coding

It is usual for a traffic-light colour coding system to be used to assess key indicator performance against. Typically this RAG (red, amber, green) system is used: red is below target, amber is below target but not seen as a major issue, while green is on or ahead of target. Some organizations add "blue" as a measure of breakthrough performance (that is well ahead of target) as in the Ashghal case example in Chapter 3.

Within the RBPM approach we have adopted a scoring methodology designed to be simple and to effectively communicate exceptions and beaches in tolerances. The scoring methodology uses a RAGAR (red, amber, green, amber and red) approach, with a scoring range of 0–3 (Figure 5.5).

This method is used as it communicates indicator status and exceptions more effectively than the more conventional RAG approach, which typically adopts a scoring range of 0–10. From our observations, we have found that managers often find it difficult to relate the RAG score to the underlying value. For instance, what exactly does 8.4 really mean? How much better is 8.3 compared to 7.8? Often this type of question distracts from monitoring and analysing underlying trends. At the end of the day, what really drives management action – a score or the actual status of the indicator?

We believe that it is the actual status and generally this can be expressed in three ranges – on-track (green – within tolerance), off-track (red – outside of tolerance) and somewhere in between (amber – currently out of tolerance but only by a relatively small margin which might indicate a temporary blip or the beginning of a worrying trend).

This approach is designed to move thinking beyond the traditional "red is bad and green is good" thinking and encourage a more intelligent discussion around indicators. The RBPM scores have the following meaning:

3 – The indicator is within tolerance – no action required.
2 – The indicator has moved out of tolerance – monitor trends, action may be required.
1 – The indicator is out of control – take action.

For example, indicator A has a baseline of 10. Threshold 1 is set at 25% and threshold 2 is set at 50%. Therefore an actual status between 7.5 and 12.5 will be green, an actual status of 5–75 and 12.5–15 will be amber and anything less than 5 or greater than 15 will be red.

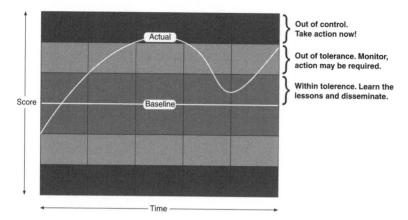

Figure 5.5 **RAGAR model**

In addition to creating confusion, the use of a RAG approach has the potential to encourage the wrong behaviours to emerge as people start "chasing an absolute target", whereas the RAGAR approach promotes a culture where people seek to operate within tolerances but recognize that, although there will be variances over time, the organization need to operate within the tolerances expressed within a suite of indicators.

The risk of doing well

Importantly, this method also acknowledges that the organization can have "too much of a good thing". For example, normally most organizations would suggest that they cannot have too many sales, therefore they set a sales target and as long as it is hit, they do not worry if and to what extent it is exceeded (indeed in most cases exceeding sales targets will be deemed a good thing). If an organization has adopted a performance-only approach to strategy execution, that focus on hitting or exceeding performance targets is understandable and generally rewarded and not usually thought of as a reason for punishment (how many people get fired for exceeding targets?). However, embedding risk management into the strategy execution process means that questions begin to be asked about the risks of over-selling (something that might surprise many).

For example, consider a revenue indicator. A traditional performance-only mindset would generally see higher revenue growth as always positive. While this is usually the case, the RBPM scoring challenges management to think through the consequences of excessive growth and consider the risks introduced to the business due to this growth. For example, if you are growing much faster than expected, will your customer service objectives be met? Do you have the right capacity in your call centres? Are you taking on high-risk clients? What is the root cause of this excessive growth? Is your sales team mis-selling? Are you taking on excessively risky business? Are you operating outside of risk appetite levels? Consider how the world might look today if financial services organizations had been asking such questions in the years before the Credit Crunch.

Conclusion

The RBPM scoring methodology is designed to be simple to understand while communicating a powerful message, highlighting exceptions and challenging management to work through these and determine the right set of actions. When the key indicator scorecard and RAGAR approach are used in combination, or to support other strategic tools such as the Strategy Map and Risk Map or appetite alignment matrix, organizations gain a richer view of the present and likely future health of the enterprise. A new type of conversation begins to take place.

6 Managing Performance

Within the RBPM approach, we define Managing Performance as the continuous process of monitoring objectives and their KPIs, identifying root causes of underperformance and making adjustments.

Introduction

In Chapter 4 we explained that the critical linkage between strategy execution and risk management is made at the objective-setting stage, where a risk appetite level is set for each objective: this enables the board and executive to indicate the level of risk they believe to be acceptable for the pursuit of individual objectives.

Defining and setting the risk appetite by objective is important for a number of reasons. The overriding value is that it ensures that risk appetite is formally embedded into the strategy management and monitoring process.

By defining risk appetite at both the objective level and the individual risk level the organization is in a position to then aggregate and align the appetite at the individual risk level to the objective level. This enables the organization to balance its strategic ambitions and risk-taking and so set the stage for the sustainable execution of the strategy.

Managing Performance sub-components

The implementation of objectives is a core sub-component of the Managing Performance discipline of the Risk-Based Performance Management (RBPM) framework and methodology (Figure 6.1), each of which we will describe fully below.

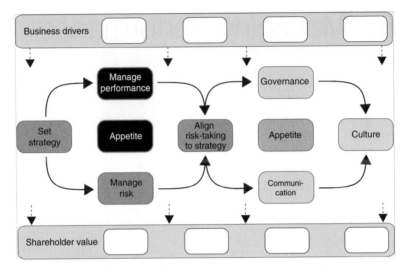

Figure 6.1 **RBPM framework**

1   Strategic Objectives
2   Key Performance Indicators (KPIs)
3   Strategic Initiatives
4   Key Processes.

Within the RBPM approach, we define Managing Performance as the continuous process of monitoring objectives and their KPIs, identifying root causes of underperformance and making adjustments.

Managing Performance works alongside the Manage Risk discipline in the operationalizing of strategic goals. To ensure that this does not simply reinforce siloed thinking in the management of performance and risk, the two disciplines are pulled together within the Aligning Risk-taking to Strategy" element of the RBPM approach, where we introduce tools such as the Appetite Alignment Matrix to help managers ensure their organizations are "operating within appetite."

Strategic objectives

Strategic objectives serve as the first sub-component of Managing Performance, and rightly so. Organizations *must* define objectives before they consider KPIs and their targets, and initiatives, as according to the conventional Balanced Scorecard approach. Within the RBPM approach to managing performance, we add "processes" as a critical sub-component. This is because strategy is executed by driving change (initiatives) or via day-to-day activities (processes). Therefore, once the organization has completed the strategic-level work to define their objectives, they must also define their change portfolio (initiatives) and process architecture (processes).

For each objective on the Strategy Map (which describes the causal relationship between objectives) there is a set of processes and initiatives which are aligned to the objective and support its delivery. This also assists from a risk management point of view as it enables organizations to understand both the strategic and the operational risk associated with a particular objective or set of objectives.

In this chapter we will not describe the value of creating a Strategy Map, which is covered in Chapter 3, but rather the best-practice process by which to identify and describe the strategic objectives that make up the map. As examples of well-constructed Strategy Maps, see Figures 6.2 and 6.3. Readers are also directed to the HML Operational Risk example in Chapter 2, the Ashghal (Qatar) Strategy Map in Chapter 3 and the Saatchi and Saatchi example below (Figure 6.4).

Objectives crystallize the critical capabilities and relationships that an organization must master in order to deliver to its vision and mission and that are then filtered through the lenses of key drivers and the business model.

Using the Strategy Map as a visual guide, the selection of strategic objectives begins by identifying the key financial objectives (or the stakeholder equivalent within the public or not-for-profit sectors) and using these as guides for selecting "supporting customer" objectives. Then, through a causal logic, customer goals guide the choice of objectives within the internal processes, which in turn inform those within the learning and growth perspectives.

The Balanced Scorecard: deceptively simple

That's the process, so let's discuss how to define the individual objectives. Firstly, it is our observation that organizations are often seduced by the apparent simplicity of defining objectives, and indeed the overall scorecard system. It is after all simply a matter of identifying a collection

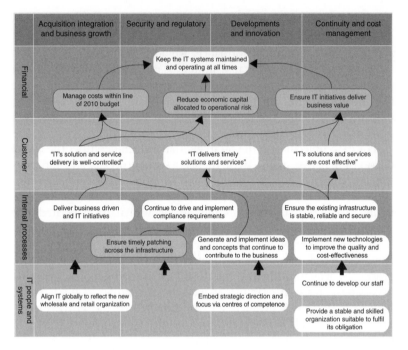

Figure 6.2 **An example Strategy Map**

of objectives and supporting measures, targets and initiatives. How hard can that be?

The fact is that a Balanced Scorecard is *deceptively* simple, which is why a significant percentage of Balanced Scorecards that we see deliver limited value to management teams; and so is why many scorecard programmes eventually wither and die – 3–5 years is a ballpark guesstimate – or at best become reduced to little more than a data collection and reporting exercise that is essentially divorced from strategy. Too often the creation of the scorecard system is given to a relatively junior person or team that has little or no knowledge of the framework or methodology. "It's simple, just do it!" seems to be the prevailing order from the senior team.

The fact is that the identification of the objectives that make up the Strategy Map requires the involvement of an expert facilitator. This might be an external consultant or an internal resource that is fully conversant with the theory of the strategy management and the Balanced Scorecard, supported by demonstrable practical experience.

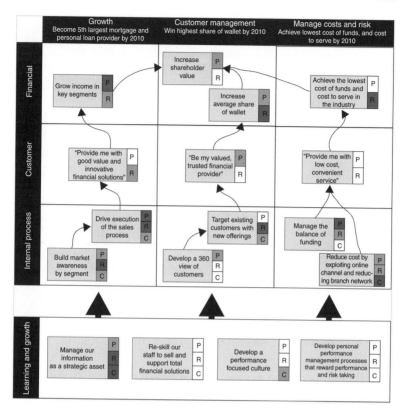

Figure 6.3 **An example Strategy Map**

Asking the right questions

The facilitator needs to know the right questions to ask in identifying objectives, and how cause and effect works at both objective and KPI levels, as well as understanding how to overcome the not insignificant challenges of rollout. In short, the facilitator must know what works, what doesn't and the pitfalls to avoid.

Oftentimes engaging external support is sensible because this should bring independence and neutrality. A skilled external facilitator is able to bring together individual views without getting involved in politics or pushing their own agenda. This is a point that should not be underestimated. It is rare for internal people to be able to remain completely outside of the politics of the organization. They either do not

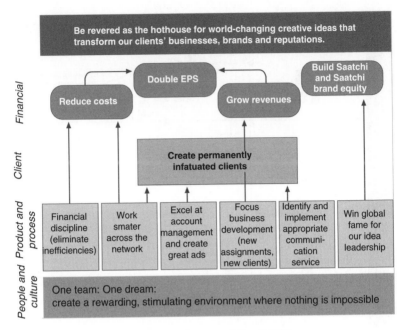

Figure 6.4   **Saatchi and Saatchi Strategy Map (1998)**

have enough perceived authority to challenge the views of the senior team or they are seen to have their own strong interests or agendas: a finance director, for example, might have the authority to lead a scorecard effort but might push their own agenda and make the scorecard too finance-oriented (this is also true of IT or HR directors, as other examples). Conversely, performance analysts might have the independence but not the authority required to influence the scorecard design process or to challenge senior managers.

In dispatching their duties, the facilitator must be armed with the appropriate strategy documents (including the identified key drivers, etc.) and based on this and their scorecard knowledge shape a set of questions to pose to the senior team (who have ultimate responsibility for delivering the strategy).

The capability to formulate and ask the right questions (and then do a proper analysis and evaluation) is critically important, as an early phase of a best-practice approach to scorecard creation is to hold one-to-one interviews with each member of the senior team to tease out what each individual believes to be the key strategic outcomes and enablers, and what they think the organization does well and not so well.

In order for these interviews to be valuable, they *must* be anony-mous. A common mistake is for organizations to create the Strategy Map from scratch in a workshop setting involving all the key person-nel. Unfortunately this tends to lead to a map that is shaped based on the views of the most dominant and outspoken members of the group and therefore primarily represents a personal or functional view, or conversely leads to a map on which all views are captured and so is neither focused on what really matters strategically or ultimately useful. Anonymity ensures that key personnel can express their views in a safe and confidential environment. They can say what they really think!

From our experience, it is important that a standard template of questions is used to collect the insights from the senior team, as doing so invariably means that a clear picture emerges with regard to the organization's general strengths and opportunities for improve-ment. Moreover, what also tends to emerge is a general, high-level understanding of the critical capabilities and relationships that an orga-nization must master to deliver to the strategy. Where there is usually some divergence is regarding the *priority* capabilities and relationships – unsurprising as functional heads typically see their own outcomes as well as processes and learning requirements as taking precedence – and in the description of what those capabilities and relationships look like.

The question set used should be small and focused (perhaps three to four questions per perspective – or per theme, if felt to be more appropriate) and the interview should take no more than one hour. Questions should be open and not closed (such as "describe what value means in the eyes of the customer" rather than "do we satisfy the cus-tomer?") and should be formulated and sequenced so that the answers from each question provides insights into the ones before. Think about cause and effect in question creation.

Moreover, it is important that in these sessions there is no discussion on KPIs or even initiatives. This interview is about clarifying strategic priorities and identifying the capabilities that the organization has or must develop. That said, given that the facilitator has been granted one-to-one access to senior managers we would take the opportunity to ask two questions related to risk, one about appetite and one about risks themselves, as described from the perspective/theme viewpoint, such as "how would you describe your risk appetite for the achievement of your objective?" and "what are the greatest risks in maintaining value in the eyes of the customer"? This will provide useful data for helping to shape the key risks that are assigned to objectives. It also makes sure that the importance of risk is highlighted at the start of the strategy implementation phase; so further ensuring that risk does not become a simple add-on later, with all the dysfunctional thinking and behaviour that might cause.

An objective-setting workshop

With the interviews completed, the facilitator then synthesizes the findings into a first draft Strategy Map. But note that during this phase (and throughout the complete scorecard creation process) a small staff team (perhaps two or three in total drawn from different functions, who should be selected for their commitment to collaborative working as much as their domain expertise) are involved. This is particularly important when an external consultancy is engaged, as the organization must be able to manage scorecards without external support once the consultancy period is over: this should be a contractual deliverable in any consultancy project.

In a workshop setting the draft Strategy Map is presented to the senior team for refinement and approval. The facilitator must use their skills to ensure that this is about making changes that can be anchored back to the original senior management interviews, rather than see wholesale and inappropriate changes made that are based on the narrow observations or opinions of the one or two most vocal team members – which is exactly what the original interviews strive to avoid. That said, in the final analysis it is the Chief Executive Officer (CEO) (or the most senior member of the unit) who must put their stamp of approval on the map, as they assume ultimate responsibility for the strategy and therefore the content of the Strategy Map.

Depending on the level of buy-in and changes made, it often makes sense to schedule another workshop to sign off the final map. The second workshop should be about two weeks after the first strategy mapping workshop. This allows the changes to be made and the new map to be circulated so people can discuss it with their teams and "compare the map with reality".

Understanding key terms

Whether using external support or internal resources, an oft-noted problem with objective selection is the continued confusion regarding key terms: between *objectives and initiatives; initiatives and key indicators* and *objectives and key indicators.* The failure to properly distinguish the two has led to the design of many poor Strategy Maps and scorecards. And this distinction must be understood by the expert facilitator from the outset (although it is unusual for an organization hiring an expert to know that there is an issue here).

Differentiating objectives from initiatives

Beginning with objectives and initiatives, at the simplest level an objective describes *what* the organization wishes to achieve (a statement of strategic priorities) while an initiative describes *how* the organization will deliver the objective (the action programmes launched). For example, "implement a customer relationship management CRM system" is not an objective – it is an initiative to support an objective such as "excellent customer communications". Similarly, "implement a project management system" is an initiative to support an objective such as "excellent project management practices". As a general guide, if progress is measured according to the completion of tasks or milestones then it is an initiative; an objective is tracked through KPIs. When initiatives are large enough, the classic project management KPIs of on-time, within budget and to quality will likely also be used.

Differentiating key indicators from initiatives

This brings us to differentiating initiatives from key indicators. A key indicator tracks progress to a strategic objective through targets that can alter month by month or quarter by quarter (whatever the reporting cycle might be) depending on a number of variables – key indicators are not stable. For example, customer satisfaction scores can vary based on a host of factors – 85% this month might alter to 80% or 90% or whatever in the next. An initiative is a project or action that needs to be completed and is tracked through milestones of completion of tasks. For example, an initiative might be to implement a CRM system and month by month this will increase from, say, 20% to 30% to 40%. The score generally moves in one direction.

Differentiating objectives from KPIs

In the same vein, organizations often fail to differentiate objectives from KPIs. For instance, "improve customer satisfaction" is routinely found within the customer perspective of a Strategy Map. But we would argue that customer satisfaction is a KPI, not an objective. A customer objective should describe what success looks like "in the eyes of the customer". Customers rarely buy a product or service simply to be satisfied, but for some other purpose, such as because they are emotionally attached to the brand of the supplier. This is typical for organizations that prosecute a strategy based on product leadership; people buy a designer label or a particular make of car (such as a Ferrari) because of the brand promise. Similarly, people might buy from one supplier because of their environmental credentials (such as the cosmetics provider Body Shop). Satisfaction with the service, or even product quality, is just one part of the story.

Organizations should really take the time to think through what constitutes value to the customer. Immediately defaulting to customer satisfaction as an objective means that a golden opportunity to hold a discussion about what really drives value to the customer is missed. A skilled facilitator should make sure those conversations take place.

Objective description

Such conversations are useful for many reasons, one being that they can help shape full objective descriptions (or statements). Due to the limitations of space, the definitions of a strategic objective that appears on a Strategy Map are of necessity kept to perhaps 3–5 words; "improve the customer experience" or "create a high-performing culture" being two popular examples. Although useful for ease of reference and communication, such definitions provide no insights into what is meant by terms such as "customer experience" or "high-performance culture". An objective statement is therefore required to fully describe what the objective means and how it will be delivered. For example, the objective statement for "improve the customer experience" might read, "We will target the young mid-high income segment, which are looking for an efficient convenient, innovative banking experience. We will accomplish that by offering low cost, high value services through our exquisite online banking experience."[1] As we can see, such a statement describes who the customer is, the value proposition and the delivery mechanism.

Objective desired state

Such statements can then form the basis for creating a "desired state", which describes what a good state will look like if the strategic objective is delivered and operationalized. Consider the desired state for the "excellent management of knowledge" objective on the Ministry of Works, Bahrain corporate scorecard:

> Knowledge will be effectively learnt and developed and then richly shared, re-used and leveraged across the organization. It means that the right information finds its way to the right people who need it, at the right time when they need it. In order for this to happen, people's attitudes and their practices need to be in tune with known good practices for better sharing and management of knowledge, and they need to be supported in their knowledge work by leading edge tools and systems that support effective management of knowledge. This implies not just Knowledge Management specific tools and systems, but the whole underlying information systems required should be effective. The staff would be supported by a culture that encourages good knowledge management practices. A culture that is open, encourages, recognizes, and rewards the sharing of knowledge, rather than the hoarding of knowledge: a culture where the best kinds of open fruitful dialogue and learning takes place.

This knowledge management desired state was designed as a narrative that told the story of the objective. A key reason for this design was that as the organization progressed the narrative provided a strategic anchor for discussing how well the organization is progressing towards the objective, and should be considered alongside desired states for other theme objectives. Such a discussion cannot be galvanized through just talking about performance to KPIs.

Objective accountability

It should also be stressed that for the Strategy Map to be an effective management tool, it is critical that someone is held accountable for the delivery of strategic objectives. At the corporate level this should be a member of the senior management team. It is the senior team that is accountable for the delivery of the strategy and so, logically, must be responsible for the delivery of strategic objectives. This is true at the Ministry of Works. Indeed, the strategic objective "win and maintain stakeholder support" is owned by the Minister of Works, His Excellency Essam Khalaf.

As a further example, when Saatchi and Saatchi Worldwide (as early as 1997) built their first Strategy Map, which it called CompaSS, ownership was firmly assigned at the top of the organization

(Figure 6.4). The Global CEO owned the corporate map, regional CEOs (such as for Asia-Pacific) owned perspectives and a selection of Country CEOs owned objectives. Assigning such high-level ownership ensured that things got done and the strategy got delivered (from near bankruptcy in 1997 the organization used the scorecard as the central tool to transform into a highly successful and profitable organization; for example it hit very stretching three-year targets it had set itself and communicated to Wall Street six months early).[2]

Performance Scorecard

Within the RBPM approach, a Performance Scorecard is used to track progress towards the objectives on the Strategy Map. The Performance Scorecard presents the organization's (or business unit's) objectives, the accountable person for each objective, Appetite Alignment status, Aggregated Objective Score (based on the underlying KPIs), KPIs and KPI score.

The Performance Scorecard is designed to enable a management team to focus on the performance of the organization with each of the accountable people speaking to their objectives. The Performance Scorecard also shows progress towards KPIs. An example Performance Scorecard is shown in Figure 6.5.

Selecting KPIs

We will now discuss how to select KPIs. Firstly, the expert facilitator and their team then (and *strictly* only then) move on to the selection of KPIs once the Strategy Map is complete. As with the selection of objectives, this comes complete with a raft of challenges that are not always readily apparent – and reinforces the deceptive simplicity of the Balanced Scorecard.

Both financial and non-financial

A primary reason for building a Balanced Scorecard is that it houses financial and non-financial performance perspectives, so it is critical that as much attention is expended on identifying non-financial KPIs as on financial ones.

Performance scorecard

Objective	Exposure	Appetite	Effectiveness	Accountable	Responsible	Perspective	Theme	KPIs	KRIs	KCIs
Increase shareholder value	■	■	▫				●	●	○	
Grow income in key segments	■	■	▫					●	○	○
Increase average share of wallet	■	▫	▫					●		○
Lowest cost of funds and cost to serve	■	▫	▫					○		
Good value and innovative solutions	■	▫	▫							○
Valued, trusted financial provider	■	▫	▫					●	○	
Low cost, convenient service	■	▫	▫				●		○	○
Drive execution of the sales process	■	▫	▫				●	●		
Build market awareness by segment	■	▫	▫				●	●	●	
Develop a 360 view of customers	■	▫	▫				●	●		○

Figure 6.5 **An example Performance Scorecard**

But there is no escaping the fact that it is generally much more difficult to identify non-financial KPIs than their financial counterparts. For legal and accounting reasons we have a long history of using and reporting financial metrics. Double-entry bookkeeping, for instance, was invented in the 13th century by Venice merchants and subsequently formalized by the Italian monk Luca Pacioli in the 1494 book *Summa de Arithmetica, Geometrica, Poroportioni et Proportionaltie*.[3] We have more than half a millennium of experience and knowledge in defining the financials. This isn't true for non-financials. And we have very little experience of measuring some of the areas that will be critical in moving forward, such as around global and collaborative working.

As one example of the challenges we currently face, many score-cards include objectives around creating high-performance cultures or knowledge management: it is notoriously and frustratingly difficult to identify meaningful KPIs for both – but that doesn't mean we should use the level of challenge as an excuse to settle on KPIs that are at best tenuously linked to the objective. The facilitator and their team must expend the time and effort to really think through the key data that are required to inform the senior team as to how well they are progressing to any non-financial objective and so will determine the KPI (the objective statement and desired state will be used to guide this thinking).

There is also a large (and seemingly ever-growing) repository of online advice from KPI libraries and other such forums to draw from: blogs and LinkedIn being two further examples. But a golden rule is: do not simply pick and plug and play a KPI; it must properly represent the key information requirements.

KPI cause and effect

As with objectives, there should be a cause and effect relationship between KPIs. The targets for outcome KPIs will only move up and down, at least to any significant level, if there are also changes to the lower level enabler KPIs (for example, a change in a KPI related to customer management is required to drive changes to a KPI such as customer satisfaction). It is not unusual for KPIs to be identified for individual objectives without any reference to other objectives or their KPIs. This is a fundamental error.

For cause and effect to be understood, KPI selection must start at the outcome level. When selecting lower level theme KPIs the facilitator and their team must ask themselves how these enabler KPIs will drive changes at the outcome level.

But changes in outcome statuses will likely be subjected to a time delay. For this reason the organization must develop capabilities in *reading* a scorecard: what is the past, present and likely future story that is being told?

Strategic versus operational KPIs

It is also important to stress that strategic performance indicators are different from those required to monitor operational performance. Too many scorecards confuse the two. While with operational measures it is desirable to get closer and closer to "real time" measurement, this is not required for strategic KPIs. Strategic KPIs are not monitored day by day, and certainly not hour by hour. Strategic KPIs are more about monitoring progress toward achieving a new and different envisioned destination, as opposed to just doing things better, and they typically don't change that often. More frequently we are seeing strategic KPIs monitored on a Balanced Scorecard and operational measures monitored on an operational dashboard.

The following provides some good practice tips for selecting and using KPIs.

Common definitions

To be useful for aggregation, comparison and best-practice sharing, measures should be commonly defined organization-wide. Typically this is an early and difficult challenge as it is not unusual to find that performance is measured in many different ways across the enterprise. For example, we observed one organization that had a KPI for on-time delivery. Whereas in one part of the company on-time delivery was calculated from when the order was received, another unit's calculation was from when the order was processed. In practice they had two different KPIs, and any performance comparison was misleading and not providing the senior team with useful data to identify performance gaps.

In an ideal world over 90% of reports and information would come from a central repository, such as a data warehouse, as a single source of truth. Note that a "single source of truth" is a concept and does not necessarily mean one single data warehouse in a physical sense, but is a single place where particular information is sourced. The goal is to inculcate common metrics definitions and consistent data sources that ensure consistency and quality of information.

Do not repackage

It is also important that organizations choose strategic KPIs that truly do support strategic objectives and are not simply a repackaging of measures that are already in existence. From our experience, it is not surprising for up to 50% of preferred measures to be unavailable on launching a Balanced Scorecard system. Organizations then have to either create the KPI from scratch, or if data sourcing would prove too time-consuming or expensive opt for proxy measures (a close assimilation). That said, too many organizations default to proxies that are far from close assimilations. To continue the illustration above, although it might be difficult to identify Impactful KPIs for an objective such as "effective knowledge management", defaulting to something like "the percentage of employees that have access to a shared drive" is not good enough on its own.

Driving the right behaviours

The facilitator and supporting team must also ensure that selected KPIs do not drive inappropriate behaviours (this holds true for all indicator types) and this is not always as evident as is thought. As a true story, one global pizza delivery firm had a KPI around time to deliver product to the customer. They supported this by a promise to the customer that if the food was not delivered within a certain timescale then the food would be free. This worked well until one day a restaurant had a problem with the ovens, a delivery was dispatched late and the delivery boy (about 18 years old) got on his motorcycle and drove as quickly as possible to meet the delivery deadline. He crashed and died.

As a further example, many organizations have KPIs around site injuries. Although these should be tracked, the danger is that if care is not taken, rather than encouraging greater safety it simply leads to people not reporting the more minor injuries as they did previously. Typically, therefore, the KPI score improves, while in reality performance might not have changed or even deteriorated. As the true performance is now masked managers have poorer information to inform their conversations. Driving inappropriate behaviour is particularly likely when indicator performance is linked to bonuses.

KPI ownership

As with strategic objectives, ownership and accountability should be assigned to KPIs, as well as key risk indicators (KRIs) and key control indicators (KCIs) and also for initiatives. This is crucial for the operationalizing of the strategy and assuring that the organization is operating within appetite. As an example, the Ministry of Works in Bahrain has more than 170 owners assigned to objectives, KPIs and initiatives. But assigning ownership is not enough in itself; it must be accompanied by accountability.

Plan to overcome resistance

A problem that many organizations face is that the process of assigning ownership – and most particularly accountability – is that it often leads to resistance to the KPI.

The plain truth is that most people have a natural fear of measurement because they are afraid it will expose their weaknesses and shortcomings. People in positions of influence in organizations have often succeeded against a certain set of KPIs and the measures effectively define the rules of the game in the organization. Those in positions of power understand the rules of the game well, so they may resist if they fear they can't succeed under the new set. Moreover, at lower levels employees might resist because they do not want their superiors to gain insight into their work.

As a consequence, there can be a tendency for managers to push for metrics with which they feel comfortable and are sure they can succeed against. Overcoming such resistance requires the constant communication of the fact that the purpose of KPIs is to identify performance improvement opportunities and not to name and shame. For this reason, within the RBPM methodology we encourage the usage of a RAGAR (red, amber, green, amber, green) approach to indicator monitoring and reporting which assesses performance to thresholds rather than absolute targets. This approach promotes a culture where people seek to operate within tolerances but recognizes that although there will be variances over time, broadly the organization needs to operate within the tolerances expressed within a suite of indicators.

Actionable

It is also important that KPIs are actionable. KPIs that are nice to know but do not trigger step-change performance improvement typically have no place on a Balanced Scorecard. For instance, if an organization has an objective to retain talent and has clearly defined what constitutes talent and has an agreed common enterprise-wide KPI, and the measures shows that strategically critical employees are walking out the door, (which actually also serves as KRI and should therefore be managed through risk management activities) then this should trigger an intervention. Simply put, we have a strategic objective, the KPI indicates we are failing to meet that goal and so we do something about it (either as a short-term action or a longer term strategic initiative).

City of Christchurch, New Zealand case example

As an example, the City of Christchurch, New Zealand is a recognized exemplary user of the Balanced Scorecard (its Strategy Map, which it simply calls a "Plan on a Page", is shown in Figure 6.6). As with the Ministry of Works in Bahrain it is a member of the prestigious Palladium Hall of Fame (an honour bestowed by the originators of the Balanced Scorecard on those that can demonstrate

Plan on a page
Executive team

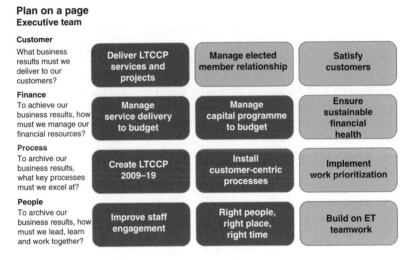

Customer
What business results must we deliver to our customers?

Deliver LTCCP services and projects

Manage elected member relationship

Satisfy customers

Finance
To achieve our business results, how must we manage our financial resources?

Manage service delivery to budget

Manage capital programme to budget

Ensure sustainable financial health

Process
To archive our business results, what key processes must we excel at?

Create LTCCP 2009–19

Install customer-centric processes

Implement work prioritization

People
To archive our business results, how must we lead, learn and work together?

Improve staff engagement

Right people, right place, right time

Build on ET teamwork

Figure 6.6   **City of Christchurch Strategy Map**

breakthrough performance through the usage of the scorecard). The City of Christchurch has customer-focused strategic objectives within both its customer and learning and growth perspectives. Through an annual assessment against the Malcolm Baldrige criteria (a quality management framework that assesses performance against various categories such as leadership, strategic planning and customer focus) see figure 1.4 it realized that it was not performing as well against customer performance criteria as it would like (a KPI on its scorecard). As a consequence it launched a comprehensive council-wide customer service training course and mandated that all employees attended. The initiative was monitored by the senior team as part of their monthly scorecard review. When Christchurch completed their next Malcolm Baldrige assessment they significantly improved their score to the customer criteria, which was then reported as an improved as a KPI on their scorecard. As well as showing the importance of taking action, it also highlights the role of target-setting, to which we now turn our attention.

Selecting targets

Naturally, any chosen KPIs must be supported by targets (although amazingly this is not always the case!) and these should be set over the lifetime of the strategic plan. The purpose of setting these targets is to set a course by which performance to the targets rises on an upward trend throughout that timeframe. But there are some rules regarding the selection of performance targets that need to be understood.

Stretching but achievable

Firstly, organizations need to be clear about the criteria for setting targets. Basically, targets should be stretching but achievable. There is little point setting a long-term on-time delivery target of 80% if present performance is 75%. That said, targets should not be so ambitious that everyone knows they are simply unachievable: for instance, setting a target of 95% to be achieved during the next quarter is pointless if the present performance level is 50%. Any lack of credibility regarding targets will damage the integrity Balanced Scorecard system as people refuse to take it seriously and buy-in recedes. It will also provide powerful ammunition to those with a strong personal desire to derail the scorecard process.

Moreover, setting stretch targets also highlights the already cited issue around encouraging inappropriate behaviours. For example, it was aggressive sales targets that led to issues in UK financial services, such as mis-selling of payment protection insurance on mortgages.

Relative performance targets

It is also important to think in terms of relative performance targets. Organizations typically set targets based on what they think they can do, but increasingly leading companies are setting relative targets as they're much more concerned about where those in their industry are moving to. For example, setting a target of 85% on-time delivery in a year's time is of little value if the competitors are already at 95%. In such instances, an organization might need to set targets that many think to be unachievable, but in doing so invest significant time and resources in driving breakthrough performance over a relatively short time.

Benchmarking

In understanding relative performance we must discuss benchmarking. The customer-facing KPIs used by Christchurch City Council were based on benchmarks drawn from the extensive performance database of organizations assessed against the Malcolm Baldrige criteria (the same holds true for the European Foundation for Quality Management Excellence model – see figure 1.5). From both frameworks, benchmark data can be secured against the universal database (that is, all industries and sectors and in all geographic regions) or more narrowly (specific industries, etc.). Moreover, organizations such as the US-headquartered Hackett Group[4] has a rich database of benchmarks for support functions such as finance, HR, IT and Procurement. A good consultant will likely bring with them a useful arsenal of benchmarks.

Trending

Furthermore, in setting targets organizations must be cognizant of how trending works, and the role of control limits. Consider this example (which is based on a real-life occurrence). A UK-based housing estate was experiencing serious criminal-related incidents on a Friday evening (connected with the local bars) that required police intervention. There was not a permanent police presence during this timeframe, so in order to reduce crime it was decided that this had to be rectified. On the Friday before the police made their presence felt there were eight serious incidents. On the first Friday with a police presence there were 11 such incidents. Plotted against a scorecard this tells us that performance *went down* (in that incidents went up) when the police were present. This seems to suggest that the police presence had no impact, and perhaps made things worse.

Trending tells a different story. In the 10 weeks prior to the police intervention the number of incidents ranged from eight to 20 (with 14 being the average). Therefore, eight was the lowest number that could reasonably be expected. This can serve as the control limits that provide the data of what performance looks like without any intervention. In the 10 weeks after the deployment of the police, their lowest number of incidents was two and the highest 11, with the average being six. As we can see the police intervention was a success, but not if we only looked at the first two data points.

Organizations need to know control limits so that they avoid making expensive interventions – perhaps through initiatives – if the scorecard shows that performance to a customer satisfaction score has fallen from 82% to 76% in a quarter (which feasibly could change a traffic light colour from yellow to red and so trigger an exception report) when in fact it is no more than a natural variation.

Returning to the work of the external facilitator and their team, it is they who will complete the field work of identifying KPIs and their corresponding targets. But again these need to be presented to the senior team in a workshop setting for refinement and signoff. The facilitator must use their skills to ensure that powerful voices do not drive the removal of challenging KPs or the easing of stretching targets.

Strategic initiatives

It is through strategic initiatives (along with processes; see below) that strategy execution takes place. It is through strategic initiatives that breakthrough performance change is achieved.

Initiatives should be kept to the vital few that really drive the significant change required to improve the KPI score and ultimately therefore the delivery of the strategic objective. Strategic initiatives are not about incremental performance improvement. In organizations for which project management is a critical capability, it is not unusual for strategic initiatives to be managed according to the established project management approach. Gate reviews, where the project must pass an assessment against milestone criteria in order for investment to be approved for the next stage, and other such techniques will be used. However, this will likely only apply to large projects and not smaller initiatives that might be strategic in nature but delivered over a reasonably short timeframe, say six months to a year.

Describing a strategic initiative

It is important to be clear as what an initiative is and what it isn't. Without this clarity, organizations often end up with a long list of initiatives that are part genuine initiatives and part actions and part business as usual.

For instance, "implement a CRM system" or "build a shared services organization" are genuine strategic initiatives, meaning that they are initiated to drive significant change. An action might be to conduct a customer survey or appoint a customer service manager; that is, they are tasks that are required for the successful delivery of an objective but will not in themselves deliver breakthrough performance improvement. Actions might appear as tasks within a strategic objective. Creating an annual business plan is something an organization has to do on a regular basis; therefore it is business as usual and not a strategic initiative.

As a rule of thumb, any initiative should require at least two quarters to be delivered, otherwise there is little point placing it as a major item on the scorecard and it is more appropriately managed as an action.

A strategic initiative is also a one-time event, is unique and has a start and end date. Within the RBPM approach we use the terms "initiative" and "sub-initiative". For instance, "transform the organizational culture using the RBPM approach" might be an initiative, whereas "framework design", "change management" and "technology procurement" might be sub-initiatives. Oftentimes sub-initiatives will be handled by different parts of the organization. Housing them together as sub-initiatives (alternatively called child-initiatives) that support a parent and are managed holistically is a powerful way to drive cross-functional collaboration and a consistency of purpose. Once completed, the initiative is taken off the scorecard.

Prioritizing initiatives

We have stated that initiatives should be kept to the vital few. As well as providing the clarity required to tell the performance story there's another, more practical reason for keeping the number down. Unlike the selection of strategic objectives or KPIs, choosing initiatives means committing what might be scarce financial and human resources (and in these post-Credit Crunch days, scarcity is certainly the day-to-day reality facing most organizations).

So let's consider how to prioritize initiatives.

Candidate identification

Within facilitator-led brainstorming sessions with cross-functional teams from across the business, candidate initiatives can be identified. The teams will be provided with a definition of an initiative, with examples and criteria for their selection, such as "drive breakthrough performance change against one or more strategic objectives".

Identify all existing initiatives

All existing initiatives within the organization need to be identified, which will require the facilitator and their team to spend time with functions and departments to determine which major initiatives are under way; but at this stage the primary interest is in identifying those that drive corporate change and not those that are driving local, operational improvements.

Choose the preferred initiatives

Next, for each strategic objective simply list the initiatives (candidate and existing). This is a relatively straightforward exercise, but one that can deliver immediate benefits as it:

(a)   Shows just how many initiatives are under way enterprise-wide (the sheer number and aggregate cost might surprise many of the senior leaders).
(b)   Enables a first discussion as to "why" these initiatives are in progress (the benefits) and therefore allow senior managers to comment on how they see the initiatives linking (or not) to strategic goals.

Indeed it is not unusual, when a systematic exercise is completed that links initiatives back to the Strategy Map, for the number of strategic initiatives presently under way within the organization to reduce substantially. This is because some initiatives might well have historically been launched for good reasons but are no longer strategically relevant. There's another bunch of initiatives where there's overlap and several departments are unknowingly tackling the same issue: in such cases teams can be brought together to form one team or one or more initiatives might be simply killed.

As a caveat, although initiatives should generally be tracked back to one or more strategic objectives under RBPM, we also look to ensure that we catch and manage all important initiatives, regardless of their alignment to objectives; this is because we develop an understanding of not only the alignment of initiatives to objectives but also the risk picture related to the organizational change agenda. For this we need to capture an extra level of initiative detail. Capturing strategic initiatives is absolutely critical, but is not enough.

Crucially, at the corporate level, the initiative prioritization process should involve the senior team. This is especially important because it is only at the initiative level that money is spent. And there is little point in a lower level team "agreeing" a set of strategic initiatives that might or might not be approved by the senior team.

Resource allocation

Next there needs to be a cost breakdown for each of the strategic objectives. As part of this it is important to map the required resources to the intended initiatives.

Initiative selection templates

There are a number of templates available for guiding an organization through the initiative selection process, two of which we now show – one from a consultancy and the other from an organization.

Palladium example

Figure 6.7 shows a template originated by the Balanced Scorecard specialist consultancy Palladium that shows how to map initiatives against strategic objectives on the Strategy Map. It shows where objectives have no aligned initiatives and others than have more than one initiative. The most powerful initiatives are those that impact more than one objective and will typically receive preference over others. This template needs to be supported by a more granular description of initiative selection, which takes us to the second template.

Ashghal case example

Figure 6.8 shows an initiative template that is used by Ashghal, Qatar's Public Works Authority. This template is applied for every initiative that is to be considered for funding and thus appearing on the scorecard. The template comprises an initiative description as well as timelines (milestones and tasks). It also includes an assessment of the initiative against several key criteria.

▷ **Alignment**: impact on strategic objectives
▷ **Value/benefits**: financial and intangible (Environmental, Social and Cultural. Sustainability)

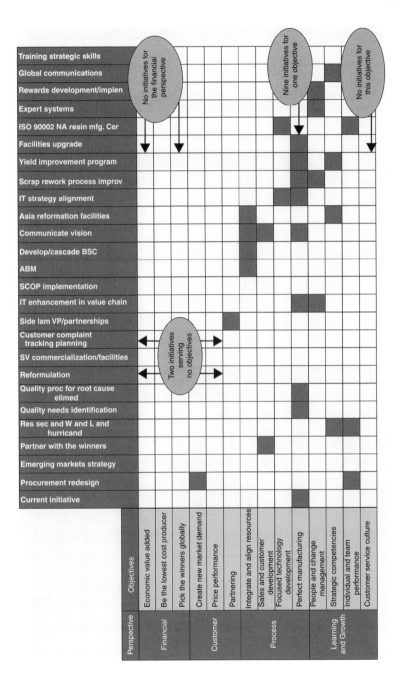

Figure 6.7 **Mapping Initiatives to Objectives, Palladium**

Initiative details	
Initiative name	
Initiative owner/sponsor	
Project manager	

Initiative description

Timelines

Major tasks/milestones	FY2009				FY2010				FY2011				FY2012			
	Q1	Q2	Q3	Q4	Q1	Q2	Q3	Q4	Q1	Q2	Q3	Q4	Q1	Q2	Q3	Q4
1.Initiation																
2.Planning																
3.Implementation																
4.Phase 1																
5.Phase 2																
6.Phase 3																
7.Phase 4																
8.Testing																
9.Monitoring and control																
10.Closeout																

Assessment of risk/difficulty to implement

	FY2009	FY2010	FY2011	FY2012
FT staff hours rqd	2.5	2	1.5	
$ Capital costs rqd	200,000			
$ Other costs rqd	30,000	30,000	30,000	
Total cost	M	H / M / L assessment of the above costs in total (for this business plan period)		
Duration	M	H / M / L assessment for this business plan		
Tech complexity	M	H / M / L assessment		
Org. complexity	M	H / M / L assessment		

Assessment of benefits

$ Return (saved/made)	M	H / M / L assessment
Intangible benefits	M	H / M / L assessment

Assessment of strategic alignment

Level of alignment	M	H / M / L assessment
% Strategic impact	M	H / M / L assessment

Figure 6.8 **An example initiative template**

▷ **Difficulty**: Duration (Time to implement the Project) Cost (Cost to Implement the Project) Organization Difficulty (Stakeholder Involvement/Breadth and Depth of Change) Technical Difficulty (Uniqueness, Sensitivities, Scarcity of Resources, Materials, People)

Assessment against these criteria is used for all initiatives, be they performance improvements or risk-focused mitigations. But note that the final score generated does not in itself decide which initiatives will go forward. The final order is decided by the senior team, who might accept initiatives that more costly and difficult than others, for instance, due to the initiative's strategic importance and the organization's appetite for risk.

Manigent approach

A further example – and an approach used by many Manigent clients – is to look at the capital expenditure requirement, the business impact (what objectives is the initiative enabling?), level of risk of the initiative and time (man days) involved. Each of these dimensions is given a maximum of 100 points and then a cut-off value is agreed: for example, 260. Any initiative below the 260 threshold will not progress to execution. For this we use an Initiative Alignment Matrix (Figure 6.9).

The Initiative Alignment Matrix enables the organization to define the relative strength of alignment between the initiatives and the

	Objectives					Risks			Controls	
	Objective 1	Objective 2	Objective 3	Objective 4	Objective 5	Risk 1	Risk 2	Risk 3	Control 1	Control 2
Initiative 1	25%									
Initiative 2			50%		75%		25%			
Initiative 3		100%								
Initiative 4		50%		50%		50%			50%	

Figure 6.9 **An Initiative Alignment Matrix**

strategic-level objective, risk and/or control. We recommend using percentages to represent the strength of the alignment:

▷ 100% – Very strong alignment
▷ 75% – Strong alignment
▷ 50% – Moderate alignment
▷ 25% – Weak alignment
▷ 0% – Very weak alignment

Each initiative must be aligned to a strategic objective, risk or control or a combination of all three – meaning an operational process can be in place to enable the achievement of an objective, to enable the management of a strategic risk or to enable a control to be implemented effectively.

Using the Initiative Alignment Matrix, an organization can align a single initiative to multiple objectives, risks and/or controls using the percentages above.

However, the CEO always has the final say in which initiatives are or are not funded.

Processes

The final sub-component of the Managing Performance component of the RBPM framework considers processes. Invariably, when executing strategies the day-to-day performance of the existing processes require some levels of improvement if the organizational objectives are to be delivered. Moreover, other operational issues will emerge that require changes to be implemented within the business to correct current or projected performance gaps; this is why consistent monitoring is core to successful strategy execution.

As a brief descriptor, processes are the day-to-day activities that an organization undertakes to deliver on its strategy. For example, an organization might have a strategic objective relating to excellent customer service. Processes aligned to this objective might be, for example, the client on-boarding process or the client management process. Importantly, and as a key differentiator from initiatives, processes are a set of ongoing or repeated activities.

According to the classic Balanced Scorecard approach, "strategic" processes are mentioned only in the internal process perspective. However, because we are including risk – strategic and operational – we need

	Objectives					Risks			Controls	
	Objective 1	Objective 2	Objective 3	Objective 4	Objective 5	Risk 1	Risk 2	Risk 3	Control 1	Control 2
Process 1	25%									
Process 2			50%	75%		25%				
Process 3	100%									
Process 4		50%	50%	50%				50%		

Figure 6.10 **A Process Alignment Matrix**

to take the definition of processes to another level of detail and map out all the organization processes and align these to objectives.

In the world of operational risk, we have had experience developing "front-to-back" diagrams which are large process flow diagrams that show how a "product" and related information flow through a business process; for example, how a trade moves from the front office, through the middle office and ends up at the back office of a bank. To effectively do this we need to have defined the processes, to overlay the risks related to each process and then overlay the associated controls.

We recommend the use of a Process Alignment Matrix (Figure 6.10) for ensuring alignment of processes with strategic goals. It is used and deployed in exactly the same way as the Initiative Alignment Matrix except, of course, that the goal is to align processes rather than initiatives and demonstrate the impact of business change on objectives, risks and/or controls.

Benefits of alignment

We use percentages in the Process Alignment Matrix and the Initiative Alignment Matrix for a number of reasons:

▷ It creates debate and challenge within a team as they seek to agree the relationship between the operational level processes and initiatives and the strategic-level objectives, risks and controls.
▷ It indicates the relative strength of alignment, therefore helps in deciding and prioritizing the real "key" processes and initiatives

from a holistic viewpoint, taking account of performance, risk and compliance perspectives.

▷ It enables the incorporation of operational considerations within any scenario, regression or similar modelling that might be conducted. Operations can use statistical techniques to validate the strength of alignment between the strategic level and the operational level, and of course this then provides the opportunity for scenario analysis at the strategic level to be cascaded down to understand the impact at an operational level.

Conclusion

This chapter has described how to "manage performance" according to the RBPM framework and methodology. Based on, and building on, the classic Balanced Scorecard, we introduced new dimensions such as the heightened importance of processes and, of course, the role that appetite plays at the objective-setting phase. We also paid attention to explaining the "watch-outs" or the common pitfalls to avoid when building a Balanced Scorecard.

What this chapter has done is explain how to manage "with one eye on performance". In the next chapter we explain how to manage "with one eye on risk." But, as with humans, we require both of these eyes to be working in synch for optimal results. 20–20 strategic vision is the ultimate goal.

7 Managing Risk

In the context of Risk-Based Performance Management, risk management is about understanding and exploiting opportunities and threats (the risk the organization faces in pursuit of its objectives), and the continuous monitoring and management of those risks to ensure the organization executes its strategy while "operating within appetite".

Introduction

The preceding chapter explained the Managing Performance discipline of the Risk-Based Performance Management (RBPM) approach (Figure 7.1). This chapter focuses on the Managing Risk discipline. While the previous chapter focused on strategic objectives, this one considers key risks and key controls; while in Managing Performance we looked at Key Performance Indicators (KPIs), here we pay attention to Key Risk Indicators (KRIs) and Key Control Indicators (KCIs). In this chapter we also explain how to assess risk.

As an introduction, in the context of RBPM we describe risk management as being about "understanding and exploiting opportunities and threats (the risk the organization faces in pursuit of its objectives), and the continuous monitoring and management of those risks to ensure the organization executes its strategy while 'operating within appetite'." We define risk as: "The uncertainty of future events that will impact on the achievement of objectives, either positively (opportunities) or negatively (threats)."

But before elaborating on these definitions and describing how they are applied in a practical setting, we provide some historical context for the emergence of risk management.

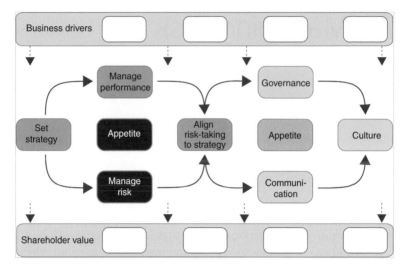

Figure 7.1   **RBPM framework**

The Risk Management discipline and function

As a discipline and function, Risk Management is a relatively recent addition to an organization's stable of management tools. It first began to appear within organizations in the 1940s and 1950s with a narrow approach to quantifying and mitigating financial risks (evolving out of earlier work in managing insurable risk). But it wasn't until the 1960s that the field was actually named, largely through principles and guidelines that were developed by Robert Mehr and Bob Hedges, widely acclaimed as the founding fathers of risk management. Mehr and Hedges laid down the following steps for the risk management process:

▷ Identify loss exposures
▷ Measure loss exposures
▷ Evaluate the options for handling risk

     ▷ Risk assumption
     ▷ Risk transfer
     ▷ Risk reduction

▷ Select a method
▷ Monitor results[1]

As we can see, Mehr and Hedges established a risk management process that was exclusively focused on handing "pure risk"; that is risk for which there is either a loss or no loss – such an owning a house, which might burn down. With "pure risk" there is little, or no, upside in managing the risk, with the primary goal being to essentially remain where you are (no loss). Managing risk is all about mitigation – reducing the likelihood of the downside (Box 7.1 outlines a modern-day approach to managing loss events).

Box 7.1   Managing Loss Events

One aspect of risk management which has gained increased regulatory attention in recent years is Risk Events, also known as Operational Losses or Loss Events. While improvement in Loss Event capture and monitoring is often driven by a regulator, we believe that by taking a structured approach which is focused on creating business value, Loss Events Management can be a powerful driver of change and value within an organization.

In simple terms, a Loss Event is an event in which a risk materializes which results in a loss (or near-miss) and that can be either economic or non-economic. Examples of an Operational Loss Event include losses resulting from processing errors, fraud, industrial accidents, etc.

The business benefits of developing a robust Risk Events process include:

- Significantly improving organizational reputation and standing with regulators, shareholders, employees and customers, due to being able to both more effectively response to events if they happen and lessen the likelihood of such events materializing in the future.
- Reducing operational losses and creating a "no surprises" culture. As an example, Manigent client HML (see Chapter 2) reports a 94% reduction in the value of errors and a 63% reduction in the volume of errors.
- A significant reduction in regulatory capital for operational risk for those banks that use the Advanced Measure Approach (AMA) under Basel II.[2] A key requirement for a bank to be able to use AMA is that they must have a robust Loss Data database for use in modelling their capital requirement.

Within the overall RBPM approach, Loss Event management has an important role to play. Clearly, improving the management of Risk Events has a direct impact on the bottom-line performance of organizations and within RBPM we are able to link Risk Events to Strategic Objectives or Operational Enablers via key risks. Additionally, Risk Events data can be used as a base for scenario analysis exercises where the impact of multiple events within a scenario can be modelled to understand the impact on the organization's ability to deliver its strategic objective. We have developed an 8-step process for managing Loss Events.

Step 1 – Loss event capture

The first step in the process is ensuring that Risk Events are captured in a structured and consistent way across the organization. This means that everyone in the organization should be aware of what a Loss Event is and the importance of capturing Risk Events. Staff should be engaged by the risk management team as part of their ongoing embedding and enabling activities related to the risk management process. It is important that a culture is created which ensures that Loss Event capture is not restricted to the risk management team but becomes everyone's responsibility.

Step 2 – Estimation

During the Estimation step, someone from either within the business (a Risk Champion) or within the risk management team should review and "sense check" Risk Events as they are captured to ensure that the details of the Loss Event are in line with expectations given the type and nature of the event and the Risk Event has been recorded in line with the organization's policies. In particular, it is important to ensure that the values related to the Loss Event are as accurate and consistent as possible.

The Estimation step is really about completing the Registration step and ensuring that the data entered from across the organization is consistent, correct and forms a robust basis for decision making. How a Risk Event is managed through to resolution should be largely determined by the information captured about the event in the Registration and Estimation steps.

Step 3 – Investigation

The Investigation step is an information-gathering step in the process which should be undertaken if the risk event meets a set of predefined criteria which aim to align the scale of the investigation to the scale of the risk event. For example, a risk event resulting from an error applying an interest rate to an individual mortgage will be treated very differently from a risk event resulting from the systematic and repeated setting of an incorrect interest rate across an entire mortgage book. The first might be simply a case of human error on a given day which should be detected by organizational controls, whereas the latter could be a case of fraud where controls are systematically circumvented.

Ideally investigation processes should be defined in advance based on the type, nature and value of the Risk Events. If they are not defined in advance, then over time a "library" of investigation processes should be developed and apply to events as they arise.

The investigation process should ensure that all the relevant stakeholders across the organization are engaged and provide input and information to the investigation so an accurate picture of the causes and consequences of the event can be developed.

Step 4 – Root cause analysis

During this step, the information gathered as part of the investigation step is analysed and the root causes of the risk event are discovered and documented. There is a range of tools and techniques that can be used to support Root Causes Analysis, such as the "5 Whys" (a question-asking technique used to explore the cause-and-effect relationships underlying a particular problem)[3] approach and Ishikawa diagram (that shows the causes of a specific event).[4] These provide a structured approach to problem solving and identify the root causes of the Loss Event. This step would normally be completed only for certain Risk Events.

Step 5 – Business impact assessment

The Business Impact Assessment step is about understanding the business impact of the Loss Event on the business. While it is common practice when analysing Risk Events to seek to determine which risks materialized and/or which controls failed, using the RBPM framework we would seek to understand the impact of individual Risk Events on the objectives of the organization, including their impact on enabling processes and initiatives. We would also seek to understand how the drivers of the organization might be influenced by a Loss Event.

This takes Risk Events monitoring beyond the traditional capital modelling area and uses this data to inform the organizational understanding of why objectives are not being achieved, thus creating a clear and powerful feedback loop from the Risk Management discipline to the Strategy and Performance Management disciplines.

Step 6 – Corrective actions

This step is all about what actions should be taken to (1) resolve any issues related to the current Loss Event and (2) ensure that the Loss Event does not occur again – or at least minimize the Likelihood of it occurring again or the impact if it does occur again.

The corrective actions might be either external or internal in nature. Consider the 2012 outage of the Royal Bank of Scotland ATM network. This Loss

Event resulted in both external and internal actions. For example, to minimize the impact of the event on the bank's reputation with clients, all clients impacted by the outage were offered compensation for the inconvenience of not being able to access their accounts. Internally, there were some actions to build additional robustness into their ATM network and into their software testing and release process (it was reported that a software bug was the cause of the ATM network failure).

Step 7 – Authorizations

In line with Discipline 6 of RBPM (Governance; see Chapter 9) a step in this Risk Events process is related to ensuring the right authorizations are in place before any suggested corrective actions are undertaken. This is particularly important where a Loss Event has potential legal implications or where compensation has been paid out. Where the corrective action involves the implementation of a business change, be that the implementation of some additional controls or the reengineering of a process, then such business change should go through an established business change approval process.

Step 8 – Management information analysis and reporting

It is vital that as Risk Events data is captured and built up over time it is analysed to identify weaknesses in controls, to recognize any reoccurring events, to make visible any data and to develop and understand the correlations between Risk Events, KRIs and Risk Assessment data. This final step enables the identification of interventions to ensure that Risk Events are managed effectively and so deliver bottom-line and stakeholder-facing benefits.

Since that time, risk management has largely continued along these lines. It has remained an immature function in most industries and sectors (with the exceptions perhaps of financial services, oil and gas, and pharmaceutical and other industries where risk simply had to be managed more formally). Even when risk management was practised elsewhere there might not have been a formal risk management function; oftentimes this was captured within the roles of the finance function.

Although executive teams might have been well aware that there were inherent risks in chosen strategies – for instance in geographic expansion or product diversification – there was little systematic analysis and conversation on how to properly articulate and manage those risks.

To an extent, this has not been surprising as historically risk has typically been defined by the corporate board and executive, using technical risk management "tools" and models that can be somewhat abstract and neither actionable nor comprehensible.

Without a language with which to communicate or models with which to implement it, risk management was not part of the day-to-day decision-making processes of senior managers, and few saw the point of trying to imbue an understanding of risk into the culture of the organization (and so the day-to-day actions of the employee-base). Risk management was dealt with by people who understood this stuff – the risk professionals squirrelled away in finance or wherever they lived (in the few sectors in which they had a home, that is). The RBPM approach brings together the language of the business (through Strategy Maps, etc.) with that of the risk professionals to create a language that the senior leaders can understand and act upon.

The birth of enterprise risk management

The 2004 release of *Enterprise Risk Management – Integrated Framework,* by the Committee of Sponsoring Organizations of the Treadway Commission (COSO) did much to simplify the concept of risk management and increase its relevance beyond narrow financial confines, explaining that risks should also be defined and managed through myriad dimensions such as operational, project, legal, environmental and, perhaps most important, strategic risks. Boards and executive teams were presented with a framework by which they could understand risk through an enterprise-wide lens and deploy risk management in a meaningful way. COSO essentially introduced the term Enterprise Risk Management (ERM) to senior teams (although the term had been used previously). ERM is defined as

> a process, effected by an enterprise's board of directors, management and other personnel, applied in strategy setting and across the enterprise, designed to identify potential events that might affect the entity, and manage risk to be within its risk appetite, to provide reasonable assurance regarding the achievement of entity objectives.

While broadening the idea of risk management, a major contribution of COSO's paper was the hardwiring of risk management to strategy and the introduction of the concept of risk appetite. Risk management, therefore, was positioned as something that really should be discussed at the board and executive levels.[5]

Although COSO (and to a smaller extent other works, such as the UK Treasury's Orange Book series) helped establish the concept of ERM, it could be reasonably argued that progress in making risk management a top-table topic of conversation had been sluggish by the time of the epoch-, and perhaps century-changing event that was the Credit Crunch. There were examples of organizations where the board and executive had "got the message" but in most cases risk was still a matter for the risk professionals.

That a failure of risk management was almost immediately identified as a primary cause of the collapse of the sub-prime lending markets (and that the impact on organizations was broader than just on those within the financial sector) elevated ERM to a front-of-mind board and executive concern. This was reinforced through a range of reports from governance and regulatory bodies (see Chapter 9). For instance, COSO's 2009 white paper *Strengthening Enterprise Risk Management for Competitive Advantage* stated that the crisis forced boards to re-examine their approach to risk oversight. The paper reported that boards had begun to ask executive teams probing questions, such as:

▷ "What are management's processes for identifying, assessing and managing top risk exposures?"
▷ "How does management's process for managing risks consider whether risks being taken in the pursuit of objectives are effectively monitored to be sure they are within acceptable levels?"
▷ "What processes does management have in place to identify emerging risks affecting objectives and the related changes in risk prioritization in a rapidly changing environment?"
▷ "How is management monitoring key risks related to core strategic objectives?"

In some organizations, COSO stated, executive teams were struggling to answer these questions due to there being a minimal structure or definition as to how the organization approaches risk oversight. The paper explained that when risk management was underdeveloped, the concepts surrounding risk and risk management would likely be ill-defined; therefore there might be little agreement amongst executives about what constitutes risk for the organization and so boards would have difficulty in being assured that these risks were being managed to acceptable levels. "Boards of directors can be left wondering whether the organization's risk management processes are effectively identifying the organization's key risk exposures affecting key strategies and objectives," the paper noted.[6]

ISO31000

The 2009 release of the ISO31000 standard *Risk Management – Principles and Guidelines* further strengthened the argument that organizations had to become much more systematic about risk management. As part of this argument, the standard provided a useful definition of risk management, as well as describing a risk management framework and a risk management process.

▷ Risk management was defined as "coordinated activities to direct and control and organization with regard to risk".
▷ A risk management framework was defined as a "set of components that provide the foundations and organizational arrangements for designing, implementing, monitoring, reviewing and continually improving risk management processes throughout the organization" (Figure 7.2).
▷ A risk management process was defined as "systematic application of management policies, procedures and practices to the tasks

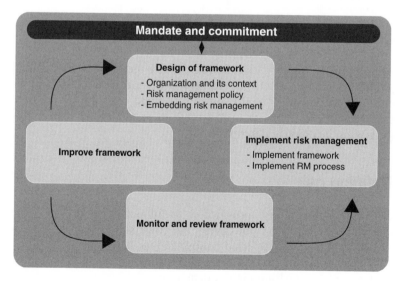

Figure 7.2 **Risk Management framework from ISO3100**

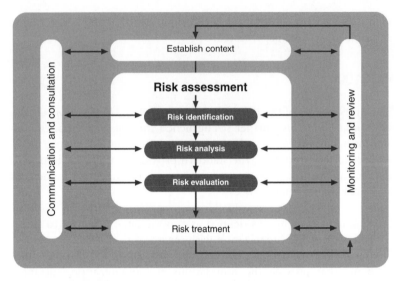

Figure 7.3 **Risk Management process from ISO3100**

of communication, consultation, establishing the context, identifying, analysing, evaluating, treating, monitoring and reviewing risk" (Figure 7.3).[7]

Our definition of risk management

Although very useful – and the reason why the ISO31000 standard is a key foundation of our RBPM approach – the ISO3100 definitions excluded any mention of risk appetite (an odd omission, as we have stated elsewhere). For risk management in particular, we believe this leads to an incomplete description.

Defining risk

The ISO standard also provided a useful definition of risk: "the effect of uncertainty on objectives". An effect was further clarified as "a deviation from the expected positive and/or negative".

The notes to the ISO3100 standard further explained the meaning of the words used within the risk definition.

▷ Objectives can have different aspects (such as financial, health and safety, and environmental goals)

▷ [Risk c]an apply at different levels (such as strategic, organization-wide, project, product and process)

▷ [Risk i]s often characterized by reference to potential event and consequences, or a combination of these

▷ [Risk i]s often expressed in terms of a combination of the consequences of an event (including changes in circumstances) and the associated likelihood of occurrence

▷ Uncertainty is the state, even partial, of deficiency of information related to understanding or knowledge of an event, its consequence, or likelihood.[8]

ISO's focus on uncertainty is worthy of further analysis. The fact is that the purest definition of risk is actually the "threat" side of how we (and many others) use the term. The Oxford Dictionary, for instance, defines risk as "a situation involving exposure to danger".[9] However, when we talk about risk we are actually talking about uncertainty. Most people, when challenged, would agree that risk is made up of threats and opportunities, yet due to structure and perceived priorities just about every risk management function is almost exclusively focused on the threat side. The RBPM methodology, and specifically the Appetite Alignment concept, speaks to the general use of the term "risk" in that it challenges risk functions and senior management to think about the upside – particularly important where the organization is not taking enough risk.

These clarifications point to how we define and manage risk, to which we now turn our attention.

Identifying and defining key risks

For risks to be effectively managed, organizations must first identify what those risks are. Within the RBPM approach we define the key risks: those which are the most significant to the organization – the biggest potential threats and/or opportunities. These key risks are defined at the level of the strategic objectives. By doing so we can manage the risks – both the upside and downside – related to particular aspects of defined strategic goals.

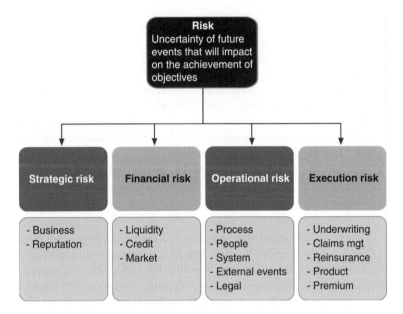

Figure 7.4 **Categories of risk**

There are various techniques that can be used to develop a list of
key risks. However, the general approach is to generate a long list of
potential risks against risk categories and then conduct an assessment
to understand which risks should be deemed to be key, non-key and
emerging. The risk type will influence how the risk is managed. These
categories typically focus on risk areas relating to strategic, financial,
market, operations and reputation, but an organization must define
its categories according to its own requirements; we provide two such
examples below.

Within the RBPM approach, we use the "uncertainty" element of
managing risk as part of our describing of categories (Figure 7.4).
As examples:

▷ **Strategic risk:** uncertainty related to strategic choices (such
  as misreading of the external environment or external change,
  wrong/uncompetitive business model, setting poor objectives).
▷ **Execution risk:** uncertainty related to execution of the chosen
  strategy (a failure to deliver business objectives).
▷ **Operational risk**: uncertainty related to processes, people, technology, change, etc. (such as mis-selling, fraud, process failures,

inability to deliver change and IT projects, mishandling of employee issues).

▷ **Financial risk**: uncertainty related to capital invested and capital due (capital invested in geographies, plant, partners, product development or a customer's ability to meet their obligations).

If deemed valuable, these categories can be further refined into subcategories. Consider the example of Nigeria's National Insurance Commission (NAICOM), which has a mandate to ensure the effective administration, supervision, regulation and control of insurance business within the country. As shown in Figure 7.5, NAICOM has the following risk categories: strategic, financial, operational, insurance and hazard. As three examples of sub-categories: risks for strategic are business and reputation; for financial they are liquidity, credit and market; for hazard they are natural, act of God, accidents, civil disruption and health and safety). As we can see from the figure, the question is asked: "within these categories, what risks exist"?

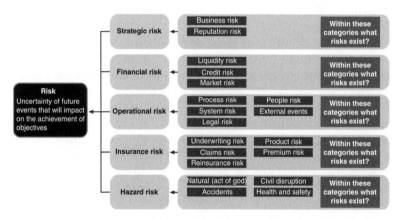

Figure 7.5 **NAICOM categories of risk**

The Risk Bow-tie

In thinking about and defining risks, it is also important to be clear about what might potentially cause that risk to happen (such as lack of policies and procedures, inadequate activity management or external events) and the consequences should it materialize (direct, indirect or

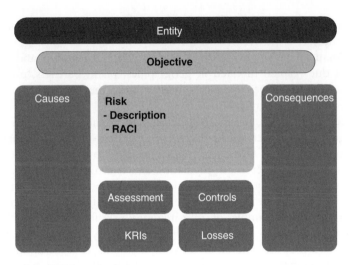

Figure 7.6 **The Risk Bow-tie**

intangible). The Risk Bow-tie is a valuable tool that can be used for this purpose (Figure 7.6).

During the identification phase of the process, the Risk Bow-tie can be used as a "thinking tool" to encourage a high quality conversation around risk, and enables a clear definition to be created, while capturing and recording the various causes and consequences related to the risk. This helps overcome a commonly seen issue within risk management where risk definitions are a confused mix of causes, events and consequences, all wrapped up in a definition with no structure.

When using the Risk Bow-tie in a risk identification and definition process, start by focusing on events that could either prevent or ease the achievement of objectives. Once these have been listed, start to develop as many potential causes as possible that will lead to the event happening and therefore the risk materializing.

Creating this "long list" of causes will help clarify thinking about the risk and form the base of a consolidated list of causes that should be documented alongside the risk. This process should be repeated for consequences (or the process can be done "horizontally" with causes and consequences defined together).

Capturing a set of causes and consequences as part of the definition of a risk leads to making a better risk management framework and derives more value from the process. The reasons for this include:

1   It assists in the risk assessment process, as those completing the
    risk assessment can review the causes and consider how they have
    changed or may change over the assessment period.
2   It helps develop a fuller picture of the risk environment, including
    the potential consequences of the risk materializing.
3   It leads to a better definition of leading KRIs and preventive key
    controls based on a robust and well thought-out set of causes while
    also leading to the definition of better lagging KRIs and detective
    key controls.

Risk identification template

Based on our client experiences, we have found that when defining a
risk it is useful to use a template that helps the senior team to think
in terms of what, where, when and how, and then (and only then)
the resulting impact. This is articulated as "the risk of (*what, where,
when*)...caused by (*how*)...resulting in...(*impact*)".

Consider these two examples from the healthcare industry.

▷ The risk of *financial deficit at end of year* caused by *decreased
  in-patient activity and revenue*, resulting in *rationalization of service
  offerings.*
▷ The risk *of exceeding A&E waiting times*, caused by *increased
  demand and staff vacancies*, resulting in *not meeting community
  expectations and adverse patient outcomes.*

In assigning risks to objectives, the question should be asked: which
categories are relevant and within those categories, which risks are relevant to key objectives? Therefore, key risks must only be chosen if they
have impact on objectives. If they are deemed critical enough for the
senior team to track on a regular basis then questions should be asked
about the completeness of the Strategy Map.

   Also note that that a risk should not simply be defined as the con-
verse of the objective; for example, supporting an objective of employee
engagement with a risk defined simply as employees not being engaged
is not useful or helpful.

   On a regular basis, these "key risks" need to be reviewed, with a
level of challenge from the board, to ensure that they really are the main
threats to the business. Additionally, as the strategy is executed there is
the potential for other risks to emerge, which must also be monitored

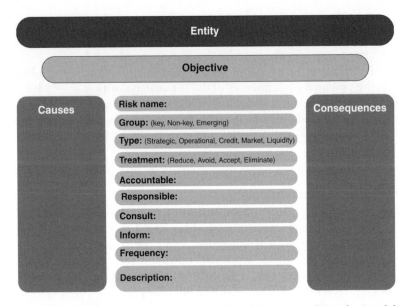

Figure 7.7 **Documenting risks from the risk name through to risk description**

and managed accordingly. Figure 7.7 shows how risks can be documented for each entity from the risk name through to risk description (as with objectives, risks need to be fully described).

Risk assessment

With key risks defined, the next step is to assess whether or not that risk will materialize and the effect on the organization if it does. This assessment can be completed through an Impact and Likelihood (or Probability) Matrix. Used by many organizations in both the commercial and government sectors, this simply plots on a vertical axis the consequence to the organization if the risk materializes and on a horizontal axis the likelihood of its happening. The point where consequence and likelihood meet determines the risk's position on the matrix (the Risk Heat Map) and therefore the level of urgency for risk mitigation.

For example, consider Figure 7.8. On this 5×5 Risk Heat Map, likelihood is rated from "rare" to "almost certain" and impact from

Assessment: Impact/Probability matrix
Reflects all (residual) risks and controls.

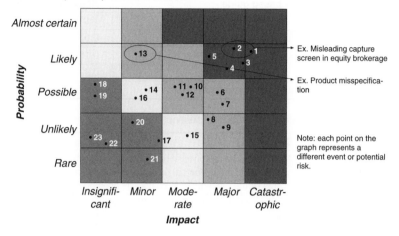

Figure 7.8 **An example Risk Map**

"insignificant" to "catastrophic". Each number on the matrix represents a different risk. Those risks placed toward the top right-hand side of the matrix – and so assessed as likely/almost certain as well as major/catastrophic are the risks that will be immediately dealt with and so might be reported to the board/executive team on a very frequent basis – weekly or even daily.

Likelihood versus impact Risk Heat Maps are to a large extent subjective, in that the insights and knowledge of the senior team and other experts have an important role in assigning ratings. Collecting such insights is right and proper, but best practice is to take a semi-quantitative approach.

Public sector case example

Consider this likelihood rating example (shown in Table 7.1) from a large public sector organization, which is pursuing a very aggressive strategy in transforming the nation it serves as well as the organization itself. As shown, the likelihood risk is described according to a time horizon with an annual probability assigned. For example, possible is described as "about once in a 5-year planning period", with an annual probability of 20% (within the range of 15–30%).

Table 7.1   Example risk likelihood rating

Descriptor	Time based guide	Annual probability
Rare	Once or less in a 20-year period	< 0.05
Unlikely	About once in a 10-year period	$0.05 < 0.1 < 0.15$
Possible	About once in a 5-year planning period	$0.15 < 0.2 < 0.3$
Likely	About once every 2 years	$0.30 < 0.5 < 0.8$
Almost certain	About one or more times per year	> 0.8

Table 7.2   Risk categories and their descriptions

Risk category	Description
Community disruption	Assessment based on level of disruption to service in terms of geographical area affected, time over which the disruption occurs or the percentage of customers affected.
[Strategic Supplier] delay	Number of primary or secondary [strategic suppliers] that fail or amount of time for which their key milestones are delayed.
Health and safety	Assessment of impact as it relates to deaths, disability, illness and the level of government intervention or inquiry.
Finance	Financial impact in terms of percentage of annual operating budget, absolute value, or number of financially unviable primary and secondary [strategic suppliers].
Environment and heritage	Assessment of level of impact on environmental features and ecosystem function in terms of the geographical area affected and the time over which the effect occurs; or effect on flora or fauna; or length of time over which environmental damage lasts.
Governance and compliance	Assessment of the level to which concerns and reprimands are raised within the organization and to the government including any loss of confidence and the level of reprimand.
Reputation	Assessment of level and extent of media coverage or damage to [nation's] brand, or level of effect on relationships with partners and voicing of concerns by stakeholders.

Table 7.2 shows an abridged version of the organization's impact definitions. The impact of risks against the categories are scored on a range from 1 (minor) through 2 (material), 3 (serious), 4 (severe) to 5 (catastrophic). As one example of the wordings of the scores, consider reputation. Catastrophic is defined through three events:

▷ Consistent extreme (months) negative international media attention
▷ Nation's brand damaged with loss of international event hosting rights

▷ Strategic partners refuse to associate with the company due to damaged reputation'
▷ Consistent active opposition by stakeholder groups Minor is defined as
▷ Adverse local media attention (days)
▷ Key partners raise potential reputation issues

In this organization, key risks are aligned to strategic objectives and the risks are assessed against the appropriate risk categories. The highest score against any category (likelihood x consequence) is the score plotted on the Risk Heat Map.

Note too that all of those risks deemed catastrophic are monitored closely, even if the probability is unlikely or rare. Unlikely does not mean that the risk isn't going to materialize; organizations will be misusing a likelihood versus impact matrix if they believe that unlikely/rare risks can be ignored. Furthermore, likelihood should be reassessed on a regular basis (perhaps monthly). Levels of consequence also need to be reviewed, but on a less frequent basis (perhaps annually). But in today's continuous turbulent times the periodicity of the review will be determined by the dynamics of the sector or industry.

Four Perspective Risk Map

While a Risk Heat Map is a well-known tool, within the RBPM approach we use a Four Perspective Risk Map to bring key risks together, enabling their visualization in relation to each other. This is designed to work with the Strategy Map and has the added benefit of providing an "organizational-wide" view and a "perspective" view of risk. See Figure 7.9.

The Four Perspective Risk Map enables organizations to focus on risks in specific perspectives and explore the relationship between risks across perspectives and to identify risk clusters. For example, one organization that uses the Four Perspective Risk Map focuses attention on the risks within the outcome perspectives – financial and customer – as a starting point for their monthly risk review. The senior team explores the causal relationship between objectives, using both the Strategy Map and Four Perspective Risk Map, believing that taking this approach enables them to manage and monitor the delivery of their strategy, while ensuring they operate within their risk appetite – the central goal of the RBPM framework.

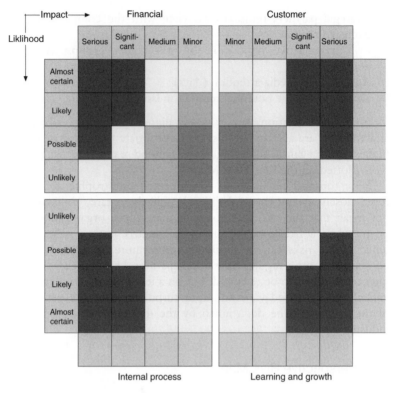

Figure 7.9 **Four Perspective Risk Map**

The Four Perspective Risk Map helps senior teams to answer the following questions:

▷ What is the level of our risk-taking?
▷ Are our risks clustering together?
▷ Where are our main exposures?

Based on this information, mitigation plans, priorities, risk treatments and potential scenarios can be debated and agreed upon.

Our experience using the Four Perspective Risk Map has shown that it has a powerful effect on the quality of conversations around risks as it challenges front-line and risk management staff to be very clear about the definition of the risk. Often we have seen risks redefined to increase the clarity of the definition once the Four Perspective

Risk Map has been used, because too often risks are defined as the consequence of the risk materializing rather than as the risk event itself.

KRIs

Just as performance to strategic objectives is tracked via KPIs, key risks are monitored through KRIs. A KRI dashboard, which reports KRI performance to key risks, is shown in Figure 7.11.

KRIs are used to answer the question: "How is our risk profile changing and is it within our desired tolerance levels?" KRIs provide an early signal of increasing risk exposure in various areas of the organization. A KRI might simply be a key ratio that the board and senior management track as indicators of evolving problems, which signal that corrective or mitigating actions need to be taken. On other occasions they might be more complex, aggregating several individual risk indicators into a multidimensional risk score regarding emerging potential risk exposures. As explained in COSO's 2009 white paper *Strengthening Risk Management for Competitive Advantage*:

> KRIs are typically derived from specific events or root causes, identified internally or externally, that can prevent achievement of performance goals. Examples can include items such as the introduction of a new product by a competitor, a strike at a supplier's plant, proposed changes in the regulatory environment, or input price changes.

COSO goes on to say that the development of KRIs that can provide relevant and timely information to both the board and senior management is a significant component of effective risk oversight, and that KRIs should be developed by teams that include the professional risk management staff and business unit managers with a deep understanding of the operational processes subject to potential risks. "Ideally, these KRIs are developed in concert with strategic plans for individual business units and can then incorporate acceptable deviations from plan that fall within the overall risk appetite of the organization."

COSO provides this useful overview of well-designed KPIs. They should:

▷ Be based on established practices or benchmarks
▷ Be developed consistently across the organization
▷ Provide an unambiguous and intuitive view of the highlighted risk
▷ Allow for measurable comparisons across time and business units
▷ Provide opportunities to assess the performance of risk owners on a timely basis
▷ Consume resources efficiently[10]

As examples of KRIs, a strategic objective within the learning and growth perspective of a financial services organization might be defined as "continuously improve application processing accuracy". A key risk might be described as "failure to achieve standards of processing accuracy due to inexperienced staff". A leading KRI might be "key employee retention rate", while a lagging KPI might be "number of loan processing errors due to inexperienced staff".

In the public sector case example above, and looking at the reputation category, a sophisticated media tracking solution is used to track global, regional and national coverage and is reported as a key indicator against a reputation objective.

Risk tolerance

An important function of KRIs is that they help translate risk appetite into operational risk tolerances (which are expressed as thresholds around the indicators). If the organization has a high/extreme appetite it would be expected that the threshold would be wider allowing for greater levels of variation away from the defined baseline; whereas a low risk organization is going to have tight thresholds to promote a higher level of control. This is shown in Figure 7.10, which shows actual against baseline and where that sits with regard to tolerance. Performance is displayed using Manigent's RAGAR (red, amber, green, amber, green) traffic light reporting system.

It is worthwhile spending a little time in explaining tolerance. This is because there is still much debate and confusion as to what it is and how it relates to and differs to risk appetite. COSO's 2012 paper *Understanding and Communicating Risk Appetite* provided this useful

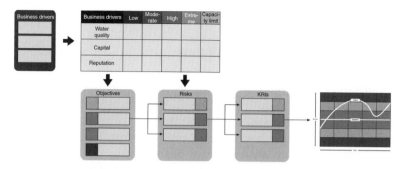

Figure 7.10 **Translating risk appetite into risk tolerance**

definition of risk tolerance, which is broadly aligned with the position we hold within the RBPM approach:

> The acceptable level of variation relative to achievement of a specific objective...

> In setting risk tolerance, management considers the relative importance of the related objective and aligns risk tolerances with risk appetite. Operating within risk tolerances helps ensure that the entity remains within its risk appetite and, in turn, that the entity will achieve its objectives.

Aerospace supplier case example

The COSO paper provided an example from an Aerospace supplier to illustrate the relationship between risk appetite and related risk tolerances.

The company, the paper explained, had set a high-level objective to grow revenue and operating earnings by 8% per year through working with customers to improve products and market share. Because of the long-term nature of its supply arrangements and product development, the company communicated the broad parameters of its risk appetite, which then cascade into risk tolerances relating to operations, reporting, and compliance, as shown below. As part of its Risk Appetite Statement the company stated, "While the company seeks to grow at this rate, acquisitions should not put the company's capital structure at risk. There is a low risk appetite for allowing the capital structure to be so leveraged that hinders the company's future flexibility or ability to make strategic acquisitions."

Tolerance levels were described thus:

Operations tolerances

▷ Near zero risk tolerance for product defects
▷ Low risk tolerance for sourcing products that fail to meet the company's quality standards; low, but not zero, risk tolerance for meeting customer orders on time, and a very low tolerance for failing to meet demands within x number of days
▷ High risk tolerance for potential failure in pursuing research that will enable the company's product to better control, and increase the efficiency of, energy use

Reporting tolerances

▷ Low risk tolerance concerning the quality, timing and accessibility of data needed to run the business
▷ Very low risk tolerance concerning the possibility of significant or material deficiencies in internal control
▷ Low risk tolerance related to financial reporting quality (timeliness, transparency, GAAP, etc.)

Compliance tolerances

Near zero risk tolerance for violations of regulatory requirements or the company's code of ethics.

Such tolerance levels should be reported through KRIs, and the COSO paper advises that risk tolerance must be expressed in such a way that it can be mapped into the same metrics the organization uses to measure success. "Because risk tolerance is defined within the context of objectives and risk appetite, it should be communicated using the metrics in place to measure performance. In that way, risk tolerance sets the boundaries of acceptable performance variability."[11]

Our definitions of risk appetite and risk tolerance

In defining risk appetite and risk tolerance, our thinking is most closely aligned to the COSO approach in that:

Risk appetite – the amount and type of risk that an organization is willing to accept, and must take, to achieve their strategic objectives and therefore create value for shareholders and other stakeholders

Risk tolerance – the acceptable level of variation of risk-taking in the pursuit of a specific objective

This means that we use risk appetite to set the boundaries of acceptable risk-taking within the organization and we use risk tolerance in the definition of KRI thresholds which are defined per risk and used to monitor variations in risk-taking and the risk-taking environment over time.

Water company example

For example, a water company may be seeking to deliver on an objective of "Delivering clean and safe drinking water". A risk related to this objective might be "Failure of filtering equipment resulting in a contamination". Recognizing that there is no such thing as "no risk", the water company may state it has a Low Appetite for risks related to the objective delivering clean and safe drinking water. The levels of risk appetite related to Water Quality may be defined using a Water Quality Index, so Low might be between 0 and 10 on the index whereas Extreme might be between 80 and 100.

To express risk tolerance we might define a KRI such as Water Quality Sampling Results versus Baseline. In this example we might set a Baseline for the KRI of 10 (this number is not the same as the Water Quality Index where 10 is the upper limit of Low Appetite), with Thresholds of 5% and 10%, where the KRI will be green if the results are within 5% of the Baseline, that is, +/− .5 and it will be amber if the results are between .5 and .99 and red if the results are 1 or greater. When defining these thresholds we consider the risk appetite for the risk that the KRI belongs to and use the upper threshold to express risk tolerance (we use the upper threshold as this indicates where the KRI is either inside or outside of tolerance). In this example the water company is prepared to accept a 10% variation from the acceptable level of risk-taking (meaning residual risk-taking).

We believe that by expressing risk appetite for objectives and using it to set the boundaries for risk-taking we provide the board and senior management with the tools to clearly define the amount of risk that is acceptable and must be taken to deliver the objectives while risk tolerance, expressed at the KRI level, provides a mechanism to translate risk appetite from the strategic level to the operational level. This use of risk tolerance also enables the organization to effectively cascade risk appetite through the enterprise and embed it in the day-to-day management activities, processes and decision making.

A Risk Scorecard

Within the RBPM approach, overall risk profile is tracked through a Risk Scorecard.

The Risk Scorecard includes the organization's key risks, the accountable person for each risk, appetite alignment status, aggregated risk score (based on underlying KRIs), key risk assessment data, current risk exposure, KRIs and KRI score.

The Risk Scorecard is designed to enable the management team to complete several important tasks:

▷ Assess whether the organization is operating within or outside appetite. This is achieved through analysing the appetite alignment status, which is an output of the Risk Appetite Alignment Matrix, which we explain in the next chapter as it shows how appetite versus exposure is aligned to strategic goals.
▷ Analyse and discuss risk assessment data and exposure values alongside KRI status data.
▷ Identify from the indicators any emerging risk trends.

The Risk Scorecard (an example is shown in Figure 7.11) also highlights any mixed messages that might be coming from the risk assessment results and the indicator data. Naturally they should be giving the same message but often, particularly in less mature risk management environments, they can be different, which can highlight the need for further work to embed the process and develop the knowledge, skills and culture. Each of the accountable people should be in the room and around the table and speak to, and lead the discussion around their risks.

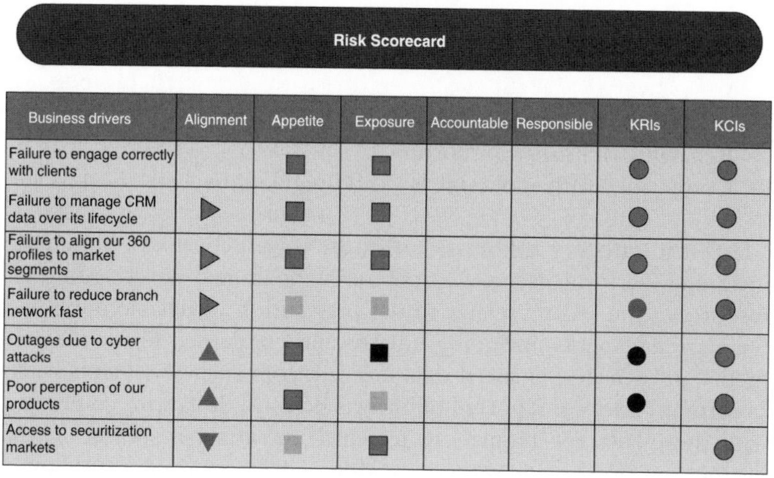

Risk Scorecard							
Business drivers	**Alignment**	**Appetite**	**Exposure**	**Accountable**	**Responsible**	**KRIs**	**KCIs**
Failure to engage correctly with clients		■	■			●	●
Failure to manage CRM data over its lifecycle	▶	■	■			●	●
Failure to align our 360 profiles to market segments	▶	■	■			●	●
Failure to reduce branch network fast	▶	■	■			●	●
Outages due to cyber attacks	▲	■	■			●	●
Poor perception of our products	▲	■	■			●	●
Access to securitization markets	▼	■	■				●

Figure 7.11 **An example Risk Scorecard**

The Risk Scorecard helps the senior management team to answer these questions:

▷ Are we managing our risks to enable the organization to deliver its objectives?
▷ Is our risk-related losses position improving or getting worse?
▷ Over time, are the risk management-related trends going in the right direction?
▷ What are the risk management exceptions we need to review and investigate?

Key controls

In managing key risks it is also important to place emphasis on ensuring that key controls are in place; we now turn our attention to this.

COSO's *Internal Control – Integrated Framework*

A major influence on the thinking around controls that appears within the RBPM approach was COSO's 1994 *Internal Control – Integrated Framework*. According to COSO, "Internal control is broadly defined as a process, effected by an entity's board of directors, management and other personnel, designed to provide reasonable assurance regarding the achievement of objectives in the following categories:

▷ Effectiveness and efficiency of operations
▷ Reliability of financial reporting
▷ Compliance with applicable laws and regulations."

"The first category addresses an entity's basic business objectives, including performance and profitability goals and safeguarding of resources. The second relates to the preparation of reliable published financial statements, including interim and condensed financial statements and selected financial data derived from such statements, such as earnings releases, reported publicly. The third deals with complying with those laws and regulations to which the entity is subject. These distinct but overlapping categories address different needs and allow a directed focus to meet the separate needs."

COSO adds that

> Internal control systems operate at different levels of effectiveness. Internal control can be judged effective in each of the three categories respectively, if the board of directors and management have reasonable assurance that

> ▷ They understand the extent to which the entity's operations objectives are being achieved.
> ▷ Published financial statements are being prepared reliably.
> ▷ Applicable laws and regulations are being complied with.

> While internal control is a process, its effectiveness is a state or condition of the process at one or more points in time.

COSO adds that internal control consists of five interrelated components. These are derived from the way management runs a business, and are integrated with the management process:

> ▷ *Control Environment* – The control environment sets the tone of an organization, influencing the control consciousness of its people ....
> ▷ *Risk Assessment* – Every entity faces a variety of risks from external and internal sources that must be assessed. A precondition to risk assessment is establishment of objectives, linked at different levels and internally consistent ....
> ▷ *Control Activities* – Control activities are the policies and procedures that help ensure management directives are carried out ....

▷ *Information and Communication* – Pertinent information must be identified, captured and communicated in a form and timeframe that enable people to carry out their responsibilities...

▷ *Monitoring* – Internal control systems need to be monitored–a process that assesses the quality of the system's performance over time. This is accomplished through on-going monitoring activities, separate evaluations or a combination of the two...[12]

RBPM definition

Within the RBPM approach, key controls are the processes, policies, practices or other devices or actions designed to affect control over the risk, and should be defined for each identified risk, with the effectiveness of the controls being regularly assessed.

Key controls can be either preventive (designed to reduce the likelihood of the risk materializing), or detective (designed to detect when a risk has materialized). They should also enable corrective action to be taken once a violation or error is detected.

Control Map

The effectiveness of key controls can be monitored through a Control Map, which assesses control performance and control dimensions on a matrix. As shown in Figure 7.12, performance is assessed on the

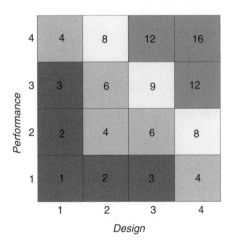

Figure 7.12 **An example Control Map**

vertical axis from 1 to 4 (where 1 equates to the control not being applied or applied incorrectly and 4 means the control is applied when it should be and in the way intended). Control design is assessed through a 1–4 rating score (where 1 equates to the controls providing little or no protection and 4 means that the control is designed to eliminate the risk entirely).

The result of the control performance and control design assessment gives a rating between 1 and 16, where 1 is in the lower left corner (and shows a very ineffective control) and effective control would be close to the top right-hand side of the map. Those that do not should be reassessed.

Through a Control Map, the senior team can focus on the questions:

▷ Are our controls effective?
▷ What does our controls environment look like?

The Control Map works alongside the Strategy Map and Risk Map to provide powerful visualization of the current state of control effectiveness.

However, some Manigent clients are beginning to use Exposure versus Control Effectiveness (Figure 7.13) and Appetite Alignment

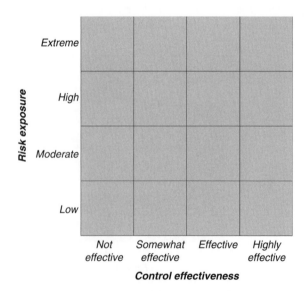

Figure 7.13 **Exposure versus Control Effectiveness Matrix**

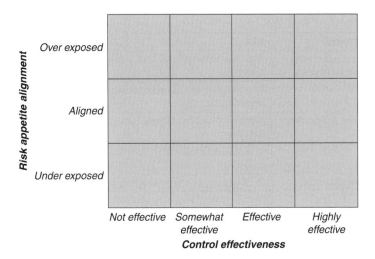

Figure 7.14   **Appetite Alignment versus Control Effectiveness**

versus Control Effectiveness (Figure 7.14) to provide more advanced visualizations of control effectiveness.

Looking at the Exposure and Appetite versus Control Effectiveness via a Control Map provides additional insight around Control Effectiveness and so helps to prioritize Control Improvement activities.

If the Control Map shows that the organization has an equal number of ineffective controls related to risks with either high exposure or low exposure, then it is clear that the improvement priorities must be the ineffective controls related to the risks with high exposure.

In a similar vein, if we consider control effectiveness in relation to risk appetite we can prioritize our control improvement activities with ineffective controls related to risks which are outside of appetite been the priority for improvement. We can also use this map to help us understand if our controls are simply too stringent and thus leading to the organization not taking enough risk to achieve its objectives.

KCIs

Key control effectiveness is monitored through KCIs. KCIs play an important role in managing the execution of strategy and management of risk as they enable the effectiveness of controls to be monitored and proactively managed. This in turn helps create an environment within

Table 7.3 Key controls and their KCIs

Key control	KCI
Reference checking for new employees	% of new employees without a reference check completed (Lagging)
	% of HR staff who are adequately trained in the recruitment process (Leading)
Payment authorization levels	Number of returned payments due to improper authorization (Leading)
	% of losses resulting from incorrectly authorized payments (Lagging)
No tailgating policy	% Failure rate of physical security testing sampling exercise
	% of incidents caused by unauthorized people being on-site

which decisions can be effectively implemented. A robust controls environment also helps create a "no surprises" culture, thus enabling the organization to remain focused on delivering their objectives while "operating within appetite". KCIs are used to answer the question: "Are our internal controls effective? Are we, as an organization 'in control'?"

In addition to assessing control, KCIs can be used to monitor changes in control effectiveness. Often organizations will use KCIs to capture data around control effectiveness on a weekly and/or monthly basis. These can then be used in trends, dashboard and other management information outputs. They also form one of the key inputs into the control assessment process, which is commonly completed on a less frequent basis (monthly/quarterly). Table 7.3 illustrates how KCIs can be set for key controls.

Controls Scorecard

Overall control effectiveness is tracked and reported through a Controls Scorecard, which includes the organization's key controls, the accountable person for each control (using the RACI system), aggregated Control Score (based on the underlying KCIs), Key Control Assessment data, KCI data and KCI score.

As with the performance and risk scorecards, the Control Scorecard (an example is shown in Figure 7.15) brings focus to and informs the management conversation and decision making, in this case around

Control Scorecards					
Business drivers	**Appetite**	**Account-able**	**Respon-sible**	**KCIs**	**Effective-ness**
Compliance policy and process framework	■			●	▫
Four eye check	■			●	■
ATM outsourcing contract	■				▫
Online change control process					▫
Compliance policy and process framework	■			●	■
Product committee and exec challenge to take account of TCF outcomes	■			●	■
Copy of T and C scheme in place	■			●	▫
Liquidity and financial forecasting	■			●	■
Continous credit scoring process					■
Two-stage checking process				●	▫

Figure 7.15 **An example Control Scorecard**

the controls environment and effectiveness within the organization. Control Scorecards answer the questions:

▷ Is our controls environment effective in enabling us to mitigate and manage risk?
▷ Are we meeting our compliance and regulatory obligations?
▷ Over time, are the control effectiveness trends going in the right direction?
▷ What are the control effectiveness exceptions we need to review and investigate?

Initiatives

As a final note on controls, just as we capture strategic-level risks and controls associated with each objective, we should define operational level risks and controls for each initiative.

We will not explore initiatives here as they were covered in the previous chapter and the same process holds true for selecting and managing initiatives to improve performance to KPI as well as to mitigate risks, as defined through KRIs ort KCIs. The value of a common approach is that the senior team can easily see and monitor how the organization is improving with "one eye on performance" and "one eye on risk."

Conclusion

This chapter has focused on the Managing Risk discipline of the RBPM framework and methodology. This supports the Managing Performance discipline explained within the previous chapter. But although described separately, for strategy and risk to be fully integrated, as required for succeeding in these "continuous turbulent times", it is important that organizations understand how to "align risk-taking with strategy", which we focus on in the next chapter. In doing so, the management of risk becomes not just an enabler of strategy execution, but an integral part of the complete strategy management process. The siloed view and narrow mandate of risk management might well become a thing of the past.

8 Aligning Risk-Taking to Strategy

Appetite Alignment is the process of continuously aligning current risk exposure to the defined risk appetite, which by implication encapsulates the strategy of the organization. To translate into simple terms, it is about understanding whether the current level of risk-taking is aligned to the chosen business strategy, that is, are we operating within appetite?

Binding together strategy and risk

We define strategy as "to develop a sustainable (and defendable) position which enables the organization to achieve its objectives while operating within defined risk appetite boundaries". Within the Risk-Based Performance Management (RBPM) framework and methodology, risk appetite is the glue that binds together strategy and risk. We define risk appetite as "the amount and type of risk that an organization is willing to accept, and must take, to achieve its strategic objectives and therefore create value for shareholders and other stakeholders" (Figure 8.1).

It is the emphasis on risk appetite that makes RBPM particularly appropriate for managing in "continuous turbulent times". Bringing strategy and risk closer together is right and proper and fundamentally important, but it is working with the parameters of appetite – the amount and type of risk that an organization is willing to take in pursuit of its strategic objectives – that will enable organizations to both establish the controls and inculcate the agility that are required in today's markets. In short, it is through appetite that we are able to effectively align risk-taking with strategy, which is Discipline 4 of the RBPM framework and methodology and the focus of this chapter.

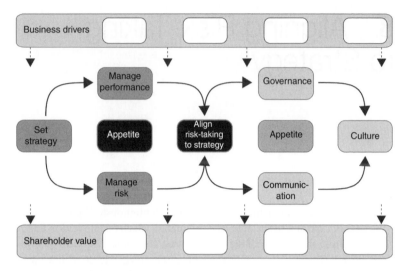

Figure 8.1 **RBPM framework**

Aligning Risk-taking with Strategy is a combination of disciplines 1 to 3 (Setting Strategy, Managing Performance and Managing Risk, which can be described as the "hard" disciplines). But it also sets the tone for the other three disciplines (Governance, Culture and Communication: the so-called "soft" disciplines).

Appetite and set strategy

Discipline 1 focuses on developing a clear organizational strategy, which is formed through the careful consideration of the performance ambitions of the board and executive team as well as the understanding of key business drivers and using these drivers as the starting point for defining of the organization's risk appetite. Within this discipline the shaping of a Risk Appetite Statement is central to beginning the process of aligning risk-taking with strategy. The importance of risk appetite is set at the outset.

Appetite and managing performance

Discipline 2 focuses on the importance of managing performance – that is, monitoring and managing the delivery of the chosen strategy. Tools such as the Strategy Map and Performance Scorecards are important here. The setting of risk appetite at the strategic objective level continues the process of embedding appetite into key management processes and thus making it a part of senior management conversations.

Appetite and managing risk

Discipline 3 focuses on the importance of managing risk and the gaining of critical information as to how the organizational threats and opportunities are changing and as such how they might impact on the delivery of the strategy (either positively or negatively). The identification of Key Risks and tools such as Risk Scorecard and Control Scorecard are used within this discipline. Risk Scorecards report on the organization's level of risk exposure against appetite and control maps can be used to assess control effectiveness against risk exposure and appetite. Appetite becomes more operational.

Three maps that align risk-taking with strategy

In the Managing Risk chapter, we also introduced a new tool called the Four Perspective Risk Map, which is designed to work with both a Strategy Map and the Appetite Alignment Matrix (a further new tool which we introduce in this chapter).

Strategy Map

A Strategy Map is typically arranged according to four perspectives that are described hierarchically, with shareholder (or financial) at the apex and then flowing down through customer, internal processes and learning and growth. A slightly different hierarchy is used in the public sector. A Strategy Map describes the cause-and-effect relationships between objectives that ultimately deliver value to the shareholder. It sets out what the organization is trying to achieve.

Four Perspective Risk Map

A Four Perspective Risk Map provides a view of current risk-taking as well as insights into any clustering of risks. Key risks are mapped according to the four perspectives of the Strategy Map, so providing an at-a-glance view of the level of risk that the organization is taking in pursuance of its strategic goals.

The power of this combination is that it provides useful checks and balances with regard to the progress of the strategy: the Strategy Map might well inform the senior management team that all is going smoothly (as monitored through Key Performance Indicators [KPIs]), whereas the Four Perspective Risk Map might tell a story that the organization is exposed to the possibility of one or more Key Risks materializing that might derail the strategy effort.

Appetite Alignment Matrix

However, using these two maps together doesn't tell whole story. While both Strategy Maps and the Four Perspective Risk Maps are extremely powerful tools in their own right, both individually give a view of the current state of strategy execution (strategy map) and risk exposure (risk map); however, the third tool – the Appetite Alignment Matrix – provides further strategically critical insights, which might be described as providing the "so what". By plotting risks on the matrix at any level (be it individual risk level, groups of risk, or business units) an organization is able to understand if it is operating within appetite and taking the right amount of risk to deliver the strategy going forward.

Explaining the Appetite Alignment Matrix

This brings us to an explanation of the Appetite Alignment Matrix, which is shown in Figure 8.2, while Figure 8.3 shows how a Strategy Map, Four Perspective Risk Map and Appetite Alignment Matrix work together in providing a robust summary of the present state of strategy execution.

The Appetite Alignment Matrix was designed by Manigent to provide a simple, visual way of understanding alignment between the current level of risk-taking (based on enterprise-wide risk assessments) and the strategy as expressed by taking an aggregated view of the risk appetite levels assigned to each strategic objective.

Client engagements have shown that this tool enables the executive team to see where they are taking too much or not enough risk

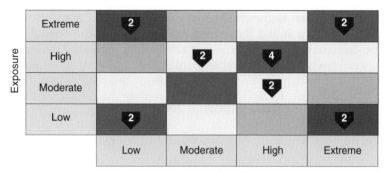

Figure 8.2 **Appetite Alignment Matrix**

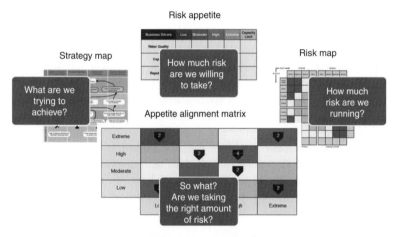

Figure 8.3 **How a Strategy Map, Four Perspective Risk Map and Appetite Alignment Matrix work together in providing a robust summary of the present state of strategy execution**

in pursuance of their objectives. It is a decision-making tool that has enabled users to generate tangible benefits, such as new revenue streams, and intangible benefits related to setting the right tone from the top of the organization and encouraging the right conversations to take place at senior and lower levels around strategy and risk management.

The Appetite Alignment Matrix plots the levels of appetite along the horizontal axis and the current risk exposure on the vertical axis. The diagonal cells from bottom left to top right show the intersection between levels of appetite and levels of exposure.

Three appetite versus exposure zones

The Appetite Alignment Matrix is articulated around three zones.

1 Optimal (Aligned) Zone (appetite and exposure and aligned)
2 Over-Exposed Zone (exposure is greater than appetite)
3 Under-Exposed Zone (exposure is less than appetite)

Optimal zone (appetite and exposure and aligned)

The main diagonal is the optimal zone, where there is full alignment between the risk appetite determined by the firm and the risk exposure induced by the business strategy. In the example matrix shown in Figure 8.4, eight risks are in the optimal zone. For two, the company has a moderate appetite and a moderate exposure. It may be, for instance, the risk of currency exchange for a business operating both in the UK and in the Eurozone that partially hedges its currency exposure. Risk and exposure are aligned for a second set of risks for which the company has both a high appetite and a high risk exposure, and a third

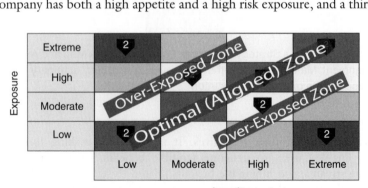

Figure 8.4 **Appetite and Exposure Alignment Matrix**

one where the company has both an extreme appetite and an extreme exposure. An example of the latter could be the risk exposure to market fluctuation for a broker or dealer. In other words, extreme risk exposure is acceptable as long as it is fully acknowledged and managed by the business.

The two other zones of the alignment matrix are suboptimal, either simply inefficient or downright dangerous.

Over-exposed zone (exposure is greater than appetite)

The upper left of the matrix is the over-exposed zone of the Appetite Alignment Matrix and should be particularly worrisome for business executives. This is the zone where risk exposure exceeds risk appetite; in short, the business is taking more risk than it is willing to take or capable of taking. This is most likely to be caused by negligence of assessing risk in the organization, either through ignorance or through a lack of risk culture that leads executives to pay little or no attention to the risks that their strategy has initiated. Examples are diverse, from entering a new market to launching a new product.

To move the risks into alignment the organization should review the treatment of those risks, asking themselves if they are best placed to manage those risks or should seek to transfer the risk via outsourcing or insurance; avoid the risk altogether, for example by changing the strategy or exiting part of the business; or seek to reduce the risk via adding additional controls or by undertaking targeted improvement projects to improve the effectiveness of the existing controls.

Under-exposed zone (exposure is less than appetite)

In the lower right of the matrix is the under-exposed zone where risk appetite is larger than the actual risk exposure. This should also be of concern to senior management, but this is rarely the case, simply because the senior team is unaware of the misalignment or its strategically negative impacts. When using this matrix and looking at alignment of appetite and exposure, business leaders typically understand the over-exposed zone, where exposure exceeds appetite, and generally know how to respond. However, the most interesting, and potentially most powerful aspect of this simple matrix is its ability to leverage benefits from the under-exposed zone, outlining where the exposure is less than appetite, that is, showing areas where the organization is not taking enough risk and therefore increasing the uncertainty around the delivery of their strategy, either by being under-exposed or over-controlled. Examples of such situations could be a credit institution not lending to its full capacity (under-exposure) or a credit card company blocking too many transactions due to over-cautious fraud system alerts (over-control). In both cases, money is lost, not through an operational risk event but in opportunity costs due to inefficiencies.

The importance of this zone should not be underestimated. It is within this zone that organizations find opportunities for cutting cost through reducing control activities or increasing revenue through exploiting market opportunities. This visual aid allows the board and executives to easily recognize where they are under-exposed, thus highlighting potential business opportunities. Consider these three examples of how organizations derived real benefits from realizing their exposure was less than their appetite.

Case Example 1: Results matching the collective "gut feel"

On a recent client engagement, the Appetite Alignment Matrix generated a very high level of senior management engagement and buy-in as the results generally matched the collective "gut feel" of the senior team, who felt certain areas of the business were not moving fast enough or had not been aggressive enough in seizing opportunities in their changing market.

Case Example 2: Identifying sectors where competitive advantage could be secured

As a further example, an organization that has implemented the RBPM approach used the Appetite Alignment Matrix to identify sectors within the market where they have a competitive advantage due to their superior risk management capabilities. The organization was then able to enter these new market sectors at the same price point as the existing players but generating superior margins because it would not incur the "standard" amount of risk-related losses and was, therefore, able to allocate less regulatory capital to this new business unit than its competitors.

Case Example 3: Reducing the cost of controls

Yet another organization used the Appetite Alignment Matrix as a key tool in a profitability exercise. It was able to identify parts of its business that were being over-controlled, particularly via manual controls. This resulted in a significant headcount reduction, as manual control activities were discontinued as the forecast level of risk was still within appetite.

The Appetite Alignment process

Appetite Alignment is the process of continuously aligning current risk exposure to the defined risk appetite, which by implication encapsulates the strategy of the organization. To translate into simple terms, it is about understanding whether the current level of risk-taking is aligned to the chosen business strategy, that is, are we operating within appetite?

Central to the Aligning Risk-taking with Strategy discipline is the use of an Appetite Alignment Process. This process is designed to show the steps an organization should go through on a regular basis to monitor and manage the alignment of risk-taking to risk appetite and by implication, the alignment of risk-taking to business strategy. This process shows where the Appetite Alignment Process interacts with the "hard" RBPM disciplines of Strategy, Performance and Risk Management.

The Appetite Alignment Process is made up of nine steps:

1 Review business drivers
2 Review strategic objectives
3 Review risk appetite
4 Review business performance
5 Review key risks
6 Conduct a risk assessment
7 Review appetite alignment (this is where we deploy the Appetite Alignment Matrix)
8 Act to correct misalignments
9 Continuous monitoring and review

The first three steps of this process are strategic and would normally only be reviewed in depth on an annual basis unless there is a major change in the business or its operating environment (the Credit Crunch is one obvious example where organizations both within and outside the financial services sector had to review their strategy due to a seismic shift in their business environment).

During the annual review, the organization's board and executive team should take an in-depth and fundamental review of the strategy of the organization and the dynamics of the industry and consider business drivers, the performance and continued relevance of strategic objectives, and revisit the amount or risk that they are willing and required to take to achieve those objectives (risk appetite).

However, while this in-depth session is an annual event, this does not mean that the board and executive should complete the review, leave it and then forget about it until the following year. Rather, reviews should be held on a quarterly basis with the board and executive team focusing on emerging threats and opportunities and asking themselves if the assumptions etc. on which they set strategy are still valid, what changes are emerging that could impact on the strategy and ordering interventions to keep the strategy on track and/or resetting appetite levels.

We will now consider each of the nine steps in turn.

Review business drivers

When reviewing Business Drivers, organizations should consider both their internal and external operating environment and, importantly, consider their business model and the assumptions inherent in their business model. This step is about identifying the fundamental drivers of success of a particular organization in a particular industry and understanding how they can be used to drive success in the organization. Understanding the business drivers is vital when setting objectives and defining risk appetite.

Review strategic objectives

At this stage the organization should be challenging itself on both the current objectives and the thinking behind each of those objectives, and the hypothesis around how the relationships that exist between objectives ultimately drive success.

Review risk appetite

Here the organization should ensure that given the drivers of their particular industry and business, and given the objectives they are trying to achieve, they have correctly set the risk-taking boundaries within which the executive team will execute the strategy. This means that the risk appetite must be set so that it reflects the level of risk that the board (which represents the shareholders) thinks is acceptable in order to achieve the expected returns. This puts the risk/reward relationship right at the centre of the performance conversations being held between the board and the executive team. And when using the RBPM approach, conversations around risk and reward sometimes lead to a reappraisal and refocusing of appropriate risk appetite levels.

As an example, one of the authors recently conducted a risk appetite exercise with the CEO and CFO of a small bank in the UK. At the end of the exercise, the CEO made the observation that he now recognized the importance of understanding risk appetite in the context of strategy – he had not considered this in the past or how to do it. He also said that his board had always considered the organization to be one with a low appetite for risk. However, applying the RBPM approach to risk appetite and explaining this clearly to the board would lead them to conclude that they were actually a moderate to high appetite organization and this would result in their allowing executives to put forward business plans that would call for high risk-taking in certain areas. Without such an approach he firmly believed that such plans would be rejected outright (especially in the current economic environment), as the board would not be able to properly evaluate the required level of risk-taking and lacked the tools to link risk appetite setting to the business strategy.

After the completion of a follow-up education and awareness exercise with the board, more aggressive business plans were indeed proposed and accepted by the board.

Review business performance

At this stage the organization should be asking itself if it is delivering the level of business performance that will enable it to achieve its strategic objectives. For most organizations, this is typically about reviewing performance from the perspective of "did we hit our targets?" and if not, why not. However when asking why not, few organizations would answer this question with the response that they either took too much or too little risk. Often when performance is under discussion, risk-taking is left as a separate conversation, which is a flawed approach. The issues of performance and risk are closely linked and should not be separated, as we stress repeatedly throughout this book.

When reviewing performance, rather than simply accept the "traditional" reasons for non-performance such as "Our sales team have not hit their numbers" and "The economy is slow", senior teams should add to that conversation questions around "Are we taking enough risk with our brand? Could we take more risk within our Research and Development or innovation processes to drive the next big thing?" Also organizations should be challenging the number and type of controls they have in place. Are they over-controlling the business to such an extent that it cannot effectively execute?

Review key risks

At this stage, risks should be reviewed to ensure that the organization has captured and is tracking the most appropriate and important risks facing the organization. Again an annual, in-depth review is important; however, given the rate of business change, a more frequent review of the risk the organization manages is important to capture emerging risks that must be either managed or exploited.

Conduct risk assessment

Conducting risk assessments is central to the risk management process. Equally it is a vital activity in the Appetite Alignment process as the level of risk exposure is an output from the risk assessment process and is a critical input into the Appetite Alignment step.

Review appetite alignment (this is where we deploy the Appetite Alignment Matrix)

Described fully above, the Appetite Alignment Matrix is designed to provide a simple but powerful visualization of whether or not an organization's risk-taking is aligned to its risk appetite, and by implication, its strategy.

Risk Appetite is set per strategic objective (or operationally, per process or initiative) per organization unit, whereas risk exposure is based on the residual risk exposure from the risk assessment process.

In addition to focusing on risks, it is also possible to use the Appetite Alignment Matrix to evaluate the alignment of risk-taking and risk appetite by plotting objectives, processes, initiatives or even business units onto the matrix.

Act to correct misalignments

This is where corrective actions, incremental process improvements or larger strategic initiatives are deployed to correct any appetite misalignments.

Continuous monitoring and review

The review of the Appetite Alignment Matrix, and the initiatives and actions related to it, should become part of the day-to-day monitoring and review process within the business. It is where aligning risk-taking with strategy becomes "the way we do things around here" – put another way, an ingrained part of the organizational culture.

Aligning risk-taking to strategy: From the technical to the cultural

As explained thus far, the Aligning Risk-taking to Strategy discipline is a key part of the "left half" of the RBPM framework. It serves to pull together the technical elements of RBPM – the Setting Strategy and Managing Performance and Managing Risk disciplines. Moreover, it is through the Aligning Risk-taking to Strategy discipline that we are able to properly visualize and exploit the idea that risk has an upside as well as downside, which although now widely stated is still poorly understood. This is largely due to a lack of tools with which to describe what managing the upside of risk might look like. The Appetite Alignment Matrix makes this possible.

But the work in ensuring that that risk-taking is aligned to strategy does not end when the technical piece is complete. Alas, there much more work to do and some would say much tougher work. These challenges are found in the disciplines within the right half of the RBPM approach: Governance, Culture and Communication, which we focus on in the following chapters.

Governance, whether by the board or internally though the Responsible, Accountable, Consult, Inform (RACI) approach, does much to ensure that risk-taking aligned to both strategic and operational goals is embedded into the very fabric of the culture and that proper communication tools are used to ensure that a risk-aware culture takes hold. This is critically important, for as we have said previously and will say again, "Culture eats strategy for breakfast and risk for lunch." Put starkly, fail to take into consideration and indeed master the "soft" aspects of implementing an integrated approach to strategy management and risk management and all the hard work completed in getting the "hard" bits right will likely count for nothing.

9 Governance

> Governance is the processes and practices which define the strategic, operating and decision-making boundaries of an organization (or organizational unit) and how decisions are made and implemented.

Introduction

Governance is the first of the so-called "softer" disciplines within the Risk-Based Performance Management (RPBM) framework and methodology (Figure 9.1). The other two are Culture and Communication, which we discuss in the next chapter. We purposely use the term "so-called" because they are only softer inasmuch as organizations rarely have formal processes and procedures for managing these disciplines and embedding them deep inside the organization. In practice, each of these disciplines provides a wealth of challenges that can derail the implementation of any performance management framework, and perhaps more quickly than any of the so-called harder disciplines, which come replete with a history of institutionalized processes and checks and balances.

This chapter describes the role that governance plays in successfully executing strategy and managing risk. We will show how the RBPM approach enables an integrated approach to governance by delivering a number of outputs that support good governance and decision making at an enterprise level. Moreover, the RBPM approach is structured so that good governance can be cascaded through, and embedded deep inside the organization via the RACI (Responsible, Accountable, Consult and Inform) model.

Governance and the Credit Crunch

But at the outset it is worth considering why governance has suddenly been elevated to front-of-mind status for boards and executive

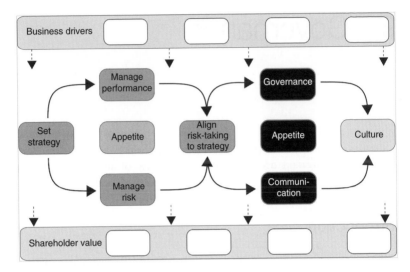

Figure 9.1 **RBPM framework**

committees. As we explained in earlier chapters, at the time that the Credit Crunch first raised its head (2008) the general consensus amongst experts and regulatory bodies was that risk management was essentially "sorted", especially for banks. It was something that we really had little need to spend much time worrying about. By the same token, there was a general belief that governance was well established and working effectively in most large organizations. After all, governance codes such as the Cadbury,[1] Greenbury[2] and Turnbull[3] codes had been in existence since the 1990s and provided robust guidelines for the structure and responsibilities of corporate boards. Governance was also believed to have been "sorted" by experts and regulatory bodies alike.

It was therefore something of a surprise that a failure of governance was quickly identified as a major contributory cause of the Credit Crunch, as much research suggests. More pointedly, many experts and reports have stated that the main failings of corporate boards were that they poorly understood and therefore managed their organization's risk profile and exposure. As we explained in Chapter 1, an early analysis of the causes of the Credit Crunch by the US Association of Chartered Certified Accountants (ACCA) reported that corporate governance was one of five main areas that led to the Credit Crunch (risk identification, remuneration and incentives, accounting and financial reporting, and regulation were the others). ACCA also claimed that a systematic failure in that the responsibility of boards to provide strategic oversight and direction, to ensure a strong control environment and to challenge the executive appeared to have been inadequately discharged. "We need to ask what inhibited banks' boards from asking the right questions and understanding the risks that were being run by their managements," the report's authors stated.[4]

Other works and reports since have been equally damning. For instance, the article *The Corporate Governance Lessons from the Financial Crisis* by Grant Kirkpatrick concludes that the financial crisis can be to an important extent attributed to failures and weaknesses in corporate governance arrangements. When they were put to a test, Kirkpatrick argues, corporate governance routines did not serve their purpose of safeguarding against excessive risk-taking in a number of financial services companies. A number of weaknesses were apparent, he claimed.

> The risk management systems have failed in many cases due to corporate governance procedures rather than the inadequacy of computer models alone: information about exposures in a number of cases did not reach the board and even senior levels of management, while risk management was often activity rather than enterprise-based.

As Kirkpatrick rightly says, "These are board responsibilities", adding that in other cases, boards had approved strategy but then did not establish suitable metrics to monitor its implementation. "Company disclosures about foreseeable risk factors and about the systems in place for monitoring and managing risk have also left a lot to be desired," he says.[5]

Royal Bank of Scotland case example

Failures of corporate governance in the management of risk were named as key shortcomings in the UK's Financial Services Authority's December 2011 report *The Failure of the Royal Bank of Scotland* (RBS), as we explained in the case report in Chapter 4. The report described a whole raft of poor decisions by the RBS management and board. Among the most striking was the decision to go ahead with the ABN AMRO acquisition in 2007, which played a significant role in RBS's failure. The board decided to go ahead with the acquisition on the basis of due diligence which was clearly inadequate relative to the risks entailed. With incredulity, the report stated that "Many readers of the Report will be startled to read that the information made available to RBS by ABN AMRO in April 2007 amounted to 'two lever arch folders and a CD' and that RBS was largely unsuccessful in its attempts to obtain further non-publicly available information".

The FSA report continued that it was evident that in pursuing its aggressive strategy RBS was exposed to a plethora of high risks. The FSA analysis also raised serious questions about the effectiveness of the RBS board's role in relation to strategy.

> Given the scale of RBS's ambitions for growth, in particular during 2006 and into 2007, it is reasonable to expect the Board to have assured itself that the growth strategy was accompanied by a very high degree of attention to the associated risks. In retrospect, this was not clearly and demonstrably the case.

From the perspective of the RBPM framework it is particularly notable that the FSA reported that the RBS "Board, Remuneration Committee and Nominations Committee Performance Evaluation" 2006 report (so pre-dating the Credit Crunch) said that directors felt there was insufficient input to and review of risk appetite at board level and that the board needed to articulate its risk appetite.[6]

Poor risk oversight – Research findings

To be fair, RBS was far from unique in the failure of its board to provide the required risk oversight. For instance, the report *Risk Management Lessons from the Global Banking Crisis of 2008* by the Senior Supervisors Group started that there was little evidence of board involvement in setting and monitoring adherence to firms' risk appetite, reporting that risk appetite statements were generally not sufficiently robust, rarely reflecting a suitably wide range of measures and lacking actionable elements that clearly articulate firms' intended responses to losses of capital and breaches of limits.

"Most firms acknowledged some need for improvement in their procedures for setting and monitoring risk appetite," the report noted, adding that while boards of directors reportedly approve risk appetites and strategies as articulated by management, most firms did not present much evidence of active board involvement in overseeing the setting or

monitoring of the company's risk appetite or of board understanding
of the firm's current risk position relative to its risk appetite.

> In several cases, firms admitted a disparity between the risks that the firm
> took and those that the board perceived it to be taking. Many firms indi-
> cated that they are in the process of revamping the way information is
> presented to their boards and that they were expanding the range of met-
> rics for measuring risk appetite. Several firms that had previously calibrated
> limits to capital metrics were now focusing more on the level of quar-
> terly earnings. Conversely, other firms were now paying more attention
> to tail risks' (the possibility of rare events happening). These additional
> areas of focus, as well as the intense market interest in financial institu-
> tions' risk profiles since the onset of the crisis, underscore the need for
> firms to apply multiple measures of risk appetite, to develop a range of per-
> spectives, and to consider a broad distribution of possible outcomes. These
> changes also suggest a need for firms to consider further what manage-
> ment actions are realistically feasible for restoring capital or reducing risk in
> adverse environments.[7]

Board oversight – post-Credit Crunch

So has the board's oversight and management of risk improved in the
few years that have followed the onset of the financial crisis?

Ernst & Young's 2010 report *Making Strides in Financial Services
Risk Management* found that surveyed firms (62 firms participated in
the study online and/or by telephone, which resulted in 60 online
survey responses and 35 interviews) reported that boards were more
actively engaged and involved in risk policy setting and governance
than in previous years and were spending more focused, higher quality
time on risk issues. Overall, 83% of respondents reported an increase
in board oversight of risk, with 42% indicating a significant increase
in board involvement. In particular, the study noted, board members
have become better informed on risk-related topics. Respondents credit
enhanced training programmes to keep the board abreast of emerging issues impacting risk; increased transparency, quality and frequency
of reporting; more regular meetings; and more in-depth discussion of
enterprise-wide risk.

Crucially, many firms said that setting strategic direction and playing
a key role in the development, approval and oversight of risk appetite
are now considered to be board responsibilities and emerging issues

such as capital allocation, new business risks and compensation have become higher priorities on the board's agenda. The majority of the firms surveyed (86%) have separated risk from their audit committees and established a distinct risk committee to ensure independence and an adequate focus on each of those critical areas. Firms reported that boards are conducting deeper dives into matters that in previous years did not reach their agendas – requiring more sophisticated, in-depth and frequent reports and analysis.[8]

Defining governance

It's worth pausing here to explain what we mean by the term "governance". Given the central topics covered in this book, strategy execution, risk appetite, risk management, etc., it might be reasonably expected that within this context, we might mean corporate governance. However, although it is of course a central element, we argue that just focusing on corporate governance limits the application and effectiveness of governance. Rather, within the context of RBPM a broader governance approach is embedded which resolves around establishing clear strategic boundaries and accountabilities, and cascading these deep inside the organization.

As a starting point, there is a number of well established and well known definitions of corporate governance that help to shape our understanding of what enterprise-wide governance should look like.

The UK Corporate Governance Code

The *UK Corporate Governance Code* (2010) states that "The purpose of corporate governance is to facilitate effective, entrepreneurial and prudent management that can deliver the long-term success of the company." Included within this code is a definition of corporate governance from the 1992 *Corporate Governance Code* produced by the Cadbury Committee, which is perceived by many as the classic definition:

> Corporate governance is the system by which companies are directed and controlled. Boards of directors are responsible for the governance of their companies. The shareholders' role in governance is to appoint the directors and the auditors and to satisfy themselves that an appropriate governance

structure is in place. The responsibilities of the board include setting the company's strategic aims, providing the leadership to put them into effect, supervising the management of the business and reporting to shareholders on their stewardship. The board's actions are subject to laws, regulations and the shareholders in general meeting.[9]

The King Report

Around the same time that the Cadbury Committee was first formalizing the UK Corporate Governance framework, South Africa's *King Report on Corporate Governance*, the first of three ground-breaking reports, was issued (King I, 1994), which was subsequently followed by King II in 2002 and King III in 2009. The *King Report on Corporate Governance* has been cited as "the most effective summary of the best international practices in corporate governance".[10,11,12]

Unlike most corporate governance codes the King Code is non-legislative, and is based on principles and practices. The philosophy of the code consists of the three key elements of leadership, sustainability and good corporate citizenship. It views good governance as essentially being effective, ethical leadership. King believes that leaders should direct the company in order to achieve sustainable economic, social and environmental performance. It views sustainability as the primary moral and economic imperative of this century; the code's view on corporate citizenship flows from a company's standing as a juristic person under the South African constitution, which should therefore operate in a sustainable manner. As examples, key principles from King II included directors and their responsibility; risk management; internal audit; integrated sustainability reporting; accounting and auditing. King III includes several emerging trends such as alternative dispute resolution, risk-based internal audit, shareholder approval of non-executive directors' remuneration and the evaluation of board and directors' performance.

ASX Corporate Governance Council

In Australia, *The Corporate Governance Principles and Recommendations* produced by the ASX Corporate Governance Council defines corporate governance as "the framework of rules, relationships, systems and processes within and by which authority is exercised and controlled in corporations". It encompasses the mechanisms by which companies, and those in control, are held to account. Corporate governance influences how the objectives of the company are set and achieved, how risk is monitored and assessed, and how performance is optimized.

This standard also includes eight principles of good corporate governance:

1   Lay solid foundations for management and oversight.
2   Structure the board to add value.
3   Promote ethical and responsible decision making.
4   Safeguard the integrity of financial reporting.
5   Make timely and balanced disclosure.
6   Respect the rights of shareholders.
7   Recognize and manage risk.
8   Remunerate fairly and responsibly.[13]

OECD Principles of Corporate Governance

The Organization for Economic Cooperation and Development (OECD) has also set out some guidance around corporate governance in the document *OECD Principles of Corporate Governance*, 2004. This document states that "Corporate governance involves a set of relationships between a company's management, its board, its shareholders and other stakeholders. Corporate governance also provides the structure through which the objectives of the company are set, and the means of attaining those objectives and monitoring performance are determined."

In addition, this document sets out five principles of good corporate governance:

1   The corporate governance framework should promote transparent and efficient markets, be consistent with the rule of law and clearly articulate the division of responsibilities among different supervisory, regulatory and enforcement authorities.
2   The corporate governance framework should protect and facilitate the exercise of shareholders' rights.
3   The corporate governance framework should ensure the equitable treatment of all shareholders, including minority and foreign shareholders. All shareholders should have the opportunity to obtain effective redress for violation of their rights.

4 The corporate governance framework should recognize the rights of stakeholders established by law or through mutual agreements and encourage active co-operation between corporations and stakeholders in creating wealth, jobs, and the sustainability of financially sound enterprises.

5 The corporate governance framework should ensure that timely and accurate disclosure is made on all material matters regarding the corporation, including the financial situation, performance, ownership, and governance of the company.[14]

Other approaches

While the UK, much of the European Union, South Africa and many of the commonwealth countries have taken a "comply or explain" approach, and more lately an "apply or explain" approach to corporate governance, the US has tended to enact corporate governance through a detailed set of rules. This was particularly so under the 2002 Sarbanes–Oxley act, which set new standards for financial reporting and included areas such as accounting oversight, auditor independence and enhanced financial disclosures.[15]

Additionally in the US, the corporate governance framework is not defined in a single piece of legislation or code; rather it is to be found in a range of different laws and regulations, at both federal and state levels.

In addition to the corporate level, governance frameworks can be applied at more operational levels within the organization. Commonly deployed/referenced governance frameworks include

▷ Project Governance – the management framework within which project decisions are made.

▷ IT Governance – the leadership and organizational structures and processes that ensure that the organization's IT sustains and extends the organization's strategies and objectives.

▷ Data Governance – the exercise of decision making and authority for data-related matters. Or for a longer definition, Data Governance is a system of decision rights and accountabilities for information-related processes, executed according to agreed-upon models which describe who can take what actions with what information, when, under what circumstances and using what methods.

The authors' definition of governance

The definitions above show that Governance is a wide-ranging concept which by common practice is applied to specific levels (e.g., corporate), or specific areas (e.g., project governance) of the organization or its activities.

Based on an extensive review of available literature as well as feedback from client engagement within the context of RBPM, we have created the following simple definition of governance: "Governance is the processes and practices which define the strategic, operating and decision-making boundaries of an organization (or organizational unit), and how decisions are made and implemented."

This definition is deliberately designed to be broadly applicable to support a governance process that can be cascaded from the strategic level of the organization (corporate governance) to a more operational level (project, IT, data and process governance, etc.).

Setting of boundaries

Our definition speaks of the setting of boundaries. At the corporate level, these boundaries are set through a clear definition and understanding of the organizational business model, through the clear definition of long-term goals (3–5 years) and short-term objectives (12–24 months) and through the clear definition and understanding of the organizational risk appetite. Once these elements have been defined by the board and senior executive they should be cascaded through and embedded within the organization.

Decision making

This definition also touches on decision making, both how decisions are made and how they are implemented within the organization. The RBPM approach, with its emphasis on the integration of strategy and risk management, and specifically risk appetite, provides a strategic framework for boards and senior executives to ensure that from a strategic direction and risk-taking perspective they can meet their corporate governance obligations.

This definition is important to, and enabled by, the central concept behind the RBPM approach: risk appetite should be a central part of an organization's strategy, and should be embedded in their strategic execution process while "operating within appetite".

The RBPM approach, with its emphasis on the integration of strategy and risk management, and specifically risk appetite, provides a strategic framework for boards and senior executives to ensure that from a strategic direction and risk-taking perspective they can meet their corporate governance obligations.

Governance and risk management

The importance of risk oversight as a governance imperative has also been highlighted in several of the works above as well as others. Risk management features heavily in two areas within the *OECD Principles of Corporate Governance*:

Disclosure and transparency

The key item here is the recommendation to disclose material information on foreseeable risk factors, including disclosure on the system for monitoring and managing risk. These foreseeable risks may be industry-specific, geographical, a commodity dependency, environmental liabilities, derivatives, financial market risk such as interest rates or currency and off-balance sheet transactions.

Responsibilities of the board

The board is responsible for reviewing and guiding risk policy. Risk policy is seen as closely related to corporate strategy. Boards should specify the types and degree of risk that a company is willing to accept in pursuit of its goals. It must manage risk to meet the company's desired risk profile.[16]

A further report by the UK's Institute of Directors (IOD) stated that the Credit Crunch has emphasized the importance of risk management as a board-level responsibility and the board's important role in aligning risk to strategy and of risk appetite. According to the IOD the role of the board is threefold:

▷ Evaluate risk associated with the corporate strategies.
▷ Define the risk appetite of the company.

▷ Ensure that appropriate resources are identified for risk identification, avoidance and mitigation.[17]

Moreover, the report *Research into the Definition and Application of the Concept of Risk Appetite* found that the most popular answers to that question posed to survey interviewees "if you have a risk appetite statement, indicate why this was developed" were "improved board risk oversight and risk governance" (71%) followed by "communicate expectations for risk-taking to managers" (54%). The board is primarily responsible for creating the Risk Appetite Statement and for overseeing its execution.[18]

The importance of the board's oversight of risk appetite also tops the list in the October 2009 National Association of Corporate Directors Blue Ribbon Commission report, *Risk Governance: Balancing Risk and Rewards*. The 42-page report distils the key elements of board risk oversight down to six concise goals:

> While risk oversight objectives may vary from company to company, every board should be certain that
>
> 1   The risk appetite implicit in the company's business model, strategy, and execution is appropriate
> 2   The expected risks are commensurate with the expected rewards
> 3   Management has implemented a system to manage, monitor, and mitigate risk, and that system is appropriate given the company's business model and strategy
> 4   The risk management system informs the board of the major risks facing the company
> 5   An appropriate culture of risk-awareness exists throughout the organization
> 6   There is recognition that management of risk is essential to the successful execution of the company's strategy[19]

As much as anything these six points suggest the importance of embedding risk management principles and practices deep inside the organization. This is central to the RBPM approach.

The RACI model

To cascade and embed governance, we deploy the RACI model within the RBPM approach.

RACI is a governance and decision-making model that is wrapped around the objectives, processes, initiatives, risks and controls that appear within the RBPM framework and methodology. RACI is a model for identifying functional areas, key activities and decision points where ambiguities exist. It usage means that differences can be brought into the open and resolved through team effort and it enables management to actively participate in the process of systematically describing objectives, activities and decisions that have to be accomplished, and to clarify the responsibility that each holds in relation to those objectives, activities and decisions.

Responsible – this refers to the person(s) who is/are doing the work to deliver an item within the RBPM framework – deliver an objective(s), a process(es), an initiative(s), manage a risk(s) and/or ensure the effectiveness of control(s). This is the person(s) who is/are focused on action and implementation – the "doer(s)".

Accountable – this refers to the person who is ultimately accountable for the delivery of an item within the RBPM framework, an objective(s), a process(s), an initiative(s), managing a risk(s) and/or ensuring the effectiveness of a control(s). This person holds Yes/No authority and only one accountable person can be assigned to an item. This person is "where the buck stops".

Consult – this refers to the person(s) who is/are to be consulted before a major decision is taken in relation to an item within the RBPM framework (Objective, Process, Initiative, Risk and Control). There should be a two-way dialogue between the Accountable and Consult roles. The Consult is/are the person(s) that you "keep in the loop".

Inform – this refers to the person(s) who is/are to be informed after a major decision has been taken in relation to an item within the RBPM framework (Objective, Process, Initiative, Risk and Control). The Inform is/are the person(s) that you "keep in the picture".

The RACI process is rolled out through six steps:

1 Introductory meetings are conducted to inform key management of the purpose and requirements of the process.
2 Decision and function lists are developed, analysed and collated into a master function list.

3   Responsibility workshops are conducted to agree upon function definitions and to assign codes that describe the type of responsibility each role will have toward each function. The output is a responsibility chart.

4   The responsibility charts are documented and reproduced to distribute to all participants and interfacing organizations.

5   The communication and reinforcement of the new role definitions are accomplished through meetings with all individuals and departments involved.

6   Follow-up is conducted to ensure that relationships defined in the process are being adhered to and to encourage participants to live the roles.

Benefits of RACI

Our experience of using RACI as an intrinsic part of the RBPM approach has been very positive. Typically, our clients report that applying RACI in their organizations presents some early challenges, simply because it is a different way of thinking about governance and decision making and it forces a level of rigour that has previously been missing. However, when it is in place they report that the RACI framework is a very powerful driver of change and extremely usefully in establishing the right strategy-focused, risk-aware culture.

Importantly, our clients have reported significant benefits from deploying the RACI framework, including: assists teamwork by charting roles and responsibilities in a consistent manner; providing clarification of roles and responsibilities; identifying accountabilities; eliminating misunderstandings and encouraging teamwork; reducing duplication of effort; improving communication by establishing "consult" and "inform" relationships. Moreover, clients report that embedding governance using the RACI framework clarifies communication around strategy and risk management, and plays an important role in shaping an organizational culture that instinctively "operates within appetite".

One of the aspects of the RACI framework that we particularly like, and the reason we embedded it in the RBPM methodology, is that it is simple to understand and quick to apply, something that is also appreciated and recognized by our clients. This was demonstrated within one of our clients where we introduced the RACI framework. Working for the Chairman of a large professional services organization in London, UK, we introduced the RACI framework to the senior leadership team and their direct reports. At the same time, during a two-day off-site, we introduced a new Strategy Map, Risk Map and Risk Appetite Statement.

While many of those present had been actively engaged in the development of the Strategy Map, Risk Map and the Risk Appetite Statement, the RACI framework had only been discussed at the most senior level. Within two weeks of this off-site and the introduction of the RACI framework, one of the executives involved with the project travelled to Australia to work with their Sydney office. On his return, he burst excitedly into the project room and told the project team that the Australian executive team had adopted the RACI framework after one of their members had visited the UK the week before! They had found the project material on an internal website and applied it locally. This sent a powerful signal to the UK office and also to the project team – it energized the team to drive this forward and make it successful. Later both the UK and Australian executive teams reported a significant improvement in decision making, both in terms of quality and speed, and subsequent improvements in business results. Figure 9.2 shows how the RACI model works.

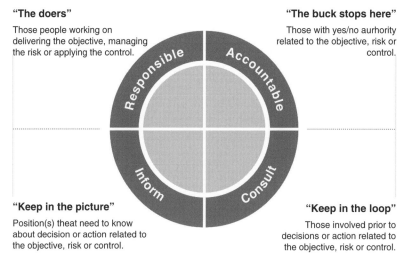

"The doers"
Those people working on delivering the objective, managing the risk or applying the control.

"The buck stops here"
Those with yes/no aurhority related to the objective, risk or control.

"Keep in the picture"
Position(s) theat need to know about decision or action related to the objective, risk or control.

"Keep in the loop"
Those involved prior to decisions or action related to the objective, risk or control.

Figure 9.2   **How the RACI model might support a Strategy Map**

Conclusion

This chapter has explained the role that governance plays in the RBPM framework and methodology. It has stressed that governance is not just a corporate responsibility, while stating the board must dispatch their duties much better than has previously been the case – to avoid shortcomings such as those that were laid bare for the world to see as a result of the Credit Crunch. Governance has to be an idea and a practical framework and process that is understood deep inside the organization. The RACI model is a powerful technique for driving this understanding and the application of good enterprise-wide governance.

Moreover, the RACI model plays an important part in creating a strategy-focused, risk-aware culture. In the next chapter we explain in detail what a strategy-focused, risk-aware culture looks like and why it is critical for the successful deployment of the RBPM framework and methodology.

10 Culture and Communication

Culture eats strategy for breakfast and risk for lunch.

Introduction

There is perhaps no harder part of any change management programme (which a Risk-Based Performance Management [RBPM] implementation certainly is) than changing, or at least shaping the correct, culture (Figure 10.1). Those Balanced Scorecard and risk management engagements that fail normally do so not because of technical construction issues but because of cultural reasons – a resistance to performance being closely monitored and measured (so a fear of accountability and transparency) and an unwillingness to change established management processes and behaviours. And the authors of this book have never encountered a client who said they communicated too much during a performance management implementation – "communicate, communicate, communicate" is quite possibly the advice most widely offered by practitioners and consultants when asked to list the critical success factors (CSF) of a performance management/change programme. Senior management support is the only other CSF that might be as high on the list of importance.

Cultural and communication issues are equally powerful potential blockers to successful implementation of a risk management programme. Cultural reasons, most notably when linked to compensation packages, are routinely blamed for any irresponsible behaviour that led to the Credit Crunch. Whether or not the compensation link is as important as claimed, it is safe to argue that many organizations encouraged (or at best turned a blind eye to) the development of a culture where high-risk investing was the norm. It is equally safe to state

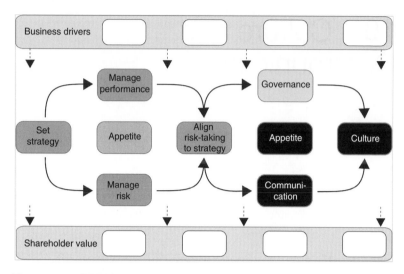

Figure 10.1 **RBPM framework**

that very little attention was paid to the communication of notions such as risk appetite or tolerance levels, even in the banking industry, which purportedly has the most sophisticated and robust risk management processes and systems of any industry or sector: fail-safe, many believed.

Moreover, and somewhat worryingly, banking hiccoughs since (such as the JP Morgan Chase example mentioned in earlier chapters) appear to have been at least partly the result of an inappropriate culture being allowed to flourish. After all, that one of the key people at the heart of the JP Morgan Chase failure went by the name of the London Whale, or Lord Voldemort (after the evil character in the Harry Potter books) due to the size of the bets he made, hardly points to a culture that encouraged the deployment of a risk appetite that was sensible and sustainable. Moreover, an article in the *New York Times* stated that individuals amassing huge trading positions were not effectively challenged, and there were regular shouting matches and difficult personality issues.[1]

With the RBPM approach combining – and integrating – both performance management and risk management strands, it is little wonder that Culture and Communication are two of the seven disciplines. We cover culture and communication together because they are so closely intertwined – planned and effective communication is a critical part of a culture change programme; both communication and culture change focus on influencing/changing behaviour and represent the two main pillars of change management.

Part one: Culture

We will start with culture. When implementing RBPM a primary objective is to shape a strategy-focused, risk-aware culture, and communication is a critical influencer of success. As a measure of the "softness" of culture, heed the words of the celebrated management thinker Peter Drucker: "Culture eats strategy for breakfast."[2] We would expand this to read "Culture eats strategy for breakfast and risk for lunch." Whatever's actually eaten first, the fact is that culture is perhaps the ultimate strategy and risk management tool: get the culture right and objectives will more likely be achieved and risk managed. Get the culture wrong and failure will be just about inevitable; even though ultimate failure might well be preceded by a period of stunning financial success, as we have seen with many organizations that suffered catastrophic failure.

An aligned and appropriate culture is a prerequisite for a strategy that is successful and sustainable. Indeed we strongly argue that culture should be treated as an organizational asset, as important as any other. Indeed culture is a substantial determinant of whether a firm is able successfully to execute its chosen strategy within its defined risk appetite.

A strategy-focused, risk-aware culture

We use the term "a strategy-focused, risk-aware culture" to describe the type of culture which has the dexterity to simultaneously remain focused on delivering a clear set of objectives while scanning broadly to identify threats and opportunities which may help or hinder the achievement of those objectives. People within such a culture operate within a clearly defined and communicated appetite for risk that is aligned to the corporate strategic goals.

Financial services research

It is notable that the origins of our thinking that led to this definition stem back to a study by Andrew Smart and Manigent into how risk and performance were integrated within the banking industry: an analysis that slightly preceded the Credit Crunch. Given what happened next, it might be viewed as eerily portentous that "developing the 'right' culture and embedding performance into daily decision-making and action-taking was highlighted as a major issue facing the sector. Seven of the 21 participants from 19 organizations characterized the 'right' culture as 'open, honest and no surprises' " and four suggested that performance and risk management should be everyone's job.[3]

Ernst & Young research

The consultancy Ernst & Young's 2011 research paper *Making Strides in Financial Services Risk Management* found that in the aftermath of the Credit Crunch 92% of organizations were indeed placing greater emphasis on culture and that most had a host of initiatives under way to institutionalize a comprehensive, consistent and collaborative culture. However, only 23% reported a positive shift. The paper stated that "For many firms, making risk 'everyone's business' represents a significant shift in mind-set, policies, systems and processes, and involves a long-term commitment and investment."[4]

Seven characteristics of a strategy-focused, risk-aware culture

Recognizing the challenges of culture change, we here identify seven characteristics of a strategy-focused, risk-aware culture:

1   Driven by a compelling vision
2   Live by a clear set of values
3   Led with integrity
4   Align risk-taking to strategy
5   Established clear accountabilities
6   Engage in high quality conversations
7   Incentives are aligned to appetite

Driven by a compelling vision

Central to a strategy-focused, risk-aware culture is a compelling organizational vision: a vision that the board, executive and front-line staff understand, and are engaged in and focused on achieving. It should be a vision that unites the organization, providing direction when setting objectives at an organizational and personal level.

There are many examples of compelling visions in corporate history, including Microsoft's "A PC on every desk", IBM's simple "Think" or Amazon's "Work Hard, Have Fun, Make History". And perhaps most famous of all, President John Kennedy's vision at the beginning of the 1960s to fly a man to the moon and bring him safely by the end of the decade. NASA delivered on this vision with five months to spare.

Live by a clear set of values

Underpinning a strategy-focused, risk-aware culture is a clear set of values which are lived by everyone in the organization. Establishing a strong set of values binds the organization together in their pursuit of their vision and objectives. It also influences the organizational attitude to risk and creates an environment in which those individuals that don't fit the culture leave voluntarily.

In Chapter 3, we profiled Qatar's public works authority (Ashghal), which was integrating strategy and risk through the Balanced Score-card. Ashghal's senior team had identified three core values to help drive delivery of the corporate objectives and to shape the culture of the organization. Each value has supporting descriptions that capture behavioural expectations: We Lead with inspiration and integrity (behaviours such as "we are trustworthy, honest, open and transparent" and "we do not compromise our ethics and integrity"); We Deliver with passion and commitment (behaviours include, "we care deeply about outcomes, performance and sustainability" and "we empower and manage partners to deliver the right outcomes"); We Care with empathy and respect (behaviours include "we look to create shared value for all our customers and stakeholders" and "we take pride in our work, credibility and the corporate reputation". Head of Strategic Planning Mark Ranford noted that "The management of risk should focus the organization around achieving its strategic objectives by best recognizing and even undertaking risks that might be deemed necessary to achieve the objectives, while also avoiding risks that are considered unacceptable to the organization, its mission, vision, values and strategic objectives."

We would add, and also stress that a clear set of values creates the type of culture which enables attention to be drawn when activities are taking place which are outside of the defined risk appetite.

Leadership with integrity

Leadership is a critical component of shaping and reinforcing the required culture. Leadership with integrity is about the leaders of the organization demonstrating their commitment to the vision and values through their actions: it is also about demonstrating commitment to balancing risk and reward and "operating within appetite", that is, operating only to the boundaries set by the board's appetite statement. Such leaders will be just as concerned about taking too little risk as taking too much risk, knowing that ultimately both could damage the probability of the organization executing its strategy and achieving its vision. These leaders will also be continuously asking "What risks don't we know about? Where do the emerging opportunities and threats lie?"

Most importantly, this leadership is not confined to the board, the executive or others in "leadership" position but rather the culture is such that leadership is present and demonstrated throughout the organization.

As with everything concerned with culture, infusing the right leadership behaviour and commitment comes replete with challenges. Indeed, one of the criticisms in the analysis of the financial crisis was that the tone at the top established a culture of risk-taking and internal control mechanisms came a poor second to the demands for growth. As Citigroup's Chief Executive, Charles O. Prince, said in July 2007, "As long as the music is playing, you've got to get up and dance. We're still dancing."[5] And dance they did, all the way to a 90% fall in their share price.

The research report *Risk Management in a Time of Global Uncertainty* by Harvard Business Review Analytic Services found that of 1419 surveyed firms only one in ten respondents said their executive management was "highly effective" at creating a strong risk-aware culture. And only 40% of respondents considered their approach to enterprise risk management (ERM) to be "proactive", with an integrated process that involves the board and business and functional leaders at all levels of the organization.

Moreover, while 34% of survey respondents cited embedding a risk-aware culture as one of the most important capabilities for successful risk management in their businesses, only 11% felt they were doing extremely well at this.

Respondents overwhelmingly cited "tone at the top – the degree of support from the board and the C-suite", – as critical to establishing effective ERM.[6]

The importance of setting the right tone from the top to embed a strategy-aware risk culture was highlighted as critical by Gillian Weatherill, Head of Operational Risk at HML (see case report in Chapter 2). "Having the buy-in from the very top and their asking the questions and making the right challenges brings the right attitudes to the organization," she explains. "As one example, we do quarterly control self-assessments and our CEO sits down with all of our directors and challenges them over the control effectiveness views that have been put forward from their division. This brings a lot of focus."

Align risk-taking to strategy. Perhaps the central characteristic of a strategy-focused, risk-aware culture is that it is embedded in the alignment of risk-taking to strategy as a central part of "the way we do things around here". This is a culture that actively sets and continuously reviews its strategy and key risks from the perspective of the question: are we "operating within appetite" – is the amount of risk we are currently running enough or too much to enable us to achieve our strategy? This is a culture that views strategy execution from both a performance and risk management perspective. See also Box 10.1 for the Institute of Risk managers take on the importance of getting the culture piece right.

Box 10.1   IIR defines a successful risk culture

The 2013 report by the Institute Risk Management (IRM), which includes interviews with many of its members, went into great detail in explaining the importance of getting the culture right if risk is to be managed properly. According to IRM, "an effective risk culture is one that enables and rewards individuals and groups for taking the right risks in an informed manner."

A successful risk culture, IRM argues, would include:

1   A distinct and consistent tone from the top from the board and senior management in regard to risk-taking and avoidance (and also consideration of tone at all levels)
2   A commitment to ethical principles, reflected in a concern with the ethical profile of individuals and the application of ethics and the consideration of wider stakeholder positions in decision making
3   A common acceptance through the organization of the importance of continuous management of risk, including clear accountability for and ownership of specific risks and risk areas

4   Transparent and timely risk information flowing up and down the
     organization with bad news rapidly communicated without fear of blame

5   Encouragement of risk event reporting and whistle-blowing, actively
     seeking to learn from mistakes and near misses

6   No process or activity is too large or too complex or too obscure for the
     risks to be readily understood

7   Appropriate risk-taking behaviours rewarded and encouraged and inap-
     propriate behaviours challenged and sanctioned

8   Risk management skills and knowledge valued, encouraged and
     developed, with a properly resourced risk management function and
     widespread membership of and support for professional bodies. Pro-
     fessional qualifications supported as well as technical training

9   Sufficient diversity of perspectives, values and beliefs to ensure that the
     status quo is consistently and rigorously challenged

10   Alignment of culture management with employee engagement and peo-
     ple strategy to ensure that people are supportive socially but also
     strongly focused on the task in hand.

The report states, "Take any public meltdown (for example, MPs' expenses,
press standards, LIBOR manipulation, Enron, the space shuttle disasters) and
many of these features will be notably absent."

From the report: *Risk culture: Under the Microscope Guidance for Boards,* The
Institute of Risk Management, 2013.[7]

Within the strategy-focused, risk-aware culture risk appetite is
seen as a tool for the board to set the boundaries of the organization's risk-taking activities and to establish a shared language to
talk about strategy and risk with the executive. Risk appetite is cascaded through the organization and strategy is executed within these
boundaries.

KPMG's work *Understanding and Articulating Risk Appetite* con-
curs that a critical role of risk culture is the tone it sets for the risk
appetite across the organization. "The importance of risk culture can
never be underestimated," the authors noted. "Most major contem-
porary examples of fraud and financial failure over the past 20 years
were related to instances of flawed or ambiguous risk cultures." They
add that the definition and articulation of risk appetite has a positive
influence on organizational behaviour. "It gives managers an improved
understanding of what risk management means to their roles and helps
them to apply effective risk management practices."[8]

Establish clear accountabilities

From a strategy-focused, risk-aware culture perspective, establishing clear accountabilities is all about having a clearly defined organizational and governance structure which assigns accountability for policies, procedures and the various governance and compliance obligations to the most appropriate committee and individuals. It is also about cascading accountabilities through the organization so that individuals are named as accountable for achieving specific objectives or for managing specific risks. The use of the RACI (Responsible, Accountable, Consult and Inform) framework, as a guide to setting accountabilities at the objective and risk level, is important, and is discussed in more detail in the previous chapter, where we focus on Governance.

Ensuring that management/staff are motivated to make decisions in accordance with the organization's appetite for risk was stressed in the report *Research into the Definition and Application of the Concept of Risk Appetite* by the consultancy Marsh and the University of Nottingham, UK. "Motivating an organization's employees is never easy", the authors noted;

> however there are some practical solutions that can be utilised. Notably an organisation might decide to reflect its appetite for risk within:
>
> ▷ Staff training initiatives – which could be used to promote risk awareness and reinforce an organisation's qualitative risk appetite statements
> ▷ Incentive schemes, whereby management might be rewarded for achieving specific economic targets whilst keeping risk indicators within agreed limits
> ▷ Performance management and objective setting initiatives where staff are given objectives that are directly aligned to current risk appetite priorities.[9]

At HML, effective training has been central to inculcating a strategy-focused risk-aware culture and to building engagement. This included innovative training initiatives which people hugely enjoyed. For example, as a team development activity HML conducted a "The Weakest Link" Risk Management exercise (based on the popular TV show) as well as something similar on the equally popular show "Who Wants to be a Millionaire". "We had lots of training initiatives like that so people could realize that this could be fun as well as important to the business," says Gillian Weatherill, Head of Operational Risk.

Engage in high quality conversations

High quality conversations are a characteristic of a strategy-focused, risk-aware culture. The RBPM approach enables and encourages high quality conversations to take place because of the availability of actionable information about the current levels of performance, alongside current levels of risk-taking, and also emerging and potential risks to the current strategy. The continuous balancing of strategic ambition and risk-taking, with clear accountabilities established via the RACI framework, naturally leads to organizational conversations which challenge assumptions and entrenched views, challenge and expose any political game-playing and welcome alternative views.

Incentives are aligned to appetite

One of the most important influences on culture is the incentive regime. Many of those working within the financial services industry have pointed to the bonus culture as a key driver of excessive risk-taking, which ultimately led to the Credit Crunch. While the bonus culture may have contributed to excessive risk-taking, perhaps more important from an incentives perspective was how the bonuses and other incentives are measured. Typical incentive structures are defined rather narrowly on hitting specific performance-related targets without factoring in the amount of risk taken to achieve those targets. Should a salesperson receive his/her bonus if they hit 100% of their sales targets by mis-selling and using aggressive sales techniques when they might be exposing their organization to multiple millions of pounds worth of fines and a damaged reputation? Common sense would of course say "no"; however, the recent string of mis-selling related fines imposed by the UK's Financial Services Authority (FSA) demonstrates that many incentive packages lack common sense.

In a strategy-focused, risk-aware culture we therefore see incentive packages that are designed so that they align to the organizational risk appetite. They balance and clearly define the targets that are to be achieved and the level of risk to be taken over each period. We have seen examples where individuals have in effect their own Appetite Alignment Matrix and are measured on the alignment over a period. Other examples include the use of a combination of Key Performance Indicators and Key Risk Indicators, or a combination of objectives and key risks, to shape incentive packages and determine incentive entitlement.

The importance of aligning incentives to risk appetite was highlighted in the 2009 report *A Review of Corporate Governance in UK Banks and Other Financial Industry Entities*, often referred to as the Walker Report after the author Lord David Walker. "Remuneration structures for all . . . high end employees are appropriately aligned with the medium and long-term risk appetite and strategy of the entity," the report noted, adding that

> In essence, the obligations of the board in respect to risk should be to ensure that risks are promptly identified and assessed; that risks are effectively controlled; that strategy is informed by and aligned with the board's risk appetite; and that a supportive risk culture is appropriately embedded so that all employees are alert to the wider impact on the whole organization of their actions and decisions.[10]

In addition to paying close attention to creating the right culture (as noted above) the research report *Making Strides in Financial Services Risk Management* also found progress in revising remuneration policies and frameworks.

Overall, 78% of executives reported they have made revisions to their programmes – up from 58% in the 2009 IIF report – and 30% indicated these changes represent significant shifts to compensation systems. Of those who reported minimal revisions, the majority were smaller firms not severely impacted by the crisis.

"Fifty per cent of interviewees indicated that changes to their compensation systems were well under way, and 40% said they were close to completion of their initial rounds of revisions. The majority of firms reported a significant strengthening in the governance of remuneration policies and practices." In particular, boards have increased their involvement in policy setting and oversight, and the remuneration committees' roles and responsibilities have been enhanced to include compensation policy reviews, performance metrics, oversight of bonus pool allocations, approval of compensation plans and in general, retention of more discretion over payments.

Furthermore, many firms reported that the CRO and risk teams are increasingly involved in remuneration, providing input into the compensation framework and processes to ensure that risk is factored into compensation decisions. In addition, risk functions are more closely involved in offering opinions on existing compensation plans, establishing new policies, providing metrics for scorecards for business units and individuals and in some cases reviewing the compensation proposed for the top people in the organization. "Several firms reported adjustments to the remuneration of the control functions – reducing and distancing the variable aspects of their salaries tied to front office results and adjusting performance measures to reflect their increased responsibilities."

"Several firms indicated they have launched risk reviews of all of their compensation plans to benchmark processes, pinpoint areas to be improved and develop guiding principles that must be incorporated into every plan. As one CRO explained, "We created seven guiding principles that every plan has to have, and then we remediated every plan. We report to the board twice a year, and any new plan or modification has to be approved by risk to make certain that the principles are upheld."[11]

Part 2: Communication

Communication is an important aspect of getting the culture right. It is a key management discipline in any circumstance, and especially when large-scale change is taking place. Communication is critical when an organization is setting out to take an integrated approach to strategy and risk management and so has been included as a discipline within the RBPM approach – most notably in getting the appetite message across and in driving the correct behaviours.

Both of these truths were highlighted in the research report, *Making Strides in Financial Services Risk Management*. The authors stressed the importance of systematically communicating, implementing and enforcing risk appetite. "The definition and articulation of risk appetite drives both strategic and day-to-day business decisions, defines roles and responsibilities around risk and has a positive impact on organizational culture and behaviour," the report noted. "When a firm's risk appetite is properly defined and clearly communicated, it becomes a powerful management tool to clarify all dimensions of enterprise-wide risk and enhances overall business and financial performance."

However, they added that creating a risk framework that is meaningful to management and that translates to actionable day-to-day management at the business unit and desk level is a tough job. None of the firms interviewed for the report have reached this stage of the journey, or as one executive described it, "The nirvana of risk appetite is when it is thoroughly inculcated into day-to-day planning and thinking."[12]

The 5 "Cs" of communication

To help reach this "nirvana" communication should be an ongoing process, rather than a one-off exercise repeated on an ad hoc basis. Messaging must be a constant part of reinforcing the dos and don'ts around strategy, risk and risk appetite and the importance of balancing risk and reward. If this is not done, there is a pressing danger that decision-makers and indeed all employees might revert to inappropriate behaviours. The mantra "communicate, communicate, communicate" is commonly heard, but less often acted upon.

During the implementation of the RBPM approach, and after the approach has been operationalized, we believe that an effective communication programme should be based on these five C's

1   Clarity
2   Credibility
3   Concision
4   Context
5   Consistency

Clarity

Within the context of the RBPM approach clarity is important because the messages can easily become confused.

When communicating, we must balance the challenges of delivering a message designed to create focus around the goals and objectives of the organization, while simultaneously encouraging all staff to challenge assumptions made during the definition/selection of said objectives. It is critical to keen an "open mind" and continuously consider the risks, both threats and opportunities, around those objectives. There is also the challenge of setting out a positive and inspiring vision, with a clear set of motivating objectives while also discussing the (often negative) consequences of risks materializing.

The RBPM approach emphasizes the need to "operate within appetite" and to create clarity around risk appetite: it is important that these boundaries are communicated effectively. It is as important to communicate which strategic objectives and opportunities are not going to be pursued or managed and why, as to communicate which objectives are going to be "operating within appetite".

Nottingham University's report *Research into the Definition and Application of the Concept of Risk Appetite* is just one of many recent research reports that have stressed the importance of effective communication of risk appetite. The Nottingham University work makes clear that there is little point going to the expense of determining an organization's appetite for risk if this is not subsequently cascaded to all of its decision-makers, so that they can understand the "rules" within which they should be operating. According to the authors some of the key lessons on communication are as follows (note that clarity tops the list):

- An organization should communicate its appetite for risk clearly
- An organization should express its appetite for risk using concepts that can be understood by both the board of directors and management
- An organization should produce a formal risk appetite statement.[13]

Reinforcing the central RBPM message of operating within appetite' should be interwoven throughout all of the 5 "Cs" of communication. KPMG stated in its work *Understanding and Articulating Risk Appetite*:

> Our research strongly suggests that the effective communication of risk appetite sharpens the overall risk management effort. Internal communication of risk appetite provides the business with a clear mandate for the amount and type of risk to accept and manage and the risks to avoid. It facilitates a more considered risk-taking culture in which decisions about taking on risks reflect the capacity to manage those risks.

The report also pointed to the importance of the external communication of risk appetite in assisting in shaping realistic expectations on the part of the investors and other external stakeholders and promoting transparency and accountability.[14]

The importance of communicating risk appetite to external investors is perhaps not stated as often as it should be (see also Box 10.2). After all, among the reasons for the Credit Crunch that are not discussed too often is that investors became more and more demanding of higher and higher returns from a sector that seemed to be simply oozing with high return opportunities. As some banks began to dance to the tune of the investors, most others felt they had little choice but to put on their dancing shoes.

Box 10.2   The role of internal and external communication, according to ISO3100

The ISO31000 *Risk Management Principles and Guidelines* is an important influencer of the RBPM approach. ISO31000 explains the importance of both internal and external communication in a risk management implementation.

Establishing internal communication and reporting mechanisms

The organization should establish internal communication and reporting mechanisms in order to support and encourage accountability and ownership of risk. These mechanisms should ensure that

- key components of the risk management framework, and any subsequent modifications, are communicated appropriately;
- there is adequate internal reporting on the framework, its effectiveness and the outcomes;
- relevant information derived from the application of risk management is available at appropriate levels and times;
- there are processes for consultation with internal stakeholders.

These mechanisms should, where appropriate, include processes to consolidate risk information from a variety of sources, and may need to consider the sensitivity of the information.

Establishing external communication and reporting mechanisms

The organization should develop and implement a plan as to how it will communicate with external stakeholders. This should involve:

- engaging appropriate external stakeholders and ensuring an effective exchange of information
- external reporting to comply with legal, regulatory and governance requirements
- providing feedback and reporting on communication and consultation
- using communication to build confidence in the organization
- communicating with stakeholders in the event of a crisis or contingency.

These mechanisms should, where appropriate, include processes to consolidate risk information from a variety of sources, and may need to consider the sensitivity of the information.

Communication and consultation

Communication and consultation with external and internal stakeholders should take place during all stages of the risk management process.

Therefore, plans for communication and consultation should be developed at an early stage. These should address issues relating to the risk itself, its causes, its consequences (if known), and the measures being taken to treat it. Effective external and internal communication and consultation should take place to ensure that those accountable for implementing the risk management process and stakeholders understand the basis on which decisions are made, and the reasons why particular actions are required.

A consultative team approach may

- help establish the context appropriately
- ensure that the interests of stakeholders are understood and considered
- help ensure that risks are adequately identified
- bring different areas of expertise together for analysing risks
- ensure that different views are appropriately considered when defining risk criteria and in evaluating risks
- secure endorsement and support for a treatment plan
- enhance appropriate change management during the risk management process
- develop an appropriate external and internal communication and consultation plan.

Communication and consultation with stakeholders is important as they make judgements about risk based on their perceptions of risk. These perceptions can vary due to differences in values, needs, assumptions, concepts and concerns of stakeholders. As their views can have a significant impact on the decisions made, the stakeholders' perceptions should be identified, recorded, and taken into account in the decision-making process.

Communication and consultation should facilitate truthful, relevant, accurate and understandable exchanges of information, taking into account confidential and personal integrity aspects.

From *Risk Management: Principles and Guidelines,* ISO31000-2006, ISO 2009.[15]

Credibility

To be effective, not only do the messages need to be credible but the people and management teams delivering those messages must be equally credible. The US-headquartered Senn–Delaney Leadership Consulting coined the term "shadow of the leader" to describe how the senior team creates the culture that determines expected working practices and attitudes. Simply put, subordinates will behave in ways that mirror their leaders. For instance, if the manager (at any level) is seen to be risk-aware, then their subordinate will likely be the same. Conversely, if the manager is seen to celebrate and reward those "star performers" who take big risks, then the likelihood is that the subordinate will behave accordingly.[16]

In the context of implementing a RPBM approach, the credibility of the message is often undermined when business units or individuals are repeatedly allowed to operate outside of appetite. For example, a star trader within an investment bank is allowed to operate outside of appetite because their success over the years leads to their management believing that "their bets always come off". This type of behaviour negates the effectiveness of communication about the need to operate within appetite.

Concision

Integrating strategy and risk management to drive improved strategic execution is a significant challenge for any organization. It is made more difficult by not properly communicating these messages, alongside the myriad of other messages that employees are bombarded with on a daily basis.

Therefore, it is important that communication about the implementation and operation of the RBPM approach is concise. Each message should either provide information or explain an action. The purpose of the message should be clear and it should be easy for those receiving the message to take appropriate action.

Context

All communication must be developed while taking into account the current organizational context and environment. One of the quickest ways that credibility is destroyed and support lost for an approach, such as RBPM, is if messages reaching staff appear to be in conflict with their understanding of the situation – thus the messages being communicated come across as being out of context and are unlikely to be believed. This is a particular issue when the organization is facing economic challenges, such as job losses.

Often at the start of an RBPM implementation the focus of the communication plan will be on developing an understanding of the current situation of the organization and the need for change. Once implemented, the focus will shift to reinforcing the need to use the approach and highlighting its successes and the benefits it can bring.

Consistent

Mixed messages and inconsistency will undermine the RBPM initiative. Organizations must be consistent in their messages around strategy and risk to ensure staff and other stakeholders are engaged and on-board with the project at hand. While changes over time will be necessary, they should be communicated clearly and managed so that support is not lost and people do not become disillusioned about their role in the achievement of company objectives and management of risk.

Effective communication has been central to creating a risk-aware culture at our case study HML. "It's all about talking it through with people," says Weatherill. "We spent a lot of time in workshops and other forums explaining risk, the relationship with strategy and why it's important to the organization. Basically it's about making sure everybody is on the same journey and that they're not at a different bus stop. It's just engaging and talking." Consistency, therefore, is a watchword.

Conclusion

This chapter has explained the importance of creating a strategy-focused, risk-aware culture and the importance of getting the communication right. Moreover, we stressed that the so-called softer disciplines of Culture and Communication offer more potential bulwarks to progress than any of the other disciplines. It is telling to note just how many times we've heard senior managers say that they wish they'd spent more time on culture and communication, that they underestimated their importance at the outset of any change programme. A favourite saying of the CEO of HML is "whenever culture meets strategy, culture always wins", which is just another way of saying that "culture eats strategy for breakfast".

Culture and communication can also be heavily influenced by the appropriate deployment of technology, which we discuss in the next chapter.

11   The Enabling Role of Technology

Within the RBPM approach, we are very clear as to the role of technology and this is summed up in a single word – "enabler", an enabler for the organization and its people to achieve its objectives and deliver its strategy while operating within appetite.

Change and the role of technology

In the previous chapter we explained that when organizations implement the Risk-Based Performance Management (RBPM) framework and methodology they are essentially rolling out a major change programme (Figure 11.1). We also explained that the greatest barriers to successfully delivering the change agenda and goals are cultural. If organizations fail to get the cultural (or people) piece right then the RBPM approach will either deliver limited benefits or ultimately fail: this holds true for all change efforts.

With that fundamental fact of change management understood, organizations that are implementing a major change programme such as RBPM can then work to put in place the underpinnings that are required to deliver the change goals – such as ensuring that the organizational structure is appropriate for the strategy. Another required organizational underpinning is a fit-for-purpose technological infrastructure, which is the focus of this chapter.

Getting the technology piece right

Technology can make or break any change programme. Although not as big a potential blocker as culture, technology can be a showstopper nonetheless. When understood and deployed properly technology

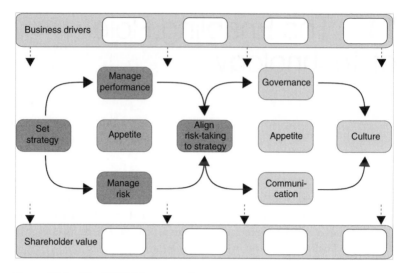

Figure 11.1 **The RBPM framework**

enables the right information to get to the right people at the right time, thus enabling proper and focused performance conversations at both the senior management and devolved levels. Technology also greatly enhances collaborative working, adeptness at which will be a competitive differentiator in the "continuous turbulent times" that will characterize globalized working in the 21st century. Furthermore, and something that should not be underestimated, technology can help drive the right behaviours and so support the inculcation of the right culture – critical to infusing the strategy-focused, risk-aware culture that is essential for succeeding with the RBPM approach.

Getting the technology piece wrong

When understood and deployed improperly, technology often becomes a barrier to change. Indeed it often becomes an end in itself – that is, the change effort is defined as a technology implementation exercise. The prevailing sense is that if you get the technology in place everything else will take care of itself, which is as dangerous as it is erroneous. What tends to happen is that there is a convoluted process to design and roll out an expensive solution that is at best partially helpful to the business (and at worse of no help whatsoever) in delivering the change agenda – and oftentimes drives the wrong behaviours. Worryingly, even in such cases, the change project (when viewed as a technology pro-gramme) is often hailed as a success, simply because a nice, new, shiny piece of technology has been delivered! However, industry evidence tells a different story. 2011 research by The Gartner Group (the world's leading IT research company) found that 28% of all large IT projects failed (over $1,000,000), as did 25% of medium-sized projects (more than $350,000)and 20% of small projects (less than $350,000) with the top reasons being:

▷ Functionality issues
▷ Substantially late
▷ Quality issues
▷ High cost variance
▷ Cancelled after launch
▷ Rejected or not implemented for other reasons

Almost half of the projects failed because they did not do what was needed (functionality) or did it too late to be valuable. The Gartner research (which is far from isolated in reporting damning statistics regarding IT project failure rates) points to a key lesson for any major programme that aims to transform the business (strategically or opera-tionally) – change must be driven by the business, not the IT function. IT has a vital role to play, but as a supporting player and not the leader or even orchestrator.[1]

Technology: An enabler of RBPM

Within the RBPM approach we are very clear as to the role of tech-nology, and this is summed up in a single word – "enabler", an enabler for the organization and its people to achieve its objectives and deliver its strategy while operating within appetite. Technology is and should always be an enabler of any performance improvement or transformation efforts.

What technology cannot do

Although technology can deliver many, and significant benefits when building the RBPM framework and implementing the methodology, there is much that technology by itself cannot do (despite the best efforts of some IT salespeople to convince business users otherwise!).

To give just a few examples, technology cannot remove or replicate the need for the in-depth and focused senior management discussion and debate that is required to decide upon the strategic goals of the enterprise, to set the risk appetite boundaries, to populate the Strategy Map, identify Key Risks etc.. Put another way, technology cannot create an organization's RBPM framework: this is exclusively the role of the senior team and is an intellectual and not a technology exercise.

Technology is not an RBPM discipline

To reinforce the message that technology's role within the RBPM management approach is as an enabler, it has not been included as a discipline with the framework. We see technology as providing the critical information and knowledge architecture and infrastructure that allows the seven RBPM disciplines to work together in delivering strategic and operational goals and for ensuring that the organization is operating within appetite. We do not see technology as an end in itself.

Integrated strategy and risk management solutions

Although there are a number of technology tools to support strategy execution or risk management implementations, it is our observation that there is a paucity of solutions that are purposefully built to integrate strategy and risk (rather than, for example, offering a risk component as a bolt-on to a strategy solution, which is becoming something of a common practice). Although organizations should take their time to identify solutions that are appropriate to their own needs, to provide appropriate enabling support, we here introduce two technology solutions that have been purposely developed to support the RBPM approach.

1   StratexSystems StratexPoint (an On-premise SharePoint App which is also available via the Cloud.)
2   Manigent's Strategy and Risk Studio (on iPad)

StratexPoint and StratexLive

As a quick overview, StratexPoint is an RBPM solution powered by Microsoft's SharePoint platform. As alluded to above, very few

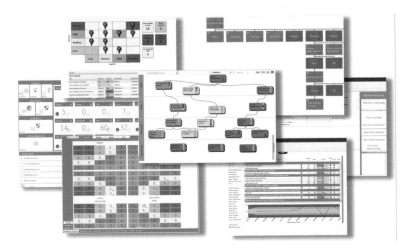

Figure 11.2 **A screenshot of the StratexSystem solution**

organizations are capable of obtaining a single enterprise-wide view of their performance and risk management information. Instead the tendency is to employ multiple tools that operate in silos; rarely communicate with one another; provide conflicting information; and contribute to poor decision-making. A core message of this book is that performance and risk are essentially different sides of the same coin and so must be managed as an integrated process with a single, integrated solution. StratexSystems provides that solution. Moreover, the StratexSystems solutions, which embed the methodology at the core of its business logic, are designed for the enterprise-wide rollout and embedment of the methodology, as shown in Figure 11.2.

Strategy and Risk Studio

The Manigent Strategy and Risk Studio iPad application is specifically designed to be an RBPM "design" application to be used in the early stage of any RBPM deployment to design the RBPM framework.

The Strategy and Risk Studio app is ideal for use in both workshops and one-to-one meetings to:

1   Provide guidance and direction to the definition of the RBPM framework

2   Capture the organization's strategy, risk appetite and risk manage-
     ment framework
3   Enable rapid prototyping and iteration of the strategy and risk
     management framework.

The Strategy and Risk Studio app can dynamically reduce the time it
takes to design the organization's strategy and risk framework. It can
also create a much more engaging experience as those involved with the
process have the ability to engage with the Strategy and Risk framework
in a very personal way (iPad app) while also having strategy and risk
guidance and "best practices" embedded within the app.

Technology and making the case for change

Together these technology solutions enable an organization to design,
roll out and manage an integrated strategy management and risk
management approach, such as RBPM.

But what is perhaps different in the view of the role of technology
taken through the RBPM approach from that generally found elsewhere is that we do not just see technology as about the technical
side of design implementation support (not to minimize the importance of the latter) but also having a critical role in embedding the
right behaviours (see below) and in making the case for change, as we
now explain.

When an organization is implementing the RBPM approach, it is
really looking to introduce significant business and culture change
around its management and decision-making frameworks and processes. And there is little doubt that many (if not most) organizations
find making change very difficult. Some of the reasons that make
change difficult include (but are certainly not limited to): people generally don't like change; they often find it difficult to see why change
is required and so legitimize their explicit or tacit resistance; they often
either cannot see the problem or if they can see the problem, cannot
see how the proposed solution will fix it or how the proposed solution
will be implemented. This uncertainty about the need for change, how
to change and what the organization is changing also almost invariably
leads to significant resistance developing with the result that "change
makers" lose power to the "change terrorists". Therefore, developing a sense of urgency and momentum early in the change process
is critical.

To get the RBPM change started, organizations need to focus on

1   Clearly making the need for change
2   Communicating a clear vision for the future
3   Setting out a roadmap which shows how the organization can successfully realize the outlined vision
4   Creating a sense of urgency to make the change happen

While there are many non-technology aspects to getting change started, the right technology in place can play a critical enabling role.

The Manigent and StratexSystems technologies provide a range of capabilities to enable organizations to quickly identify and articulate gaps in their current strategy and risk frameworks and therefore help to develop a clear understanding of the need for change and, crucially, why strategy and risk must be integrated to gain a fuller picture of performance – historic, present and future.

While each of these solutions are different in terms of architecture and value proposition, both have powerful visualization tools (the seven dashboards that we describe below) and explain fully in Box 2.1 in Chapter 2. that can be quickly loaded with data to identify weaknesses in any current frameworks. Both solutions also have strong collaboration capabilities which enable these weaknesses to be consistently communicated and socialized within the organization, thus building the case for change. These same visualization and collaboration capabilities can also be leveraged to "paint a picture" of what the future organization looks like, thereby helping to create a vision that managers and staff can "buy into". Three of the dashboards – Strategy Map, Four Perspective Risk Map and Appetite Alignment Matrix – are particularly powerful for this purpose.

With the capabilities to capture actions and initiatives, these technology solutions also provide a clear outline of the steps that the organization must undertake to deliver its change and of course what risks exist to the successful implementation of the change.

While most people do not like change, once current weaknesses have been identified and a case for change has been developed, and a clear and compelling vision of the future created with a clear set of achievable steps set out to realize the vision, people have a tendency to get behind the change initiative. Simply put, they can see the point!

As one powerful illustration, our experience in delivering RBPM engagements shows that once people begin to understand that approach and see the types of technology based outputs outlined above, their reaction is generally along the lines of "oh, that is kind of what we do now, just it is all linked up and aligned" or "this is very well structured and easy to follow". People also tend to become more engaged when the visualizations cited above are readily available on their iPad (Strategy and Risk Studio) or via the web browser (StratexPoint).

Sustaining the change effort

With the need for change established, a clear vision of the future communicated, a change roadmap in place and a sense of urgency to get started, the next challenge faced by the organization is how to actually make change happen. Again, there are a lot of non-technology requirements here, so the question we will address in this chapter is how does technology enable change to happen?

Simply, at this stage technology enables change to happen by providing the "tools" to enable the rapid prototyping of the Strategy and Risk framework, and enabling those prototypes to be shared and collaborated on across the organization.

The technology solutions enable the definition and rich visualization of the organizational structure; and once this is defined and agreed for each organizational entity, it enables the definition of objectives, risks and controls at a strategic level. Associated with each of these strategic items, indicators should be able to be defined: Key Performance Indicators (KPIs) for Objectives, Key Risk Indicators (KRIs) for Risks and Key Control Indicators (KCIs) for Controls.

To translate strategic goals into operational activities, the solutions help enable the definition of processes and initiatives (sometimes known as programmes and projects). Just as we capture strategic level risks and controls associated with each objective, we should define operational level risks and controls for each process and initiative.

Additionally, risk assessment and control self-assessment processes must be enabled via the technology solution. To support a disciplined, continuous improvement attitude in the organization, actions or tasks should be able to be defined and associated with any of the main items in the RBPM framework.

The two technology solutions have been designed to provide guidance as to the items that should be included within the RBPM framework, and support the relationships that are defined within the RBPM methodology.

Using a technology solution such as those from StratexSystems, with its enterprise level initiative and actions capabilities, has the powerful effect of enabling the RBPM implementation and change to be managed using the same technology that will be used to enable the process once the RBPM initiative moves from a project phase to a business as usual process.

Technology and culture

From our research and observations the ability to influence, shape and encourage the right behaviours is an often overlooked consideration during a technology selection process. Therefore, we are assured that culture-related considerations are central to the RBPM enabling technologies. With the RBPM methodology implemented, the role of technology changes to one which is focused on enabling the process of strategy execution and risk management to be effectively and efficiently undertaken. Ideally, the processes within the RBPM approach should be enabled in a technology solution, such as StratexPoint which is workflow driven, with notification, reminder and alerting capabilities so that these management processes simply become part of the organizational process architecture and part of "the way we do things around here", that is, part of the culture.

Embedding the RACI model

Central to inculcating a strategy-focused, risk-aware culture is that both the Manigent and StratexSystems have embedded the RACI (Responsible, Accountable, Consult, Inform) governance model within their solutions. This is a powerful driver of change and cultural change as it enables individuals to "see" their own "Line of Sight" reporting and dashboards. Embedding the RACI model within the RBPM approach and getting the processes and some key management behaviours in place is an important part of embedding the change. In particular, the Line of Sight dashboards and reporting that are enabled by the RACI model are powerful tools for embedding the change and maintaining management engagement in the process, as they provide individuals with just the information that is critically important to them as individuals. In an age of information overload, this is critical.

Visualization: The role of dashboards

Central to achieving the process and cultural changes cited above and fundamentally altering the strategy and risk conversations that take place within the organization is the use of visualization tools. Both the StratexSystems and Manigent applications include seven key RBPM dashboards.

- Strategy Map
- Four Perspective Risk Map
- Appetite Alignment Matrix
- Strategy Scorecard
- Control Map
- Risk Scorecard
- Control Scorecard

Described in Chapter 2 and more fully in the relevant subsequent chapters, these dashboards play a central role in providing regular management information which enables the execution of strategy and management of risk to be managed and monitored effectively and enable exceptions to be quickly identified and corrective action taken.

The Strategy Map, Four Perspective Risk Map and Appetite Alignment Matrix together provide a powerful summation and visualization for the senior team as to how the organization is progressing towards its strategy and whether it is operating within appetite. They enable focused conversations on the solutions required to rectify performance shortcomings or exploit emerging opportunities.

Supporting Strategy, Risk and Control Scorecards provide greater granularity around how the organization is managing performance and risk and whether this is within the appetite boundaries set by the board. Collectively, the scorecards serve as powerful day-to-day RBPM steers for operational managers and staff.

These seven dashboards are designed to enable rapid prototyping, bringing to life the RBPM framework as it emerges and develops during the deployment of the methodology. Using the technology solutions alongside the dashboards means that rather than engaging the organization during the "strategy and risk journey" using changing, unstructured ad hoc spreadsheets tools or PowerPoint slides (we outline the serious shortcomings of relying on spreadsheet tools in Box 11.1), those involved in the change process use enterprise class solutions (that are reliable, accessible and intended to be one-stop enterprise-wide solutions, rather than departmental solutions) – so the same solutions as they will use on a business as usual basis. Again, our experience implementing the RBPM approach shows that the earlier those on the front line get the technology solutions in their hands and start working with information gathered during the delivery of the change programme in workshops, one-to-one meetings, etc., the better the levels of engagement and buy-in to the change process.

For example, one organization which deployed the RBPM framework and methodology using StratexPoint found that they had to repeat large parts of their change management and training programme around the deployment of the methodology after about 18 months for about one-third of their front-line staff because the level of engagement and data quality was unacceptably low. The interesting point to emerge during a lessons-learnt session was that this one-third were almost all in the "first wave" of the deployment which was completed prior to the implementation of StratexPoint. Feedback from this group after the second round of deployment was positive and the general message was "now we have the right tools, we can do the job", that is effectively manage the execution of strategy and the management of risk.

Box 11.1   The question of spreadsheets

When considering how to support your organizational approach to strategy execution and risk management it is almost inevitable that the first option considered will be to develop a spreadsheet "solution" in Excel. This is understandable given the near ubiquitous nature of Excel, in particular its flexibility and its widespread use and acceptance in most organizations. Note too the following statement by the UK financial services regulator, the Financial Services Authority: "Spreadsheets are integral to the function and operation of the global financial system."[2]

Therefore, it could be reasonably argued that if spreadsheets are integral to the function and operation of the global financial system, why not make them an integral part of your strategy execution and risk management process? Our experience leads us to strongly recommend that organizations should resist the seductive temptations of a spreadsheet-based solution and take a more structured approach. The following are among the main shortcomings of using Excel:

Spreadsheets discourage making strategy and risk management a "front-line" concern

As we continually stress, culture is perhaps the ultimate strategy execution and risk management tool and a key principle of a strategy-focused, risk-aware culture is that strategy execution and therefore risk should be managed where it is taken, that is, on the front line. Because they are fundamentally single user, desktop applications, using a spreadsheet as the enabling technology for a strategy execution and risk management process does not enable the process to be effectively moved to the front line.

Spreadsheets are high risk

The majority (more than 90% according to some estimates) of spreadsheets contain errors, while 50% of spreadsheets that are used operationally in large businesses containing material defects.[3] It is truly ironic that so many organizations are willing to use such a high risk technology approach to support their strategy execution efforts, and simply staggering that they are willing to do so in support of their risk management processes!

Cottage industries grow rapidly

Because spreadsheets are fundamentally single user, desktop applications, when they are used for enterprise-wide processes, such as are required for strategy execution and risk management, it is invariably the case that a central team manage the "master" spreadsheet model and gather information from across the enterprise which is then input (often rekeyed) into the master spreadsheet. Once the data gathering has been completed, the analysis and reporting process begins, again often requiring significant manual intervention. All of this manual effort quickly spawns a thriving cottage industry within which jobs become protected because only a small number of individuals know how the spreadsheets work and the focus of central teams shifts from driving the process and promoting the right culture and behaviours to managing the spreadsheet system and completing its manual tasks.

Multiple versions of the truth

Because of the inherent uncontrollability of spreadsheets, and versions of spreadsheets, it is too easy for multiple versions of the "truth" to be created, which undermines confidences in the process and information being presented, which in turn leads to poor quality decision-making and failures to execute strategy and manage risk. For example, during Barclays' acquisition of Lehman Brothers a spreadsheet containing trading positions was incorrectly reformatted by a junior staff member working on the deal. This error led to Barclays acquiring 179 contracts that it didn't want. While the exact financial impact is unclear, some estimate the impact could have been north of $30 million. However, a subsequent court ruling enabled Barclays to return the unwanted contracts.[4]

Lack of collaboration capabilities

To support the mantra of enabling strategy execution and therefore risk to be managed where it is taken, the enabling technology deployed to support an integrated strategy execution and risk management framework, process and culture must enable and encourage enterprise-wide collaboration. Spreadsheet solutions nether enable or encourage collaboration, thus promoting the silo, closed approach to strategy and risk management which has been discredited.

No well-constructed approach "built-in"

Spreadsheet solutions are invariably changed over time to meet often ill-defined and changing technology requirements. Typically this leads to a lack of clarity about the approach that the spreadsheet "solution" is supporting, whereas a formally developed solution which has been subject to standard software development and lifecycle management methodologies will start with a clear conceptual approach which will then be maintained over time.

In addition to the observed issues outlined above, there is a significant volume of more formal research which points to the issues with spreadsheet use within organizations and to support business critical processes. Below are the key issues identified with spreadsheet use in the 2009 white paper on the topic, *Spreadsheets and the Financial Collapse* by Grenville J. Croll, Chair of the European Spreadsheet Risks Interest Group.

1   Fraud; mixing of the programme code and data easily enables fraud to be committed. This was a contributory factor in the AIB/Allfirst fraud/John Rusnak case.
2   Overconfidence; spreadsheet users don't systematically search for or test for errors and therefore they are overconfident in their use of spreadsheets.
3   Interpretation; translation of a business problem into the spreadsheet domain is open to interpretation (without the need to use formal business requirement approaches and gathering exercises) and can create false confidence in those making decisions based on the information within the spreadsheet.
4   Archiving; poor archiving can lead to weaknesses in spreadsheet control that contribute to operational risk; for example, the systemic failure of the Jamaican banking systems in the 1990s.

The recent financial crisis led Croll to add the following to the list of spreadsheet-related risks:

5   Assumptions; spreadsheets often rely on a series of explicit or more usually implicit assumptions. The key assumption is *ceteris paribus* – all other things being (or remaining) equal.

6   Opacity; as spreadsheets are used, they become larger, increasingly complex, badly structured with input from multiple end users (who often lack formal spreadsheet engineering training and skills), and therefore spreadsheet solutions become opaque and unwieldy.

7   Reification; once information is entered into a spreadsheet, it becomes concrete.

8   Enterprise interoperability; with the global financial system (as well as other organizations) becoming increasingly interconnected, spreadsheets and the data included in them remain closed systems.[5]

Thirteen required technological capabilities that enable effective RBPM

Of the seven disciplines within the RBPM approach, four are "hard", process-orientated and process-driven disciplines – Setting Strategy, Appetite, Managing Performance, Managing Risk, Aligning Risk to Strategy; and three are "soft" (or so-called, as getting these right is typically harder than the "hard" stuff) disciplines, Governance, Communication and Culture. Too often when selecting technology, organizations will focus on the hard, process-orientated disciplines to the detriment of the soft disciplines. We believe that this suboptimizes the strategy and risk management efforts, leading to only partial success as the culture and behaviours required for succeeding with strategy and risk over the longer term are overlooked. However, both the hard and soft disciplines must work together to deliver sustainable success; therefore, we outline the 13 main capabilities that are delivered through the RBPM technology solutions: seven focus on the hard disciplines and six on the soft disciplines.

Seven technology capabilities to support the "hard" disciplines:

1   Enable the definition and visualization of the organizational structure

2   Enable the definition and visualization of the organizational Strategy and Risk framework, including;

- Definition of Internal and External Business Drivers
- Definition of Objectives
- Definition of KPIs
- Definition of Key and Emerging Risks
- Definition of KRIs
- Definition of Key Controls
- Definition of KCIs

3 Enable the definition and visualization of operational enablers and align these to the strategy, including;

- Definition of Processes
- Definition of Process-related Risks and Controls, with supporting indicators
- Definition of Initiatives
- Definition of Initiatives-related Risks and Controls, with supporting indicators

4 Enable data to be captured, either manually or automatically, and analysed from across the organization, including;

- Risk Assessments data
- Control Self-Assessments data
- KPIs data
- KRIs data
- KCIs data
- Initiative Status data
- Action Status data

5 Enable the definition of workflow to manage update and assessment processes to automate the strategy, performance and risk management processes.
6 Enable advanced reporting, dashboarding and analytics to generate business insights, including dashboards which show the alignment between risk exposure and risk appetite.
7 Enable "red items" to bubble up so as to bring to the surface issues buried in organizational structure or data, yet avoiding the consolidation of non-weighted data that causes top-level items to be generally red or amber.

Six technology capabilities to support the "soft" disciplines:

1 Enable individuals to be empowered via the definition of clear governance structures (accountabilities and responsibilities) for each of the following;

   - Organizational entities
   - Objectives
   - Processes
   - Initiatives
   - Risks
   - Controls

2 Enable any individual to have a clear "Line of Sight" from their objectives to their team objectives and onto the overall organizational objectives.
3 Enable enterprise-wide collaboration around strategy and risk using

   - Commentary
   - Activity data feeds
   - Benchmarking
   - Alerts, notifications and remainders
   - Secure shared workspaces

4 Enable advanced reporting, dashboarding and analytics to generate business insights which enable high quality management conversations, appropriate and proportional level of challenge and which drive business decision-making.
5 Enable information to flow across enterprise boundaries to support and promote open and transparent decision-making.
6 Enable individual and team incentives to be aligned and clearly linked to risk appetite. If the individual and/or team has consistently operated within the boundaries of risk appetite this should positively influence their overall realized incentives package.

Conclusion

In this chapter we have explained that technology has a critical role to play in successfully building, deploying and sustaining an integrated strategy management and risk management approach, such as is delivered through the RBPM framework and methodology. We also explained that it should play an important role in making the case for change and helping to overcome the not insignificant, and often-times understandable resistance to change that will likely be faced by people at all levels in the organization. And to be blunt, in today's fully connected, globalized markets it is simply inconceivable to deliver enterprise-wide solutions and capabilities that are not technologically enabled.

But "enabled" is the operative word. Senior management teams must not look to technology to do their thinking for them. In recent years organizations have wasted millions of dollars on technology in the mistaken belief that it will instantaneously, or at the click of a button, solve all of their strategic, and other, management problems. Holding such a belief can lead to making the wrong decisions and buying inappropriate software, and will result in a significant waste of time, energy and money (as strongly suggested in the cited Garter research above). Rather senior managers should look to technology to enable better, more informed performance conversations – technology should inform these conversations. In the context of RBPM, it is also important that senior managers pay attention to ensuring that technology helps address the myriad culture challenges that will inevitably be faced on the road to implementation and not just focus on the technical issues. As we have stressed throughout this book, succeeding with the RBPM approach requires attention be paid to both hard and soft disciples, and all be understood through the lens of "operating within appetite", as we now summarize in the concluding chapter.

12 Conclusion and Change Roadmap

> Managing both strategy and risk through frameworks and methodologies such as Risk-Based Performance Management will play a critical role in making [continuous] turbulent times equally exciting and profitable.

Introduction

This book has introduced the Risk-Based Performance Management (RBPM) framework and methodology (Figure 12.1). The RBPM approach was conceived to plug a glaring shortcoming in how organizations (from either the commercial or public sectors) are typically managed: this being that strategy management and risk management are rarely managed holistically; rather they are viewed as separate disciplines and managed within separate silos that have little more than passing conversations with each other.

As the Credit Crunch made painfully clear (but as had already been highlighted earlier in risk management frameworks such as COSO's Integrated Enterprise Risk Management Framework) separating the management of strategy from the management of risk is not only erroneous but potentially catastrophic.[1] Organizations simply cannot successfully implement sustainable strategies without taking full and proper account of the risks they are taking in its execution. The Royal Bank of Scotland (RBS) case report in Chapter 4 paints a stark picture of how apparently "winning" strategies were actually houses "built of straw", which the big bad wolf called the Credit Crunch required little puff to blow away. From the RBPM perspective, a house, or strategy, "built of concrete" must be constructed with one eye on performance

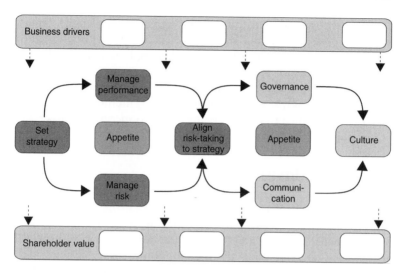

Figure 12.1 **RBPM framework**

and the other on risk to be confident of surviving whatever future tsunamis destructive economic wolves bring their way: and there is no doubt that come they will.

The size and strength of these tsunamis and the sectors that they will hit we do not know. As we stress throughout this book, we live in "continuous turbulent times", which makes prognosticating as to future economic (as well as political and social) developments fraught with danger and almost certainly riddled with what will prove to be glaring inaccuracies. What we can predict with some certainty is that the best run organizations will possess the capabilities to strategically "turn on a sixpence" and that this will be dependent on the routine collection of the best available information on both performance and risk. Critical insights and intelligence that will be delivered through approaches such as RBPM will enable organizations to respond quickly to current or emerging threats and opportunities (and as we end this book we stress that risks offer as many opportunities as they do threats – the best organizations will turn this fact into a powerful competitive advantage). The best available information will be demanded by boards of directors and executive committees and its collection, analysis and actioning will be operationalized deep inside the enterprise by employees working in purposely configured cultures that are performance focused and risk-aware.

For most organizations today, it is a significant challenge to transition from present-state to a place where executive- and non-executive directors expect such information, and where staff have the capabilities, and processes, to act upon the "golden nuggets" of mission-critical insights that are sifted from the fast flowing performance- and risk-based data that flows into and through the enterprise. The RBPM approach is designed to enable organizations to successfully make such a transition.

Change roadmap

In the previous chapters we have explained what the RBPM management framework looks like and how it fully integrates the management of performance and risk, and provided the detail of how to instil each of the seven disciplines into the organization (Setting Strategy, Managing Performance, Managing Risk, Aligning Risk-taking to Strategy, Governance, Communication and Culture within the context of risk appetite). However, as the implementation of the RBPM approach represents a significant change to "the way we do things around here" for most organizations, rollout must be planned and managed accordingly, as is the case with any major transformational change programme. For this reason, in this concluding chapter we provide a "change roadmap" that will help to strengthen initial implementation efforts, ensure institutionalization of the RBPM approach (that is, make it "the way we do things around here") and provide direction for a regular review of the effectiveness of the methodology and its deployment within the organization. The RBPM Change Roadmap comprises six phases, which we explain in turn; in doing so we will signpost the reader to the relevant earlier chapter where more detail can be found on the issues or techniques highlighted.

While these phases are presented as sequentially running in a nice tidy order, successful client engagements have taught us that the reality is often quite different and that there is a need to revisit previous phases as the organization progresses through the implementation of the RBPM approach.

1   Analyse
2   Plan
3   Mobilize
4   Operationalize

5   Align
6   Embed

Analyse

The objectives of this phase are to become fully informed of the current state of the organization from strategy and risk management perspectives (by considering both external and internal factors) and to understand the operating environment with a view to identifying how strategic execution might be strengthened via new or improved strategy and risk management processes and practices.

Making the case for change

During the "analyse" phase, the need, or case, for change should be established, along with the potential business value of undertaking the associated transformation programme, that is, before undertaking an RBPM implementation the leaders or champions must be able to clearly articulate the business benefits that the organization is attempting to deliver via the approach.

Key phase activities

The main analytical activities to be undertaken during this phase typically include, but are not limited to, the following:

▷ Strategy and Risk Maturity Assessments; various approaches exist to assess the maturity and risk management approaches in organizations, many based on the Capability Model Maturity Model, a methodology founded by the Carnegie Mellon University Software Engineering Institute (SEI) in the 1980s and since used in many industries and sectors[2]
▷ Review the existing strategy, performance and risk management documents and information
▷ Review the business environment
▷ Review of the regulatory and compliance landscape
▷ Business model review
▷ Value driver analysis

Main phase benefits

The main benefit of undertaking this phase is that a very clear picture is developed of the maturity of the organization's extant strategy and risk approaches and the desired maturity level is identified. The phase includes identifying and mapping the existing strategy, performance and risk management processes and practices. As the RBPM approach builds on existing management processes, practices and thinking, there is normally no need to take a "rip and replace" approach to an implementation. Instead, it is about becoming fully cognizant of what is already in place and planning how this can be effectively built upon via the disciplines of the RBPM framework and methodology. Organizations focus on understanding the gap between the current and desired maturity levels, the potential business value of closing the gap and likely return on investment of undertaking an RBPM implementation.

In the current environment, with a high level of regulatory change and a historically high level of regulatory fines and other sanctions, an "easy" justification for implementation of a change programme such as delivered through RBPM is to play the "regulatory card". However, while preparing for regulatory change, improving compliance to avoid fines etc., is important and can play a powerful enabling role in justifying the change programme, client engagements have shown us that if this is the sole justification, the levels of buy-in, support and motivation within the team are lower and less sustainable than if the key driver is business related – for example, reducing operational losses by x% or improving the execution of important initiatives by y%.

Plan

Armed with the knowledge and insight generated in the previous phase, the objective of this phase is to establish the foundations for successfully implementing RBPM. Within this phase there are two main activities:

1 Developing the plan
2 Socializing the plan

These activities should be done collaboratively and iteratively so that as feedback and comments on the plan are gathered through socializing, the plan is quickly adjusted (if required) to reflect the feedback. It is particularly important to rapidly incorporate feedback from key stakeholders, such as senior management and the "core change alliance" (see below).

Many organizations will have an existing, established approach to undertaking business change (that is, robust change management processes and capabilities will be well established and proven). If this is the case, we would recommend that the implementation of the RBPM approach be managed via this existing approach. Doing so will improve the likelihood of a successful implementation as people will be familiar with the change process and therefore can focus fully on the implementation of the change rather than getting to grips with a change management methodology as well as the RBPM framework and methodology.

For those organizations that don't have an existing approach to business change or are seeking some additional guidance, we would recommend that, as a minimum, the following documents be prepared ahead of any implementation:

▷ The business case supporting the implementation of the RBPM approach, which must include the measureable business value and return on investment that the implementation is expected to deliver
▷ Implementation and culture change plan
▷ Communication plan
▷ Project governance document
▷ Project plan
▷ Project Risks and Issues register

Building a "core change alliance"

A key activity that should be undertaken during this planning phase is to identify and work with key individuals who will be critical to the successful implementation of the RBPM approach, to engage them at the planning phase and to establish what we describe as "a core change alliance". This will be an informal alliance between a range of individuals who may be drawn from any level within the organization but, crucially, share a common desire to see the implementation of a robust and integrated organizational approach to strategy and risk management. Over time some of these individuals will formally be involved in the implementation of the RBPM methodology while others will remain informally involved – key members of the latter group might perhaps be drawn from the board or senior management levels who can be called on for advice or to use their influence to smooth the way when the project meets resistance (as just about all business change projects do at some point or other).

Mobilize

With the planning phase completed and the organization committed to implementing the transformational change that an RBPM initiative generates, the next phase is to mobilize the organization.

In this mobilization phase, the main objectives are 1) mobilize the implementation team and begin the rollout of the RBPM Approach and 2) mobilize the whole organization in a cultural change which will see the introduction of an integrated approach to strategy and risk management, the emergence of the concept of "operating within appetite" and the creation of a strategy-focused, risk-aware culture.

As they will likely be drawn primarily (or exclusively) from the core change alliance that was engaged during the previous two phases of the RBPM roadmap, it should be relatively straightforward to bring together and mobilize the implementation project team.

Establishing the strategic approach

Mobilizing the whole organization is clearly a more challenging task and largely depends on the chosen change management approach taken by the project team. However, a critical part of the mobilizing, and key to the RBPM approach overall, is to clearly define and establish the strategic approach with which the organization will operate. This is achieved in two interrelated parts: 1) formulating the strategy; 2) setting the strategy.

The mobilize phase starts with consolidating the knowledge and insights generated into phase 1 into a clear and concise 3–5 year business strategy, which required the establishing of clear, stretching and inspirational long-term goals for the organization. Borrowing from Jim Collins and Jerry Porras (authors of *Built to Last* and *Good to Great* – these goals should be stated in the form of BHAGs – Big Hairy Audacious Goals.[3,4] These should be goals which both excite and motivate the organization so that all employees "buy into" the strategic direction of the organization and understand (and are enthused by) the strategic journey that will be undertaken to realize the goals.

To support the setting of strategic goals, both the external environment within which the organization operates and the internal environment within the organization should be reviewed to understand the main opportunities and threats that they face, as well as the organizations key strengths and weaknesses. Established and popular tools such as SWOT and PESTEL are used here.

Articulate the chosen business model

To support the strategic vision set out in the form of strategic goals, the organization should also clearly articulate its chosen business model, that is, how it intends to create, deliver and capture value to the market. Ideally, multiple potential business models should be evaluated until the model most likely to enable the strategic goals to be achieved while taking an acceptable level of risk is identified. The state of the external and internal environment can influence what is the "right" business model. A Business Model Canvas, see Chapter 4, can be used to assist in the definition of the Business Model. A Business Model Canvas is a strategic management visual chart and template preformatted with the nine blocks of a business model, which allows an organization to develop and sketch out a new or existing business model.[5]

Each business model is likely to have different risk/reward characteristics and potentially different underlying business drivers; therefore once a business model (or potentially multiple models) has been decided on, the related inherent risks and business drivers should be clearly documented and an initial view of organizational risk appetite established.

With high-level goals established, environment strengths and weaknesses known, business model(s) clarified and business drivers documented, the next step is to distil this knowledge and insight into a clear organizational strategy which is designed to enable the organization to deliver its long-term goals. This strategy should show how the strategic goals will be achieved through exploiting environment factors, and/or leveraging a different business model from competitors, and/or more skilfully managing and exploiting the organizational risk and reward profile to sustainably deliver its strategy.

Create a Strategy Map

One of the most important parts of defining the strategy is to distil the three to five longer term goals into a strategy into executable strategic objectives which are used to communicate what the organization is trying to achieve over the next year and what its priorities are. The Strategy

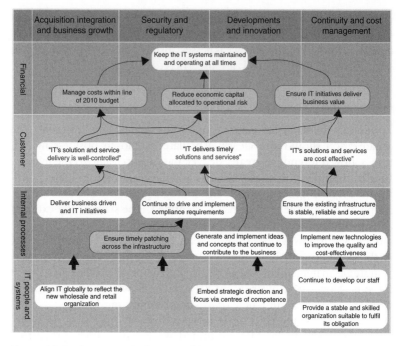

Figure 12.2 **An example Strategy Map**

Map (see Figure 12.2 and explained fully in Chapters 6 and 7) is a key tool for capturing and communicating the organization's strategy, visualizing the objectives, their relationships and organizational priorities in the form of strategic themes.

To bring greater clarity to the definition of objectives (and the overall strategy) and to generate a greater understand of the strategy, strategic risks and controls should be defined for each of the objectives (some organizations may start initially with only some objectives having risks and controls defined).

Create a Risk Map

Once these risks have been assessed, a Risk Map (Figure 12.3) can be used to visualize where the organization has exposures, what level of exposure they carry and if there are any "clusters" of risks which could indicate a systematic weakness. See Chapter 8 for more detail on Risk Maps.

Assessment: Impact/Probability matrix
Reflects all (residual) risks and controls.

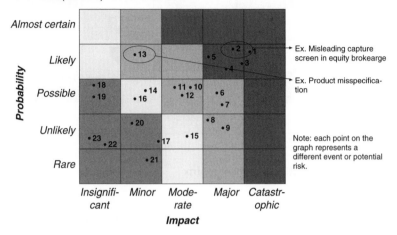

Figure 12.3 **An example Risk Map**

Set the risk appetite

A critical part of defining the strategy, and one that is often not done well (if done at all), is the organization and more specifically the board determining the organizational risk appetite. The previously defined business drivers should be used to establish a common language around risk and as a frame to set potential levels of risk that the organization is able and willing to accept. The board should decide on what level risk they are comfortable with given both the longer term strategic goals and the short-term strategic objectives. The operating environment, business model, etc., will, also influence the board's decision around the acceptable level of risk appetite.

The risk appetite should be captured and documented via the organizational risk appetite statement, which should be made up of a combination of measureable numbers and commentary to provide the meaning behind the numbers.

With the strategic objectives and risk appetite defined, there is a final set which should be taken: aligning the risk appetite to the strategy. To do this, the board should challenge itself to question if its strategic ambition, as expressed via the strategic objectives, and its risk appetite are aligned. Ensuring that there is alignment between what the organization is seeking to achieve and the amount of risk it is willing to run

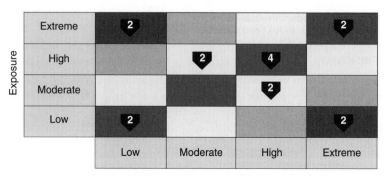

Figure 12.4 **Appetite Alignment Matrix**

goes to the heart of sustainable strategic execution (it also goes to the heart of the purpose of RBPM).

The Appetite Alignment Matrix (Figure 12.4) is a tool developed to support the alignment of risk-taking to strategy and has proven a powerful addition to the management toolbox.

It is during this phase that the implementation team will develop the initial organizational Strategy Map and alongside it a register of key risks, complete an initial risk assessment and develop an initial view of the degree of alignment between the current level of risk exposure and the desired level, as expressed in the risk appetite statement.

A series of iterations

As the organization goes through the formulation and setting stages of this phase it should expect to sequence through a number of iterations of the strategic goals, risk appetite and strategic objectives, as the board and executive work together to settle on an achievable short and long-term strategy that balances risk and reward to the satisfaction of all stakeholders. This interaction should be planned for and encouraged as it is only via engaging in the process and challenging assumptions etc. that a shared understanding of the organizational strategy can emerge so that all stakeholders, but particularly the board and the executive committee, are on the "same strategic page". This is a vital step in ensuring the process of developing buy-in and support for the strategy across the whole organization.

Operationalize

During the Mobilize phase the focus was on enthusing and mobilizing a small group of primarily senior decision-makers by engaging them in the development of a comprehensive strategic framework. In this, the Operationalize phase, the goal is to engage employees across the whole organization and to translate the strategic framework into enabling operational processes and initiatives, and their associated risks, controls, indicators, etc.

Understand the key business processes

The initial focus should be on understanding the key business processes that underpin, and are critical to the successful delivery of, strategic objectives. Related process risks, controls and indicators should be defined. Through the use of assessment and indicators, a picture of how effective the operational processes are will emerge; as part of this, gaps in the process architecture of the organization will almost certainly be identified. To close these gaps and to focus the organizational change activities, a portfolio of initiatives should be defined to structure and focus change activities. Processes and initiatives, along with their risks, controls and indicators should be documented via process and initiative registers. Risk Maps, Control Maps and Indicator Dashboards can be used to monitor and track the performance and risk status of each of the processes and risks.

Align

In the Align phase, we look to build on and bring together the nascent management framework established in the Mobilize and Operationalize phases. While the Mobilize phase focused on establishing the strategic level framework and the Operationalize phase focused on the translating the strategic into operational terms, the Align phase is about aligning the operational processes and initiatives to the strategic level objectives, risks and controls.

Align operational processes with change initiatives

During this phase the goal is to ensure that the operational activities of the organization, the business as usual (BAU) processes and change

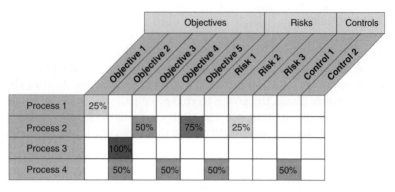

Figure 12.5 **Process Alignment Matrix**

	Objective 1	Objective 2	Objective 3	Objective 4	Objective 5	Risk 1	Risk 2	Risk 3	Control 1	Control 2
Process 1	25%									
Process 2			50%		75%	25%				
Process 3		100%								
Process 4		50%		50%		50%		50%		

	Objective 1	Objective 2	Objective 3	Objective 4	Objective 5	Risk 1	Risk 2	Risk 3	Control 1	Control 2
Initiative 1	25%									
Initiative 2			50%		75%	25%				
Initiative 3		100%								
Initiative 4		50%		50%		50%		50%		

Figure 12.6 **Initiative Alignment Matrix**

initiatives are aligned. Non-aligned activities point to opportunities to improve efficiencies and effectiveness.

There are two similar tools that we recommend deploying at this phase, the Process Alignment Matrix (Figure 12.5) and the Initiative Alignment Matrix (Figure 12.6).

The Process Alignment Matrix enables the organization to define the relative strength of alignment between the BAU process and the strategic level objective, risk and/or control. We recommend using percentages to represent the strength of the alignment:

▷ 100% – Very strong alignment
▷ 75% – Strong alignment
▷ 50% – Moderate alignment

▷ 25% – Weak alignment
▷ 0% – Very weak alignment

Each Operational BAU Process can be aligned to a strategic objective, risk or control or a combination of all three – meaning an operational process can be in place to enable the achievement of an objective, to enable the management of a strategic risk or to enable a control to be implemented effectively.

Using the Process Alignment Matrix, an organization can align a single process to multiple objectives, risks and/or controls using the percentages above.

The Initiative Alignment Matrix tool is used and deployed in exactly the same way as the Process Alignment Matrix except, of course, that the goal is to align initiatives rather than processes and demonstrate the impact of business change on objectives, risks and/or controls.

Benefits of alignment

We use percentages in the Process Alignment Matrix and the Initiative Alignment Matrix for a number of reasons:

▷ It creates debate and challenge within a team as they seek to agree the relationship between the operational level processes and initiatives and the strategic level objectives, risks and controls.
▷ It indicates the relative strength of alignment, therefore helps in deciding and prioritizing the real "key" processes and initiatives from a holistic viewpoint, taking account of performance, risk and compliance perspectives.
▷ It enables the incorporation of operational considerations within any scenario, regression or similar modelling that might be conducted. Operations can use statistical techniques to validate the strength of alignment between the strategic level and the operational level and of course this then provide the opportunity for scenario analysis at the strategic level to be cascaded down to understand the impact at an operational level.

Embed

Finally, given the nature of the transformative change that RBPM introduces, it is not surprising that the final phase of the Change Roadmap focuses on embedding the framework, processes and practices that make up RBPM.

Because each organization has its own culture and its own "way we do things around here" it is important to consider the "local" culture and to identify what has worked well in the past and what has not worked. That said, below are our recommended best practices for embedding RBPM:

1   Continuously refine the items within the RBPM framework.
2   Don't neglect the soft disciplines.
3   Deploy the right technology, early.

Continuously refine the RBPM framework

The RBPM approach should continuously be evolving and maturing within the organization. Therefore, an important part of embedding RBPM is to continuously refine the items within the RBPM framework, such as objectives, risks, controls, processes, initiatives, indicators, etc.

Nothing will undermine the approach faster than presenting information which is not relevant, out of date or simply wrong for decision-makers (either strategic or operational). Therefore, an individual(s) should be made accountable for ensuring that the items within the RBPM framework are up-to-date and regularly reviewed. As a minimum we would recommend an annual review but would encourage a quarterly review.

Don't neglect the soft disciplines

Working with organizations to implement the RBPM approach has shown that often the focus of both the implementation and the embedding of the approach is the "hard disciplines" (Strategy Management, Performance Management, Risk Management and Appetite Alignment) while the "soft disciplines" (Communication, Governance and Culture) are neglected. Maybe this is not surprising given that implementing the "hard disciplines" leads to the generation of interesting dashboards and data visualization that is regularly updated, such as Strategy Maps, Performance Scorecards, Risk Maps, Risk Scorecards, etc.

However, while the "hard disciplines" are important, without the "soft disciplines" the business benefits and the change that organizations are typically seeking when they deploy the RBPM approach will

not be realized. Additionally, the "soft disciplines" play a disproportionately important role in the embedding phase of the RBPM Change
Roadmap.

The RACI model

A critical part of the Governance discipline is deployment of the
RACI model. This sets out very clearly each individual's role in regard
to the execution of strategy and the management of associated risks.
It is important that these roles are fully understood and individuals act
appropriately.

Based on our experience implementing RBPM, there appears to
be a natural tendency to focus on the Accountable and Responsible
roles over Consult and Inform roles. However, this tendency should be
resisted because a lack of focus on the latter roles will negatively impact
on the cascading and embedding of Governance within the organization. It will also negatively impact on organization-wide stakeholder
engagement and management.

Organizations that have implemented RBPM report that defining
the RACI structure is generally one of the most challenging tasks in
the implementation process. However, they also said that it was one
of the most beneficial as one of the main challenges of RACI is that
it forces a level of clarity around accountabilities that is often absent
in organizations. Using the RACI structure to enable reporting and
dashboarding based on the individual's "Line of Sight" has a powerful
effect driving the development and embedding of a "strategy-focused,
risk-aware" culture.

Manage the culture

Culture could rightly be described as the ultimate strategy execution
and risk management tool and creating a strategy-focused, risk-aware
culture is one of the key outcomes of the implementation of the RBPM
approach.

We recommend that organizations actively define the culture that
they wish to see emerge as part of the implementing the RBPM
approach, either before or very early within the implementation. The
RBPM Maturity Model (Figure 12.7) can be used to understand the
current level of organizational maturity in relation to strategy and risk
management and the "target" level of maturity. Our experience has
shown that a Maturity Assessment can be a great catalyst for change

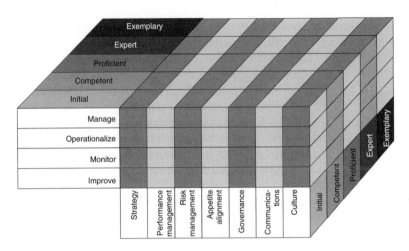

Figure 12.7   **The RBPM Maturity Model**

and for conversations around the type of culture that the organization is seeking to create. In the embedding phase, the Maturity Assessment is a great way of periodically taking stock as to where the culture is in relation to the desired state.

The importance of communication

One of the most important factors in the embedding phase is communication. Too often with change initiatives such as the implementation of RBPM, the only communication that the organization's staff receive is at the start of the process which sets out the vision, etc. Then there tends to be a deafening silence as those directly involved in the implementation become so busy and focused on the "doing" that they neglect the communication; or if the change is not going smoothly, the project team stop communicating for fear of undermining the project.

Communication is vital in the embedding phase, when staff will have important questions that require answering and to get them involved in the implementation. As one example, a Manigent client that deployed RBPM organized a series of "pizza and beer" sessions (at the end of the working day!) to enable staff to gather, socialize and create an environment for the free exchange of questions, concerns and other information around the methodology and its implementation.

The communication strategy should also seek to highlight how the organization is using and evolving the RBPM framework. For example, we recommend that a clear implementation roadmap be developed to provide guidance to the implementation team but also to provide the communications team with regular topics for communication – for example, as different business units "go live" this should be widely communicated. Also, as per the old adage that actions speak louder than words, the communications team should ensure that senior staff engagement in the RBPM process and/or implementation are highlighted across the organization: for example, as part of their RBPM implementation a client project team made a point of getting the busy, powerful CEO to sit in front of their RBPM solution and enter some commentary around certain items. Photos of the CEO actively engaging with the RBPM approach made regular appearances in communications outputs during and after the implementation.

Understand the role of technology

Chapter 11 explained that technology has a critical role to play in the successful introduction of the RBPM approach. We are not talking about spreadsheets, which have a tendency to grow into their own cottage industry, and distract resources from analysing, understanding and making recommendations and decisions based on the data – rather turning those resources into "spreadsheet jockeys" who spend their time managing the spreadsheets, manually copying, pasting and consolidating data, etc.

To effectively implement and embed the RBPM approach, we recommend that an enterprise class technology solution be deployed to support and enable the methodology and allow people to quickly and easily engage and interact with the RBPM framework.

Additionally, we recommend that organizations deploy a technology solution early in the implementation process rather than the traditional approach, which is to deploy the methodology and then deploy the enabling software. Our experience has shown that organizations can gain significant benefits through deploying software early. One client who uses the RBPM approach deployed their enabling solution (StratexPoint) approximately three months after the initial implementation of the methodology. When they completed a post-implementation review, they identified the failure to implement the software solution early as the primary cause of poor buy-in and support in certain business units (the same business units who were involved early in the implementation and were told that a software solution would be deployed in the future). Without a software solution to support the methodology early, these business units developed their own spreadsheet solutions which led to too many people being involved in maintaining the spreadsheet and not engaging in the process. Additionally, once the software solution was delivered, it led to a lot of ill feeling as many within those early business units felt their efforts to support the approach with spreadsheets was not appreciated or valued. This lead to a significant amount of implementation resource getting involved to "rework" the implementation for these early business units and to re-engage them in the overall process and approach.

The contrast with the business units who experienced the implementation of the methodology and the technology together was marked. After a year of using the methodology, these units reported significantly better engagement and buy-in, and also significantly better business results as measured by reductions in regulatory capital, reductions in operational losses, improves in the delivery of organizational initiatives and objectives (hitting performance targets).

End note: May you live in continuous turbulent times

The ancient Chinese saying "may you live in interesting times" was meant as a curse. Interesting times were characterized by turmoil, war, economic struggles, etc. In the 21st century we will live in "continuous turbulent times". For many organizations this will indeed prove a curse. But those that build the agility, the capabilities and the processes to see these times as no more than "business as usual" will reap huge benefits. Managing both strategy and risk through frameworks and methodologies such as RBPM will play a critical role in making interesting/turbulent times equally exciting and profitable.

May you live in continuous turbulent times.

Notes

Chapter 1

1 Fredrick W. Taylor, *Principles of Scientific Management*, Harper & Brothers, 1911
2 See the W. Edwards Deming Institute, http://deming.org/
3 Professor Henry Mintzberg, The Fall and Rise of Strategic Planning, *Harvard Business Review*, January–February 1994
4 James Creelman, *The Finance Function: Achieving Performance Excellence in a Global Economy*, Business Intelligence, UK, 2009
5 Globalization and the Changing UN Economy by the UK's Department for Business Enterprise and Regulatory Reform, February 2008
6 The 2011 Financial Times Global 500 Index, *Financial Times*, UK
7 Peter Hemington, The New Economic World Order: A Multipolar World Emerges, Transitions, *BDO*, May 2010
8 *The Centre for Future Studies*, Insights into the Post Recession Business Environment, Transitions, *BDO*, February 2010
9 *BBC News*, July 31, 2009
10 Andrew Pierce, The Queen Asks Why No One Saw the Credit Crunch Coming, *The Telegraph*, November 5, 2008, UK
11 *Best Practice in Risk Management: A Function Comes of Age*, Economist Intelligence Unit, UK, 2007
12 IMF Global Financial Stability, *IMF*, April 2006
13 Climbing out of the Credit Crunch, Association of Chartered Certified Accountants, 2008, USA
14 Risk Management is Dead... Long Live Risk Management, the Business Continuity Institute, UK, 2009
15 Ronan O'Sullivan and Ross McNaughton, *New UK Corporate Governance Code, Paul Hastings: Stay Current*, June 2010

Chapter 2

1 Zachary A. Goldfarb and Lisa Rein, JPMorgan Chase Execs May Depart as CEO Jamie Dimon Acknowledges "Terrible, Egregious Mistake" on Trading, The *Washington Post*, May 2012, USA

2 Andrew Smart, *At the Intersection: An Investigation into the Integration and Alignment of the Balanced Scorecard with Operational Risk Management Frameworks to Enhance Strategic Execution in the UK Financial Services Industry*. MBA Dissertation, Henley Management College, UK, 2006

3 Global Risk Management Study, Accenture, 2011

4 Dr Robert Kaplan and Dr David Norton, *Measures That Drive Performance*, Harvard Business Review, January/February 1992

5 See as examples, Dr Robert Kaplan and Dr David Norton, *The Balanced Scorecard: Translating Strategy into Action*, Harvard Business School Press, 1996 and *Creating the Strategy-Focused Organization*, Harvard Business School Press, 2001

6 Adrian Cadbury, Financial Aspects of Corporate Governance, 1992, see http://www.ecgi.org/codes/documents/cadbury.pdf

7 Attributed to *Peter Drucker*

8 *Financial Times*, August 2012, quoted from *Risk Culture: Under the Microscope Guidance for Boards*, Institute of Risk Management, UK, 2012

9 *Financial Times*, August 2012, quoted from *Risk Culture: Under the Microscope Guidance for Boards*, Institute of Risk Management, UK, 2012

Chapter 3

1 Dr Robert Kaplan and Dr David Norton, *The Balanced Scorecard: Measures That Drive Performance*, Harvard Business Review, January/February 1992

2 See as examples, Dr Robert Kaplan and Dr David Norton, *The Balanced Scorecard: Translating Strategy into Action*, Harvard Business School Press, 1996 and *Creating the Strategy-Focused Organization*, Harvard Business School Press, 2001

3 Dr Robert Kaplan and Dr David Norton (op. cit.)

4 Research by Fortune Magazine, Quoted in Dr Robert Kaplan and Dr David Norton, *Measures That Drive Performance*, Harvard Business Review, January/February 1992

5 Dr Robert Kaplan and Dr David Norton, *Creating the Strategy-Focused Organization*, Harvard Business School Press, 2001

6 Dr Robert Kaplan and Dr David Norton, *The Execution Premium: Linking Strategy to Operations for Competitive Advantage*, Harvard Business School Press, 2009

7 Darrell Rigby and Barbara Bilodea, *Management Tools & Trends*, Bain & Company, 2011

8 Aaron Crabtree and Gerald DeBusk, *The Effects of Adopting the Balanced Scorecard on Shareholder Returns Advances in Accounting*, USA, June 2008

9 See, as examples, Bernard Marr and James Creelman, *More with Less: Maximizing Value in the Public Sector*, Palgrave Macmillan, 2011. Naresh Makhijani and James Creelman, *Creating a Balanced Scorecard for a Financial Services Organization*, John Wiley & Sons, Asia, 2011

10 Professor Robert Kaplan, blog entry, December 2008

11 The Sarbanes–Oxley Act, 2002, see www.soxlaw.com/

12 Enterprise Risk Management: Integrated Framework, The Committee of Sponsoring Organizations of the Treadway Commission, 2004

13 Standards Australia and Standards New Zealand, and New Zealand Standards of Risk Management: AS/NZ 4360:2004, Risk Management, Australia, 2004

14 *The Orange Book: Management of Risks – Principles and Concepts*, Her Majesty's Treasury, UK, 2004

15 ISO31000:2009 *Risk Management Principles and Guidelines*, The International Organization for Standardization, 2009

16 ISO31000:2009 *Risk Management Principles and Guidelines*, The International Organization for Standardization, 2009

17 Andrew Smart, *At the Intersection: An Investigation into the Integration and Alignment of the Balanced Scorecard with Operational Risk Management Frameworks to Enhance Strategic Execution in the UK Financial Services Industry*. MBA Dissertation, Henley Management College, UK, 2006

18 Professor Kaplan first shared his developing ideas in a series of articles that appeared in the Balanced Scorecard Report, most notably in 2009

19 In Kaplan and Norton's January 2012 article *The Future of the Balanced Scorecard*, published in the US *CGMA Magazine*

20 In the June 2012 edition of the Harvard Business Review Kaplan, along with Harvard Business School Assistant Professor Annette Mikes, published the article *Managing Risks: A New Framework*

21 Nelson D. Schwarz and Jessica Silver-Greenberg, JPMorgan Was Warned About Lax Risk Controls, *New York Times*, June 3, 2012

Chapter 4

1 See Sun Tzu, *The Art of War, Special Edition*, translated and annotated by Lionel Giles, El Paso Norte Press, 2005

2 Quoted from Lizwe Nikala, Long Range Strategic Thinking Ability, Why CEOs Must Have It, *Entrepreneur Magazine*, February 2, 2012, South Africa

3 Dr Robert Kaplan and Dr David Norton, *The Balanced Scorecard: Translating Strategy into Action*, Harvard Business School Press, 1996

4 Michael Porter, *What Is Strategy?* Harvard Business Review, 2006

5 Michael Treacy and Fred Wiersema, *Customer Intimacy and Other Value Disciplines*, Harvard Business Review, 1993

6 W. Chan Kin and Renee Mauborgne, *Blue Ocean Strategy: How to Create Uncontested Market Space and Make the Competition Irrelevant*, Harvard Business School Press, 2005

7 Ukerto Moti, Aligning Human Capital to Execute Corporate Strategy for Public Sector Growth and Service Excellence, see http://www.academia.edu/283841/Aligning_Human_Capital_to_Execute_Corporate_Strategy_for_Public_Sector_Growth_and_Service_Delivery

8 Working paper on Risk Culture: Guidance from the Institute of Risk Management, Institute of Risk Management, UK, June 2012

9 Dr Larry Rittenberg and Frank Martens (op. cit.)

10 See http://www.reputationinstitute.com/thought-leadership/global-reptrak

11 Dr Larry Rittenberg and Frank Martens, *Understanding and Communicating Risk Appetite'*, the Committee of Sponsoring Organizations of the Treadway Commission, January 2012

12 The Failure of the Royal Bank of Scotland, Financial Services Authority, UK, December 2011

13 Dr Larry Rittenberg and Frank Martens (op. cit.)

14 Enterprise Risk Management: Integrated Framework, the Committee of Sponsoring Organizations of the Treadway Commission, 2004

15 Dr Larry Rittenberg and Frank Martens (op. cit.)

16 ISO31000:2009 *Risk Management Principles and Guidelines*, The International Organization for Standardization, 2009

17 ISO31000:2009 *Risk Management Principles and Guidelines*, The International Organization for Standardization, 2009

18 The British Standards institution, BS31100:2008

19 Dr Larry Rittenberg and Frank Martens (op. cit.)

20 Dr Larry Rittenberg and Frank Martens (op. cit.)

21 A. Osterwalder, Yves Pigneur, Alan Smith, and 470 practitioners from 45 countries, Business Model Generation, Business Model Foundry, 2010

22 Dr Larry Rittenberg and Frank Martens (op. cit.)

23 Research into the Definition and Application of the Concept of Risk Appetite, Marsh and the University of Nottingham, UK, October 2009

Chapter 5

1 Martha Lagace, *The Office of Strategy Management, Q&A with Professor Robert Kaplan*, Harvard Business School, Working Knowledge, Arch 27th 2006, Harvard Business School Press, USA

2 *Attributed to* Professor Albert Einstein

3 *Attributed to* Peter Drucker

4 *Attributed to* Peter Drucker

5 See James Creelman, *Building a Strategic Balanced Scorecard*, Business Intelligence, UK, 2003

6 Strategic Performance Management in Government and Public Sector Organizations, Advanced Performance Institute, UK, 2008

7 Bernard Marr and James Creelman, *More with Less, 2011 Performance Challenges for the UK Public Sector*, Advanced Performance Institute, UK, 2011

8 James Creelman and Jonathan Chocqueel-Mangan, *Reinventing Budgeting and Planning for the Adaptive Organization*, Business Intelligence, UK, 2006

9 James Creelman and Jonathan Chocqueel-Mangan (op. cit.)

10 Dr Robert Kaplan and Dr David Norton, *The Balanced Scorecard: Measures That Drive Performance*, Harvard Business School Press, 1996

Chapter 6

1 see www.shiftinpartners.com

2 James Creelman, *Building a Strategic Balanced Scorecard*, Business Intelligence, UK, 2003

3 Fra Lucs Bartolomeo de Pacioli, Summa de Arithmetica, Geometrica, Poroportioni et Proportionaltie, 1494, Italy. Version: Universidad Autonoma de Nuevo Leon, 1991

4 See http://www.thehackettgroup.com/

Chapter 7

1 Quoted from ERM History, Druml Group: see http://www.druml.com/management-advisory/enterprise-risk-management/erm-history/

2 Basel II The second of the Basel Accords, Basel Committee on Banking Supervision, 2004

3 See http://www.isixsigma.com/tools-templates/cause-effect/determine-root-cause-5-whys/

4 See http://en.wikipedia.org/wiki/Ishikawa_diagram

5 Enterprise Risk Management: Integrated Framework, the Committee of Sponsoring Organizations of the Treadway Commission, 2004

6 Strengthening Enterprise Risk Management for Competitive Advantage, The Committee of Sponsoring Organizations of the Treadway Commission, 2009

7 Risk Management: Principles and Guidelines, ISO31000-2006, ISO 2009

8 Risk Management: Principles and Guidelines, ISO31000-2006 (op. cit.)

9 Oxford Dictionary, see http://oxforddictionaries.com/

10 Strengthening Enterprise Risk Management for Competitive Advantage (op. cit.)

11 Dr Larry Rittenberg and Frank Martens, *Understanding and Communicating Risk Appetite*, the Committee of Sponsoring Organizations of the Treadway Commission, January 2012

12 *Internal Control – Integrated Framework*, the Committee of Sponsoring Organizations of the Treadway Commission

Chapter 9

1 Adrian Cadbury, Financial Aspects of Corporate Governance, 1992, see http://www.ecgi.org/codes/documents/cadbury.pdf

2 The Greenbury Report on Directors Remuneration, Confederation of Business and Industry, UK, 1995

3 Nigel Turnbull, Internal Control: Guidance for Directors on the Combined Code, London Stock Exchange for listed companies, 1999 (revised guide published in 2005)

4 Climbing out of the Credit Crunch, Association of Chartered Certified Accountants, 2008, USA

5 *The Corporate Governance Lessons from the Financial Crisis* by Grant Kirkpatrick

6 The Failure of the Royal Bank of Scotland, Financial Services Authority, UK, December 2011

7 *Senior Supervisors Group Risk Management Lessons from the Global Banking Crisis of 2008*

8 Ernst & Young's 2010 report *Making Strides in Financial Services Risk Management*

9 The UK Corporate Governance Code, 2010, Financial Reporting Council, UK, 2010

10 The King Committee on Corporate Governance: The King Report on Corporate Governance I, The Institute of Directors, South Africa, 1994

11 The King Committee on Corporate Governance: The King Report on Corporate Governance II, The Institute of Directors, South Africa, 2002

12 The King Committee on Corporate Governance: The King Report on Corporate Governance III, The Institute of Directors, South Africa, 1994

13 Corporate Governance Principles and Recommendations, The ASX Corporate Governance Council, Australia, March 2003

14 OECD Principles of Corporate Governance, Organisation for Economic Co-Operation and Development, 2004

15 The Sarbanes–Oxley Act, 2002

16 OECD Principles of Corporate Governance (op. cit.)

17 Dr Roger Barker, Responding to the Crisis, The Corporate Governance Perspective, Institute of Directors, UK, September 2009

18 Research into the Definition and Application of the Concept of Risk Appetite, Marsh and the University of Nottingham, UK, October 2009

19 National Association of Corporate Directors Blue Ribbon Commission report, *Risk Governance: Balancing Risk and Rewards*

Chapter 10

1 *Financial Times*, August 2012, quoted from *Risk Culture: Under the Microscope Guidance for Boards*, Institute of Risk Management, UK, 2012
2 Attributed to *Peter Drucker*
3 Andrew Smart, *At the Intersection: An Investigation into the Integration and Alignment of the Balanced Scorecard with Operational Risk Management Frameworks to Enhance Strategic Execution in the UK Financial Services Industry*. MBA Dissertation, Henley Management College, UK, 2006
4 Ernst & Young's 2011 research paper *Making Strides in Financial Services Risk Management*
5 Citigroup's Chief Executive, Charles O. Prince said in July 2007, "As long as the music is playing, you've got to get up and dance. We're still dancing".
6 Risk Management in a Time of Global Uncertainty, *Harvard Business Review Analytic Services*, Harvard Business School Publishing, USA, 2011
7 *Risk Culture: Under the Microscope Guidance for Boards*, The Institute of Risk Management, 2013
8 Understanding and Articulating Risk Appetite, KPMG, 2009
9 Understanding and Articulating Risk Appetite (op. cit.)
10 Lord David Walker, *A Review of Corporate Governance in UK Banks and Other Financial Industry Entities*, HM Treasury, UK, 2009
11 Making Strides in Financial Services Risk Management, Ernst & Young, 2011
12 Making Strides in Financial Services Risk Management (op. cit.)
13 Research into the Definition and Application of the Concept of Risk Appetite, Marsh and the University of Nottingham, UK, October 2009
14 Understanding and Articulating Risk Appetite (op. cit.)
15 Risk Management: Principles and Guidelines, ISO31000-2006, ISO 2009
16 See www.senndelaney.com

Chapter 11

1 The Gartner Group, 2011, see http://thisiswhatgoodlookslike.com/2012/06/10/gartner-survey-shows-why-projects-fail/
2 Quoted from Robert Miller, Only a Matter of Time Before the Spreadsheets Hit the Fan, *Daily Telegraph*, UK, June 30, 2005
3 See, for example, The Use of Spreadsheets: Considerations for Section4 404 of the Sarbanes–Oxley Act, PricewaterhouseCoopers, July 2004
4 John Carney, Barclays Spreadsheet Error Results in Lehman Chaos, *Business Insider*, October 16, 2008
5 Grenville J. Croll, *Spreadsheets and the Financial Collapse*, European Spreadsheet Risks Interest Group, 2009

Chapter 12

1 Enterprise Risk Management: Integrated Framework, the Committee of Sponsoring Organizations of the Treadway Commission, 2004
2 Capability Model Maturity Model, Carnegie Mellon University Software Engineering Institute, USA
3 Jim Collins and Jerry Porras, *Built to Last: Successful Habits of Visionary Companies*, HarperCollins Publishers, 2002
4 Jim Collins and Jerry Porras, *Good to Great: Why Some Companies Make the Leap … and Others Don't*, HarperCollins Publishers, 2001
5 A. Osterwalder, Yves Pigneur, Alan Smith, and 470 practitioners from 45 countries, Business Model Generation, Business Model Foundry, 2010

Index

Note: The letters '*f*', '*n*' and '*t*' following locators refer to figures, notes and tables.

ABN AMRO acquisition, 95–6
ACCA, *see* Association of Chartered Certified Accountants
advanced measure approach, 169
Advanced Performance Institute, 122
Advances in Accounting, 69
Aerospace supplier, 189–90
aggregated objective score, 148
aligning risk-taking, 213–14
alignment, benefits of, 165–6
AMA, *see* advanced measure approach
American Accounting Association, 71
API, *see* Advanced Performance Institute
appetite alignment matrix, 38*f*, 47, 117, 138, 192, 203–9, 212–13, 240, 255, 258, 276
 collective gut feel, 208
 competitive advantage, 208
 cost of controls, 209
 exposure alignment matrix, 206*f*
 exposure zones, 206
 optimal zone, 206–7
 over-exposed zone, 207
 RBPM approach, use of, 208
 under-exposed zone, 207–8
appetite alignment process, 209–13
 appetite alignment matrix, 212–13
 business drivers, 210
 business performance, 211
 key risks, 212
 misalignments, 213

 monitoring, 213
 review, 213
 risk appetite, 211
 risk assessment, 212
 steps, 209–10
 strategic objectives, 210
appetite and managing performance, 202
appetite and managing risk, 203
appetite and set strategy, 202
appetite, strategic importance, 94–100
Arab Spring, 2
The Art of War, 86–7
Ashghal, 56–61
 corporate strategy map, 57*f*, 139
 initiative sheet used by, 60*f*
 three themes of outsourcing and delivery, 61
Association of Accountants and Financial Professionals in Business, 71
Association of Chartered Certified Accountants, 19, 216–17
ASX Corporate Governance Council, 221–2
Australia, risk management process, 74–6

bailout, European Union, 17
balanced performance measurement, 62

balanced scorecard, 33, 54–70
  Christchurch City, 153
  components, 54
  enduring popularity of the
    Balanced Scorecard, 68–9
  execution premium, 65–8;
    alienation of organization, 67;
    monitor and learn, 67–8; plan
    the strategy, 66–7; strategy,
    65–6; test and strategy
    adaptation, 68
  financial benefits, 69
  financial impact of, 69*t*
  first generation, 62–3
  Hall of Fame, 124
  perspectives of, 49, 130
  schematic, 35*f*, 62*f*
  scorecard, 61–2
  second generation, 62–3
  shortcomings of scorecard usage,
    69–70
  strategy-focused organization,
    63–5; alienation of the
    organization, 64; continual
    process, 65; everyone's
    everyday job, 64–5; execution
    premium model, 66*f*; executive
    leadership, 65; operational
    terms, 63–4
  strategy map, 55–61
  weaknesses in, 81
Barker, Roger, 290*n*17
Basel Accords, 289
BAU, 277–9
BCI, *see* Business Continuity
  Institute
best-practice approach, 142
Best Practice in Risk Management,
  18–19
BHAGs (Big Hairy Audacious
  Goals), 272
Bilodea, Barbara, 286*n*7
blue ocean, 90
brainstorming, 110

business as usual, 157–8, 257, 259,
  277–9, 284
Business Continuity Institute, 20
business enterprise and regulatory
  reform, 12
business model canvas, 109–10

Cadbury, Adrian, 286*n*6, 290*n*1
Cadbury Committee, 220–1
Capability Model Maturity Model,
  269, 292*n*2
capital allocation, 73, 220
career development, 10
Carnegie Mellon University Software
  Engineering Institute, 269
Carney, John, 291*n*4
causality, granular understanding,
  131
cause-and-effect relationship, 33, 63,
  171, 203
CGMA Magazine, 81
Chan Kin, W., 90, 288*n*6
Creelman, James, 285*n*4, 287*n*9,
  288*n*5, 289*n*7, 289*n*8, 289*n*9
child-initiative, 158
China
  foreign exchange reserves, 13
  global GDP share, 14*t*
  market capitalization, 13
  nominal GDP, 13
China Construction Group, 13
Chocqueel-Mangan, Jonathan,
  289*n*8, 289*n*9
City of Christchurch, 153–4
  strategy map, 154*f*
C-level risk executive, 29
Climbing Out of the Credit Crunch, 19
Collins, Jim, 272, 292*n*3, 292*n*4
Committee of Sponsoring
  Organizations of the Treadway
  Commission, *see* COSO
Communication, 242–8
  clarity, 243–5
  concision, 247

Communication – *continued*
  consistency, 248
  and consultation, 245–6
  context, 247
  credibility, 246–7
  effectiveness, 247–8
  5 "Cs" of communication, 242–8
  importance, 244
  internal and external, 244–6
  ISO3100, 244–6
  key lessons, 244–5
  RBPM framework, 232
  RBPM implementation, 247
  strategic objectives, 243
CompaSS, 147
control assessment data, 198
control map, 195–7, 277
control scorecard, 46, 127, 129*f*,
  198–9, 203, 258
corporate performance management,
  27
corporate scandals, 10, 70
corporate strategy, 21, 43, 91, 225
corporate strategy map, 57–9, 110
COSO framework, 54, 71, 74, 78,
  173
  risk appetite managing, 99;
    communicate, 99; develop risk
    appetite, 99; monitor and
    update, 99
  risk management frameworks,
    71–4
CPM, *see* corporate performance
  management
Crabtree, Aaron, 69, 286*n*8
credit crunch, 1–2, 14–18, 23–4, 26,
  30, 39, 41–2, 47, 53, 69–71,
  80–1, 83, 94–5, 100, 108, 136,
  158, 174, 210, 215–16, 218–19,
  225, 230–1, 234, 240, 244, 266
  causes of, 15, 17, 19–20, 216
  consequence, 18
  cultural reason, 231
  governance, and, 215–19

IMF estimation, 17
JP Morgan Chase's success, 83
leading areas, 216–17
lessons from, 20, 24–5
reason for, 21
risk-taking drivers, 240
Royal Bank of Scotland, 94
credit enhanced training, 219
criminal-related incidents, 156
critical capabilities, 30
critical success factors, 231
CRM, *see* customer relationship
  management
Croll, Grenville J., 261, 291*n*5
CSF, *see* critical success factors
CtW Investment Group, 83
culture
  accountability, 239
  characteristic, 237
  clear set of values, 235
  compelling vision, 234–5
  conversations, 240
  definition, 237–8
  discipline, 76
  financial services research, 233–4
  incentives, 240–2
  leadership with integrity, 236–8
  strategy-focused, 234–42
customer experience, 146
customer relationship management,
  128, 145, 157, 193

dashboards, role of, 258–62
DeBusk, Gerald, 69, 286*n*8
Delaney Leadership Consulting, 246
Dell, 89
Deming, W. Edwards, 7, 285*n*2
denial, psychology of, 17–18
derivative trading, irresponsible, 24
digital technology development, 2
double-entry bookkeeping, 149

eBay, 90
economic crisis, 23

Economist Intelligence Unit, 18, 100
EFQM, *see* European Foundation for
    Quality Management
Enron Corporation, accounting
    irregularities, 70–1
enterprise risk management (ERM),
    10, 72–3, 101, 112, 119, 173–4,
    236
    see also risk management
Ernst & Young's, 219, 234, 290*n*8,
    291*n*4, 291*n*11
European Foundation for Quality
    Management, 8–9, 159
    excellence model, 9*f*, 156
Eurozone, 2, 206
execution premium, 65–8
    align the organization with
        strategy, 67
    develop the strategy, 65–6
    monitor and learn, 67–8
    plan the strategy, 66–7
    test and adapt the strategy, 68
exposure alignment matrix, 206*f*
ExxonMobil, 13

Facebook, 2
*The Failure of the Royal Bank of
    Scotland*, 95–8, 217–18
FDI, *see* foreign direct investment
feedback
    and communication
    in context of RBPM
    loop, 132, 171
    stakeholder, 77
*The Finance Function Achieving
    Global Excellence in a Global
    Economy*, 11
Financial Reporting Council, 21
Financial Services Authority, 20, 48,
    95–6, 98, 217–18, 240, 259
Financial Times Global 500 Index,
    13
first generation balanced scorecard,
    62–3

foreign direct investment, 12
foreign-exchange risk, 19
four perspective risk map, 36*f*, 47,
    185–6, 203–5, 255, 258
FRC, *see* Financial Reporting Council
FSA, *see* Financial Services Authority

Garter research, 265
GBM, *see* global banking and
    markets
GECs, *see* General Engineering
    Companies
General Electric, 13
General Engineering Companies,
    57
global banking and markets, 97
globalization, 11–14
*Globalization and the Changing UN
    Economy*, 12
Goldfarb, Zachary A., 285*n*1
Google, 88
governance
    apply approach, 223
    ASX Corporate Governance
        Council, 221–2
    board responsibilities, 225–6
    boundaries setting, 224
    comply approach, 223
    and credit crunch, 215–19
    data governance, 223
    decision making, 224–5
    definition, 220–3
    disclosure and transparency, 225
    IT Governance, 223
    King Report, 221
    OECD Principles of Corporate
        Governance, 222–3
    poor risk oversight, 218–19, 218
    post-credit crunch, 219–20, 219
    principles of, 222–3
    project governance, 223
    RACI model, 226–9
    RBPM framework, 216*f*
    risk management, and, 225–6

Royal Bank of Scotland, 217–18
UK Corporate Governance Code,
220–1
great depression, 17
Greece, European Union bailout, 17

Hackett Group, 12, 156
hard disciplines, 202, 215, 262, 280
Hedges, Bob, 168–9
Hemington, Peter, 285n7
high-performance culture, 146, 149
HML, 47–52
conceptual strategy map, 50f
operational risk, 139
scorecard indicators, 51f

IMF, 17, 19
impact and likelihood (or
probability) matrix, 182
India
global GDP share, 14t
annual GDP, 13
manufacturing exports, 13
indicators, 27, 31, 35, 48–9, 51, 82,
115–16, 120–35, 145, 150, 153,
187–8, 192, 239, 256, 263, 277,
280
behaviour and, 133
control scorecard, 129f
dashboards, 277
HML, 130
integrated set of, 124–6
KCIs, 127
KPIs, 126
KRIs, 126–7
leading and lagging, 130–3
performance conversation, and,
123–4
performance scorecard, 128f
risk scorecard, 128f
scorecards, 127–30
working, 130
industrial-age thinking, 10
Industrial and Commercial Bank of
China, 13

industrial revolution, 5–6
initiative alignment matrix, 163–6,
163f, 278f, 279
initiative selection templates, 160–3
Ashghal case, 160–3
Palladium, 160
Insights into the Post Recession
Business Environment, 14
Institute of Risk Management, 91,
237–8
integrated approach, 31–3
appetite, 32
business drivers, 31
integrating strategy, 21, 25, 247
integration models, 80–3
JP Morgan Chase, 82–3
Kaplan and Norton approach,
81–2
Manigent's financial services, 80
Volkswagen Do Brazil, 82–3
International Organization for
Standardization, 76
Ireland, European Union bailout, 17
IRM, see Institute of Risk
Management
iron-making techniques, 6
see also industrial revolution
ISO, see International Organization
for Standardization
ISO31000, 45, 54, 58, 76–81,
103, 175–6, 244, 246,
287n15
balanced Scorecard, 79
principles and guidelines, 78–9
recommendations, 76
risk management principles,
77–8
see also risk management

JP Morgan Chase, 24, 42, 82–3,
232, 285n1, 287n21
Juran trilogy, 7
see also total quality management

Kaplan, Robert, 33, 54, 87, 120,
    286*n*1, 286*n*2, 286*n*3, 286*n*4,
    286*n*5, 286*n*6, 287*n*10, 287*n*3,
    288*n*1, 289*n*10
Kaplan approach, integration models,
    81–2
KCIs, *see* key control indicators
key control indicators, 35–6, 120,
    122, 124–9, 132, 149, 152, 167,
    197–200, 256, 263
key controls, 193–5
    categories, 194
    effectiveness, 197
    control activities, 194
    control environment, 194
    information and communication,
        195
    internal control, 193–5
    monitoring, 195
    objectives, 194
    risk assessment, 194
key dashboards and management,
    45–7
key indicators, *see* indicators
key performance indicators, 33–6,
    51, 57, 59, 61, 84, 120–58,
    187–8, 204, 263
    actionable, 153–4
    candidate identification, 158
    cause and effect, 150
    describing a strategic initiative,
        157–8
    existing initiatives, 159
    financial, 148–50
    high-performance cultures, 149
    initiative selection templates,
        160–3; Ashghal case, 160–3;
        Palladium, 160
    non-financial, 148–50
    ownership, 152–3
    preferred initiatives, 159
    prioritizing initiatives, 158
    resource allocation, 160
    strategic initiatives, 157–8

strategic versus operational,
    150–2; common definitions,
    151; do not repackage, 151;
    driving the right behaviours,
    151–2
target selection, 154–7;
    achievable, 155; benchmarking,
    155–6; relative performance,
    155–6; trending, 156–7
key risk indicators, 35–6, 51, 81,
    104, 111, 120, 122, 124–8,
    131–2, 149, 152, 167, 172, 181,
    187–8, 190, 192, 200, 240, 256,
    263
    development of, 187
    function of, 188
    key employee retention rate, 188
    overview of, 187–8
key risks, 112–14, 177–82
    execution risk, 178
    financial risk, 179
    operational risk, 178–9
    strategic risk, 178
    techniques, 113
key terms understanding, 144–8
    differentiating key indicators, 145
    differentiating objectives, 145
    excellent management of
        knowledge, 147
    initiatives, 145
    objective accountability, 147–8
    objective description, 146
    objective desired state, 146–7
King Report, 221
Kirkpatrick, Grant, 217
knowledge age, 7–8, 11
KPIs, *see* key performance indicators
KRIs, *see* key risk indicators

Lagace, Martha, 288*n*1
leading indicator, 82, 131–2
likelihood rating, 183–4
LinkedIn, 11, 85, 150
Lizwe, Nikala, 287*n*2

London School of Economics, 17
loss management, 169–72
   authorizations, 172
   birth of, 173–6
   business impact assessment, 171
   corrective actions, 171
   estimation, 170
   information analysis, 172
   investigation, 170
   loss event capture, 170
   reporting, 172
   root cause analysis, 171
LSE, *see* London School of
   Economics

Makhijani, Naresh, 287n9
Making Strides in Financial Services
   Risk Management, 219, 234,
   241–2
Malcolm Baldrige criteria, 154, 156
Malcolm Baldrige national quality
   framework, 9f
Management Tools & Trends 2011, 68
managing performance, 33–7
managing risk, 37–8
Manigent, 163–4, 204, 255, 257
   see also appetite alignment matrix
Manigent Financial Services, 80, 27t
Marr, Bernard, 287n9, 289n7
Martens, Frank, 99, 288n9, 288n11,
   288n13, 288n15, 288n19,
   288n20, 288n222, 289n11
maturity model, 281–2
Mauborgne, Renee, 90, 288n6
MCI Corporation, 71
McKinsey & Co, 13
McNaughton, Ross, 285n15
Mehr, Robert, 168–9
Microsoft, 13
Middle East, protests and rebellions
   across, 2
Miller, Robert, 291n2
Mintzberg, Henry, 10, 285n3
money-losing mortgage, 83

mortgage-backed securities industry,
   16
   see also sub-prime lending
Moti, Ukerto, 90, 288n7
Motorola, 87–8
Motorola Mobility, 88
Motorola Solutions, 88

NAICOM, *see* Nigeria's National
   Insurance Commission
NatWest Bank, 94
   see also Royal Bank of Scotland
The New Economic World Order, 13
New Zealand, risk management
   process, 74–6
Nigeria's National Insurance
   Commission, 179
Norton, David, 33, 54, 87, 286n4,
   286n5, 286n1, 286n2, 286n3,
   286n4, 286n5, 286n6, 287n3,
   289n10
Norton approach, integration
   models, 81–2

OECD, *see* Organization for
   Economic Cooperation and
   Development
operational losses or loss events, 169
operational risk maturity model, 48
   see also HML
optimal (aligned) zone, 206
Orange Book, 75–6, 102f
organizational risk management, 27
Organization for Economic
   Cooperation and Development,
   222
ORM, *see* organizational risk
   management
ORMM, *see* operational risk maturity
   model
Osterwalder, A., 109, 288n21,
   292n5
O'Sullivan, Ronan, 285n15
over-exposed zone, 206

Payment Protection Insurance, 133
performance
    balanced scorecard, 139–40
    objective-setting workshop, 144
    -sapping problems, 122
    strategic objectives, 138–9
    sub-components, 137–8
performance gaps, identification of, 36
performance scorecard, 46, 127, 128*f*, 148, 149*f*, 203, 280
PESTEL analysis, 33, 106–7, 273
    elements of, 107*f*
Petrobras, 13
PetroChina, 13
Pierce, Andrew, 285*n*10
Pigneur, Yves, 288*n*21, 292*n*5
Plan operations, 67
PMCs, *see* Program Management Companies
Porras, Jerry, 272, 292*n*3, 292*n*4
Porter, Michael, 88, 287*n*4
Portugal, European Union bailout, 17
PPI, *see* Payment Protection Insurance
PricewaterhouseCoopers, 72
Prince, Charles O., 236, 291*n*5
Principles of Scientific Management, 6–7
process alignment matrix, 165*f*, 278*f*, 279
    usage, 165–6
profound knowledge, 8
Program Management Companies, 57

RACI model, 5, 215, 226–9, 230, 239, 257, 281
    accountable, 227
    benefits of, 228–9
    consult, 227
    inform, 227
    responsible, 227
    steps, 227–8

RAGAR colour coding, 134–6
    conventional approach, 134
    performance-only approach, 135
    ranges, 134
    scoring challenges management, 136
    scoring range, 134
    usage of a, 153
Ranford, Mark, 58, 235
RBPM approach implementation, 268–4
    align, 277
    analyse, 269–70
    articulate the chosen business model, 273
    communication importance, 282–3
    continuously refine the framework, 280
    culture management, 281–2
    embed, 279–84
    iterations series, 276
    left circle, 40*f*
    mobilize, 272–6
    operationalize, 277
    plan, 270–2
    RACI model, 281
    risk appetite, 275–6
    risk map, 274
    soft disciplines, 280–1
    strategic approach, 272
    strategy map, 273
    technology, role, 283–4
RBPM definition, 195–9
    Control Map, 195–7
    Controls Scorecard, 198–9
    KCIs, 197–8
RBPM framework, 3*f*, 4–5, 22, 25*f*, 30–2, 39, 41, 44–5, 48, 53, 54*f*, 70, 83, 86*f*, 100, 123–4, 138, 164, 166, 168, 171, 185, 200–2, 213, 216, 218, 227, 230, 232, 250–3, 256, 258–9, 264, 267, 270–1, 280, 282–3

aligning risk-taking, 4
  governance, 216f
  left circle, 4f, 32
  right circle, 5f, 41f
  risk appetite, 25
  sequencing, 4
  softer disciplines, 4
RBPM maturity model, 282f
RBS, *see* Royal Bank of Scotland
recession, 2, 14, 17, 107
red ocean, 90
Rein, Lisa, 285
Rigby, Darrell, 286n7
risk and business strategy, 20–1
risk and control scorecards, 47, 258
risk appetite, 22, 33, 93, 99–100,
  103, 111, 113–14, 116, 119, 191,
  205, 238
  aligning, 114
  and risk profiles, 20
  articulation of, 238, 242
  business model canvas, 109–10
  business models, 108–9
  cascading, 118
  COSO's definition, 101
  COSO view of managing, 99
  critical role of, 119
  definition, 100–1, 114–16,
    190–1, 238, 242; Orange
    Book, 102–3; RBPM, 103; risk
    management code, 103
  key business drivers identification,
    105
  key drivers, 105–7
  key risks, definitions and
    assessment, 112–14
  measurement, 116–18
  multidimensional construction,
    113f
  PESTEL analysis, 106
  purposes of, 119
  RBS's failure, 94–8
  risk levels defining, 110
  risk tolerance, and, 103–4

statement, 104–16
  strategic objectives, 110–12
  strategy, and, 94–8
  summarized statement, 116f
  summary benefits, 117–18
  SWOT analysis, 106
  tracking, 108
risk assessment, 59, 79, 182–7
  four perspective risk map, 185–7
Risk Bow-tie, 179–81
risk categories, 184t
risk event card, 82
Risk Heat Map, 59, 182, 183f, 185
risk identification template, 181–2
risk likelihood rating, 184t
risk management
  aligning risk appetite and strategy,
    72–3
  Australian standards, 74–6
  categories of risk, 178f
  corporate failures, 70–1
  COSO, 71–4
  cross-enterprise risks, 73
  definition, 73, 175–7
  discipline and function, 168–73
  emergence of, 167
  enhancing risk response decisions,
    73
  failure of, 5, 18–20, 100, 174
  first appearance, 10
  governance, and, 225–6
  identification of key risks, 177–82;
    execution risk, 178; financial
    risk, 179; operational risk,
    178–9; strategic risk, 178
  improving deployment of capital,
    73
  ISO31000, 76–80
  NAICOM categories of risk, 179f
  New Zealand Standards, 74–6
  Orange Book, 75–6
  reducing operational surprises and
    losses, 73
  Risk Bow-tie, 179–81

risk management – *continued*
  risk identification template,
      181–2
  Sarbanes–Oxley, 71
  scandals, 70–1
  seizing opportunities, 73
  steps, 168
  systematic analysis and
      conversation, 172
  uncertainty element of, 178–9
Risk Management Maturity
    Dashboards, 48
Risk Map, 45, 59, 136, 183, 185,
    187, 196, 229, 274–5, 277, 280
  example, 275*f*
Risk Master, emergence of, 26–30
  C-level risk executive, 29
  continuous improvement, 29
  decision-making processes, 28
  integrate risk management
      capabilities, 28
  measurement sophistication, 28
  risk awareness, 29
  shareholder value, 28
risk mitigation plan, 48
  level of urgency, 182
risk scorecard, 46, 127, 128*f*, 192–3,
    203, 258, 280
  accountable person, 192
  appetite alignment status, 192
  design, 192
  organization key risks, 192
  risk assessment data, 192
risk-taking aligning, 38–44,
    203–4
  appetite alignment matrix, 204
  communication, 44
  culture, 42–3
  four perspective risk map, 203
  governance, 39–42
  right circle, 39–44
  shareholder value, 44
  strategy map, 203

risk tolerance, 103–4, 111, 127,
    188–92
  Aerospace supplier, 189–90
  compliance tolerances, 190
  definitions of, 190–1
  operations tolerances, 190
  reporting tolerances, 190
  water company, 191–2
Rittenberg, Larry, 99, 288*n*9,
    288*n*11, 288*n*13, 288*n*15,
    288*n*19, 288*n*20, 288*n*22,
    289*n*11
RMP, *see* risk mitigation plan
Royal Bank of Scotland, 16, 21, 84,
    94, 171, 266
  board's role in strategy, 96–7
  cause of failure, 95–6
  credit crunch, 94–8
  failure of, FSA report, 95–8,
      217–18
  internal audit report, 97

Saatchi and Saatchi Worldwide, 147
  see also CompaSS
salary, betterment of, 10
Sarbanes–Oxley act, 71, 223,
    287*n*11, 290*n*15, 291*n*3
Schwarz, Nelson D., 287*n*21
scoring methodology, 134
  see also RAGAR colour coding
SEI, *see* Carnegie Mellon University
    Software Engineering Institute
seven RBPM disciplines, 45–7
SharePoint, 51, 252
shifting paradigms, 23
silo-working, 7
Silver-Greenberg, Jessica, 287*n*21
six sigma, 67, 87–8
Smart, Andrew, 26, 80, 233, 286*n*2,
    287*n*17, 291*n*3
Smith, Alan, 288*n*21, 292*n*5
social media, influence of, 2
soft disciplines, 4, 202, 215, 248,
    262–3, 280–1

spreadsheets, shortcomings of using, 259–62
  archiving, 261
  assumptions, 262
  cottage industries, 260
  enterprise interoperability, 262
  fraud, 261
  front-line concern, 260
  high risk, 260
  interpretation, 261
  lack of collaboration capabilities, 261
  lack of well-constructed "built-in" approach, 261
  multiple versions of the truth, 260
  opacity, 262
  overconfidence, 261
  reification, 262
StatexPoint solution, 51
Statoil, 123
strategic performance management, 289n6
strategic planning, 10, 27–8, 63, 68–9, 77, 154
Strategy and Risk Studio, 252–4, 256
strategy
  blue ocean strategy, 90
  for commercial and non-profit organizations, 90–1
  corporate strategy, 91
  definition of, 91–4
  Michael Porter's definition, 88
  operational focus, 87–8
  risk, 91
  risk appetite and, 94–8
  set, 32–3
  setting, 92–3
  strategic importance of appetite, 94–100
  Sun Tzu, 86–7
  three value-disciplines, 89–90; customer intimacy, 89–90; operational excellence, 89; product leadership, 90

strategy-focused organization, 63–5
  align the organization, 64
  execution premium model, steps of, 66f
  make a continual process, 65
  make strategy everyone's everyday job, 64–5
  mobilize change through executive leadership, 65
  principles of, 64f
  translate the strategy into operational terms, 63–4
strategy management theory, 140
strategy map, 33, 34f, 47–8, 55–61, 143
  Christchurch City, 154f
  emergence of, 63
  example, 140f, 141f, 274f
  internal process perspective, 111
  objective on, 139
  perspective of, 146
  Saatchi and Saatchi, 142f
  and scorecard, 34
StratexLive, 252–3
StratexPoint, 252–3, 256–7, 259, 283
  implementation of, 259
StratexSystems, 48, 252–3, 257–8
  see also HML
Strengthening Enterprise Risk Management for Competitive Advantage, 174
sub-prime lending, 15–17, 174
Sun Tzu, 86–7, 287n1
supporting customer objectives, 139
supporting performance, 47
SWOT analysis, 33, 106f, 273

tail-risk meetings, 39
Taylor, Fredrick W., 6, 285n1
Taylorism, 6, 10
  impact of, 6
technology and culture, 257

technology, role of
   appetite alignment matrix, 255
   control self-assessment processes,
      256
   four perspective risk map, 255
   integrated strategy, 252
   key risks, 252
   limitation, 251–2
   Manigent, 255
   non-technology aspects, 255
   RACI model, 257
   RBPM approach implementation,
      254
   RBPM enabler, 251–4
   RBPM framework, 250*f*
   risk assessment, 256
   risk management solutions, 252
   SharePoint, 252
   Strategy and Risk Studio, 253–4
   strategy map, 252
   StratexLive, 252–3
   StratexPoint, 252–3
   StratexSystems, 255
   technological capabilities, 262–4
   visualization, 258–62
total quality management, 7–11, 87,
   121
   popularity of, 8
   Xerox, adopter of, 8
TQM, *see* total quality management
training initiatives, 49, 51, 239
Treacy, Michael, 89–90, 287*n*5
turbulent times, 2–4, 14, 21–3, 25,
   39, 53, 91, 109, 120, 185, 200–1,
   250, 267, 284

Turnbull, Nigel, 290*n*3
Tyco International, 71

UK bank Northern Rock, 16
UK Corporate Governance Code,
   21, 39, 220–1
UK financial services study, 26
under-exposed zone, 207–8
*Understanding and Articulating
   Risk Appetite*, 238, 244
*Understanding and Communicating
   Risk Appetite*, 98–9, 104, 188
United States
   bankruptcy, 71
   debt issue, 2
   economic hegemony, 13
   global GDP share, 14*t*
   sub-prime lending, 15–17

Virgin Money, 16
Volkswagen Do Brazil, 82–3

Walker, Lord David, 241, 291*n*10
Walker Report, 241
Wal-Mart, 89
Water Quality Index, 191
Water Quality Sampling Results, 191
Weatherill, Gillian, 47, 130, 237, 239
Wiersema, Fred, 89–90, 287*n*5
WorldCom scandal, 71

Xerox Corporation, 8

YouTube, 2